'Reading Shabad's book, I was reminded of the early psychoanalytic writers whose personalities shone through their prose. Ferenczi, Abraham, Rank—and one could go on and on—exuded a pioneer spirit that simultaneously spoke themselves and their culture. Shabad's accounts of his origins, his visit to Moscow—where he was a child—begin this book that then moves into psycho-analytical musings of all kinds. The tone remains the same; a heartfelt sincerity and intelligence that is deeply moving and etches itself in one's own sensibility. A wonderful book.'

**Christopher Bollas**


'This is a wise, mature, and heartfelt book, a deeply affecting and memorable presentation of the struggle between the embrace of life and its inevitable pain, on the one hand, and on the other, the temptation to turn away from pain, and therefore to sacrifice one's involvement with life and the vitality such involve-ment brings with it. The argument Shabad makes is not theoretical—it is inspira-tional and legitimately profound. Shabad derives his deep and strong views from the events of his own life, both personal and clinical. The message not to avoid involvement with life, and the loss and mourning that come with it, is one that psychoanalysts and psychotherapists will find crucial to their clinical work—and not incidentally, their own lives.'

**Donnell B. Stern,** *William Alanson White Institute*


'Some authors move us, with their candor about the legacies of their early life experiences. Some impress us with their erudite philosophical references. Some enlighten us, with their profound psychoanalytic insights. Some change us, with their wisdom about love, loss, and fully embracing life. Shabad does it all! Laced with vivid clinical vignettes, this book demonstrates how existential values inform the perspective of a remarkably emotionally available clinician.'

**Sandra Buechler,** *faculty, William Alanson White Institute*

'In Peter Shabad's writing, one feels the strength of his unshakeable, all-the-way down, warrior-like bravery in defense of a human being's right to be himself or herself, and to his or her dignity and full humanity. This is why so many are consistently drawn to his work and this book is no exception. Generous, engaging, and philosophically challenging in the most accessible way, I wholeheartedly endorse *Passion, Shame, and The Freedom to Become.*'

**Elizabeth Corpt,** *MSW, LICSW, president emerita, Massachusetts Institute for Psychoanalysis*

'In the traditions of his joint muses, Kierkegaard and Nietzsche, Peter Shabad is an existentialist with a timely message of hope in the face of disavowing shame, resentment, and passivity. Here is a psychoanalytic vision that takes our existential freedom as a foundation for passionate growth and change. With compelling clinical examples and stories from his own life, Shabad charts a course through the self-thwarting choices that impede authentic living and offers the clinician a jargon-free guide for "seizing the moment" with our patients, acknowledging the precious gift of living fully today.'

**Jack Foehl,** *PhD, joint editor in chief, Psychoanalytic Dialogues, past president, Boston Psychoanalytic Society & Institute*

# Passion, Shame, and The Freedom To Become

This book examines how humans can overcome feelings of shame through self-acceptance and regain their innate passion and freedom to grow.

Peter Shabad examines in detail how self-shaming and passivity are intertwined with the fatalism of self-pity, envy, resentment, and ultimately, regret for not "seizing the vital moments" in life. From birth on, children attempt to contribute to the human endeavor through their innate passion. Parental receptivity enables a child to plant seeds of belonging, inspiring the generative passion necessary for furthering development. Exposed vulnerability due to the lack of receptivity leads to feelings of shame and self-consciousness; as human beings, we interpret our misfortunes and limitations as punishments and reverse our passion into an inhibited passivity. Shabad envisions psychotherapy as a pathway through which individuals learn to inclusively accept all aspects of their inner lives in order to embark on their journey of self-acceptance. He emphasizes the need for therapists to view patients as active agents in this process.

This book is a must read for psychoanalysts, psychotherapists, and anyone interested in developing a deeper understanding of the dynamics of shame and passion in our lives.

**Peter Shabad**, PhD, is on the faculties of the Chicago Psychoanalytic Institute, Chicago Center of Psychoanalysis, and Institute for Contemporary Psychoanalysis. He is co-editor of *The Problem of Loss and Mourning: Psychoanalytic Perspectives* (1989) and author of *Despair and The Return of Hope* (2001).

When music is played in a new key, the melody does not change, but the notes that make up the composition do: change in the context of continuity, continuity that perseveres through change. Psychoanalysis in a New Key publishes books that share the aims psychoanalysts have always had, but that approach them differently. The books in the series are not expected to advance any particular theoretical agenda, although to this date most have been written by analysts from the Interpersonal and Relational orientations.

The most important contribution of a psychoanalytic book is the communication of something that nudges the reader's grasp of clinical theory and practice in an unexpected direction. Psychoanalysis in a New Key creates a deliberate focus on innovative and unsettling clinical thinking. Because that kind of thinking is encouraged by exploration of the sometimes surprising contributions to psychoanalysis of ideas and findings from other fields, Psychoanalysis in a New Key particularly encourages interdisciplinary studies. Books in the series have married psychoanalysis with dissociation, trauma theory, sociology, and criminology. The series is open to the consideration of studies examining the relationship between psychoanalysis and any other field—for instance, biology, literary and art criticism, philosophy, systems theory, anthropology, and political theory.

But innovation also takes place within the boundaries of psychoanalysis, and Psychoanalysis in a New Key therefore also presents work that reformulates thought and practice without leaving the precincts of the field. Books in the series focus, for example, on the significance of personal values in psychoanalytic practice, on the complex interrelationship between the analyst's clinical work and personal life, on the consequences for the clinical situation when patient and analyst are from different cultures, and on the need for psychoanalysts to accept the degree to which they knowingly satisfy their own wishes during treatment hours, often to the patient's detriment.

A full list of all titles in this series is available at: https://www.routledge.com/Psychoanalysis-in-a-New-Key/book-series/LEAPNKBS

# Passion, Shame, and The Freedom To Become

## Seizing The Vital Moment in Psychoanalysis

Peter Shabad

Routledge
Taylor & Francis Group

LONDON AND NEW YORK

Designed cover image: © Photo by Jeremy Bishop on Unsplash

First published 2025
by Routledge
4 Park Square, Milton Park, Abingdon, Oxon OX14 4RN

and by Routledge
605 Third Avenue, New York, NY 10158

*Routledge is an imprint of the Taylor & Francis Group, an informa business*

*British Library Cataloguing-in-Publication Data*
A catalogue record for this book is available from the British Library

ISBN: 9780415703932 (hbk)
ISBN: 9780415703949 (pbk)
ISBN: 9781003559559 (ebk)

DOI: 10.4324/9781003559559

Typeset in Times New Roman
by codeMantra

Everyone once, once only. Just *once* and no more.
And we also once. Never again. But this having been
*once*, although only *once*, to have been of this earth,
seems irrevocable.

Rilke, 1923, *Duino Elegies,* p. 67

And so long as you haven't experienced this: to die and so to grow,
you are only a troubled guest on this dark earth.

Goethe, 1817, *The Holy Longing,* p. 61

For Alex, Ben, and Elaine

# Contents

# Acknowledgments

First and foremost, I would like to thank the patients with whom I have worked over the course of my career. They have granted me the privilege of entering into their lives and entrusted me with a care and concern for who they are. I am aware that I can be direct, straightforward, and challenging in my clinical style, but I appreciate how often my patients have had faith that in my candor I have held much goodwill for them in my heart. In allowing me to participate with the sharing of their most intimate secrets, they have taught me much about trust, openness, and the complexity of paradox in emotional and spiritual lives.

Many of my trainees and students over the years have contributed feedback that have helped shape the ideas appearing in this book. Similarly, the numerous individuals who have taken part in my Psychoanalytic/Existential study group also have greatly contributed inspiration to the thinking of this volume.

Steven Cooper, Jack Foehl, Steven Stern, Stan Selinger, and Frank Summers and I have shared enduring friendship and have been partners in stimulating conversations about all things pertinent to the human condition. I appreciate how they have contributed to this book in unknown, but real ways. My friend and colleague, Elizabeth Corpt, and I have co-chaired a Discussion Group at the annual American Psychoanalytic Meetings, which has been a venue for trying out and shaping the ideas of this volume. I greatly appreciate her continuing support of my work. I also want to thank my step-son Jeffry Kulp for his steady support of this work, as well as Josh Kulp and his wife Rachel.

I want to thank David deBoer and Drew McLeod for being valued friends. David also has been a trusted reader of this manuscript in its early stages. I am especially grateful to Sandra Buechler for her friendship and close reading of my manuscript. She has been of invaluable support to me and my work. She has provided wise counsel during this journey toward publication. I am also indebted to my copy editor, Kristopher Spring, for guiding, steering, and shaping this manuscript into publishable shape. I want to thank Kate Hawes at Routledge for her kindness and patience in waiting years for me to shape this work into book form.

My friend Mitchell Goldfarb has been my oldest and best friend for almost 60 years. Our lasting friendship began at a time when I most needed a friend. I now consider him my beloved family member. I will always appreciate my brother Steven Shabad for recommending that I read *Crime and Punishment* when I was 19 years old. Who knows if this book ever would have been written had I not been introduced to Dostoevsky's psychological genius?

I am grateful to my father Theodore Shabad for his good nature and ethic of hard work. His mantra of "get it done" helped me persevere through the more difficult times I spent in writing this book. Without my mother Leslie Shabad, this book certainly never would have happened. She, a high school graduate, had great psychological intuition and was a fount of philosophical wisdom about life. Most of all, I am forever grateful to her for her constant encouragement to express myself both in my hopes and my fears.

My sons Alex and Ben, my daughters-in-law Ally and Kristin and my grandsons Leo, Desi, Henry, and Vincent all continue to teach me the premium of love and family. That love has helped balance out my career ambitions and kept me away from the dangers of self-involvement that I warn against in the following pages.

My wife Elaine Shabad has been by my side for the past 27 years and during that time she has been a devoted partner and companion. Her unconditional love and support of my work have been with me every step of the way during the writing of this book. She has pushed and prodded me across the finish line, and I am forever indebted to her for that and her enduring warmth and generosity

# Introduction

## To Love and Lose, or Never to Have Loved at All

Did you ever say Yes to one joy? O my friends, then you said Yes to *all* woe as well. All things are chained and entwined together, all things are in love.
(Nietzsche, *Thus Spake Zarathustra*, 1889, pp. 331–332)

The world thinks it is dangerous in this way, and why? Because one might lose; the prudent thing is not to venture. And yet by not venturing it is so dreadfully easy to lose what would be hard to lose by venturing and which, whatever you lost you will in any case never lose in this way, so easily, so completely, as though it were nothing—oneself.
(Kierkegaard, *The Sickness unto Death*, 1849, p. 37)

### Loving and Leaving Moscow

In 2006, I made an emotional return journey to Moscow, Russia—the home of four and half years of my childhood. I lived in Moscow from 1961 to 1966 (ages 9–13) because my father was stationed there as a correspondent for the *New York Times*. I went to a Russian school and thoroughly immersed myself in the culture. After initially being fascinated by my alien American status that was dramatized by the fact that I never became a Young Pioneer (a youth group for future Communist Party membership), my classmates thoroughly accepted me as one of them. I learned a communicatively functional Russian, participated in scrap metal drives, and played soccer and hockey with my Russian friends.

Since my family lived in an apartment complex for foreign diplomats and journalists, I spent much time befriending children from all over the world. In the shared courtyard complex, I often played with Polish, Swedish, Hungarian, Turkish, Indonesian, and African children in an elaborate game of "Breakout"(similar to group freeze-tag), which often lasted hours on end. I alos vividly remember the sweet moment at the age of 10, when I enjoyed my first kiss with my Polish girlfriend as the '60s song "Sealed

DOI: 10.4324/9781003559559-1

with a Kiss" played in the background. For the most part, I was carefree and blithely oblivious to the tumultuous political events of the time such as the Cuban missile crisis, Kennedy's assassination, and Brezhnev's deposing of Khrushchev. I greatly enjoyed this rich life of "going on being" (Winnicott, (1956a) until it came crashing to a halt one day in November 1965.

On that occasion, after I returned home from my Russian school, my father greeted me with a grave expression on his face and said in an unusually somber tone: "Mom is very sick." When I asked what was wrong with her, he responded that she was having "strange ideas," but he did not elaborate further. When I went in to see her in her bedroom a few hours later, the curtains were drawn, and she, quite groggy, reached out to me with outstretched arms. Although I thought she must be dying, what I did not know at the time was that she was heavily sedated. It seems that many of the memories my mother had grown up with had wormed their way inside and now had caught up with her many years later.

My mother was born in Berlin and spent five years from 1933 to 1938 (ages 6–11) as a young Jewish girl living under Nazi rule. Three days after Kristallnacht, she, her mother, and older sister departed for good. In leaving Germany behind, she also bid farewell to her beloved father (who was divorced from her mother) aboard a boat in Hamburg harbor. She was never to see him again. In 1940, the Vichy police arrested my grandfather and, after spending two years in French internment camps, he was shipped off to Auschwitz in 1942. The bitter irony of it all is that my grandfather had been awarded the Iron Cross by Germany during World War I.

Many of my mother's personal demons concerning her parents' divorce and its splitting of loyalties, as well as the loss of her father with its consequent guilt, became conflated with the Cold War tensions of the time. My older brother had just left Moscow to go to Columbia University two months earlier, and that departure may well have triggered emotional memories of her final traumatic departure from her father and the guilt that she incurred thereafter. All of this finally bubbled to the surface in a paranoid episode in November of 1965 (at which time I was 13 years old). She had delusional fantasies that the KGB (the Sovier spy agency) and CIA (the American spy agency) would kidnap my brother and myself if she did not behave herself in just the right way. Although she was never hospitalized, the American embassy doctor had her heavily sedated and thought it best that she return to New York City to familiar surroundings and to be where her mother lived.

My father then made a fateful decision that was to have profound effects on the rest of my life. While escorting my mother back to New York, he thought it best that I remain in my familiar surroundings of school and friends until more was known where the family would be ultimately situated. In the meantime, I was left alone (my older brother had just departed for Columbia University two months earlier) in the care of our Russian housekeeper, Masha, with whom I was very close.

Very soon after my parents left, though, I became embroiled in a shouting match with Masha because of my fussiness over some food she had prepared for me. Things escalated, she got angry and left the house, leaving me to believe she was not coming back and that I was on my own. That evening, I went outside into the courtyard as I had numerous times before, except this time no one "had my back" at home, no one was waiting for me to return for dinner. I very much experienced what it meant to be alone, but strangely I did not feel lonely. I stared up at a clear starry night sky and uttered words to soothe myself that have framed my life perspective ever since: "Peter, as long as you don't die, you'll be okay." I derived much comfort from that thought that night, but I paid a subsequent price for the necessity of adapting to my traumatic experience of aloneness and then enclosing myself up in a relationship with myself.

Even though Masha eventually returned that evening and we exchanged a very emotional Russian reconciliation and hug, nothing was ever the same for me again. As a curtain drew on my carefree times of play and first love, I leapfrogged from childhood to adulthood in one fell swoop without ever really stopping at adolescence.

Two months later, my family returned to New York, and my life in Moscow came to an abrupt halt. My seventh-grade girl classmates gave me an engraved tea samovar and the boys gave me a soccer ball as goodbye gifts. As the car taking me to the airport left my beloved courtyard for a final time, I glanced up to see my Hungarian girlfriend (who had now supplanted my Polish girlfriend) standing on her balcony, waving goodbye at an age when she and I did not fully comprehend the difference between goodbye and farewell.

Unlike my brother, who remained emotionally tethered to his Russian friends for many years thereafter, upon my return to New York City I worked very hard to adapt to the shock of my mother's breakdown and the culture shock of dislocation to a 1966 American culture in the midst of radical change. Within the span of five short days (January 27–February 1,

1966), I went from a Russian school to a junior high public school in New York City, from the first kisses of puppy love to American girls smoking cigarettes on street corners, and from a Russian school, in which students stood up when the teacher entered the classroom, to an American school of students shooting spitballs at each other and getting up to go to the bathroom whenever they wanted. I felt as if I had been plucked out of a shared comradeship with my Russian peers and deposited in an alien time and place.

I was spontaneously drawn to old American movies of the '30s and '40s to help me make the transition from the relative innocence of my pre-pubescent life in Moscow to the adolescent jadedness characteristic of American youth in the '60s. My guilty sense—that my mother had suffered a breakdown because I had ignored her too much in my carefree play with my courtyard friends and Russian classmates—was now also accentuated by a burden of worry and care of watching over her to make sure she was doing okay.

In my haste to adapt to my new personal and cultural reality, I turned my back on my treasured experiences in Moscow, my relative fluency in Russian began to disappear, and the intense meanings of my life in Moscow faded into a dream-like limbo. Little did I know that I was incurring an existential guilt for forsaking a vital aspect of my personal heritage just because it could not endure. When the good was lost, it became too painful to feel my love for Moscow any longer, so for the sake of getting on with life with a measure of repressive equanimity, I disavowed its importance to me.

For many years thereafter, though, something inside of me about what I had left behind in Moscow kept gnawing at me. In my memory, my experiences in Moscow had transformed too much into a dream. I knew that I had to make a return visit to make it all feel real again.

When my wife and I finally arrived in Moscow in 2006, my best friend in the fifth grade, Sasha, picked me up at the airport and graciously hosted us for the four days we were there. So much had changed. The whole city was disconcertingly Western for me. Where was the Russian soul that I so dearly loved and left behind? Where was that rich sense of community and kinship (I truly loved the shared experience of exploring courtyards all over Moscow for those scrap metal drives!) that is earned through shared suffering and decidedly not through a competition to wear the latest fashions? In my consternation, I asked Sasha, "Aren't you afraid that with all this materialism, you are going to lose your Russian soul?" He responded, "Peter, did you forget how bare our shelves were then?" I found a brief reprieve to my nostalgia for all things Soviet when we visited a huge flea market, and I encountered familiar anti-capitalist posters with hammer-and-sickles that brought a warm sentimental glow to my heart.

Perhaps most disturbing was the fact that the apartment complex in which my family had lived in the '60s had gone through a fundamental makeover. The netless tennis courts of the neighboring Lebanese embassy, which we courtyard children had snuck into and transformed, with the help of many buckets of water, into a makeshift hockey rink, now seemed so small and puny. My old school was still there but locked up for the summer. So little remained as it had been!

By neglecting my beloved experiences in Moscow, I had compounded my sense of loss, and upon my return visit in 2006, my sense of self-alienation had brought in its wake a keen sense of intense yearning and homesickness for what once had been my life. I found to my disillusionment that I could not go back to the same "hunting grounds" that I had once inhabited with such emotional richness, and I could not duplicate the same experience that I had back then. Life, and I with it, in spite of wishing otherwise, had been swept along by the ongoing tides of change. It is this deceptive mirage of empty nostalgia, a past to which we can never really "go home again," which Kierkegaard (1843b) refers to as "recollection" as opposed to the committed "repetition" of fully embodied action that moves toward the future.

On the day of our departure, Sasha organized a small class reunion in my honor for a short hour before leaving for the airport. My classmates and I did much laughing, reminiscing, vodka drinking, and toasting during that hour. They informed me that they got together for a reunion each year (they were a very close-knit class who had stayed together through the 12th grade), and at each gathering they made a toast to me. For a too brief period, I was in my element again, enveloped by the collective Russian warmth I had missed so dearly. As we departed, one classmate gave me a picture of amber to symbolize how our shared experiences had never been forgotten and would be preserved forever.

Later on the airplane, as I began speaking with my wife about these last precious hours, I suddenly erupted into tears. I realized that I was crying not only for the present, but for being extracted from a togetherness long ago, an injury that I never let myself mourn. I had never really said farewell; I had renounced my beloved experiences because I could not endure their finality, leaving them to be frozen phantoms in time. But now, finally, through my bittersweet return journey, a vital era of my heritage that had been left for "dead" was brought back to emotional life.

In many traditions, wisdom means coming to terms with the ephemeral, ever-changing features of life. Perhaps one of the primary reasons that the body is viewed as burdensome in many religions is because of its essential tendency to decay and die, whereas the soul is celebrated for its everlasting quality. We devalue what is perishable. In a sense, our mortality, the decaying body itself, is the ultimate insult that makes a mockery of our pretensions to the perfection of eternity. This fatal flaw can become a source of existential shame or *sin*.

In contrast to the religious worldview, Freud (1916) suggests in his brief essay *On Transience* that it is precisely the perishable, ephemeral aspects of life that we must treasure because they are here now and gone tomorrow. Loss, far from minimizing what is short-lived, enhances the preciousness of that which will not last forever.

One religion that has attempted to directly address the suffering engendered by impermanence is Buddhism. Buddhist philosophy advocates for a stoic acceptance of the fact of change, to not become too attached to any one thing since it is that fruitlessly defiant protest of clinging to attachments against the flowing current of change that causes heartache.

These contrasting views on how the brevity of an individual life is to be valued parallel the dilemma inherent in the elemental question: "Is it better to have loved and lost, or never to have loved at all?" The question derives from Tennyson's (1850) poem *In Memoriam A.H.H*, in which he declares affirmatively: "Tis better to have loved and lost than never to have loved at all." Yet when we are traumatized by a definitive limit or overwhelming obstacle in our path, we are tempted to turn tail and "take our ball and go home." We seem to say that if we must suffer the tremendous heartache of losing, or to have nothing at all, it is better then to have nothing. In the immediate aftermath of loss, we rarely see that life does indeed go on and that time does heal at least some part of all wounds. In some form and to some degree, if we allow ourselves access to the resilient regenerative quality of our passion, we may hope and love and lose—and love again.

I, too, learned the difficult lesson from my Moscow experience that when one becomes attached passionately to a person or place, one may be ambushed suddenly by the loss of what one holds most precious. Unbeknownst to me, I resolved not to love my experiences in Moscow any longer because of the suffering entailed in losing something that could not last. In relegating Moscow to my own personal oblivion, I compounded the actual loss that I had to endure anyway. I subsequently paid dearly for my own self-immobilization.

Since I never put my body and soul in a farewell for which I was not prepared, I refused to take in and mourn the finality of my experiences into my emotional bloodstream. I therefore also was not able to use their meaningfulness to me as strength for my ongoing journey. The ghosts of Moscow were never laid to rest in their proper place in the past, memories that could have had an ever-revitalizing role to play in the ongoing continuity of my life. Instead, they became a haunting spectre, stuck in time not really of the past nor of the present.

At the same time that I numbed myself to the full emotional impact of the life and death of my time in Moscow, I paradoxically held on tenaciously to those experiences for dear life. I therefore did not fully accept the fact that I was now in New York, that the American kids my own age were quite different and more jaded than my Russian friends, and that I now had to give myself over to a very new environment. For the crucial ages of 14–19, I retreated within and passed up numerous opportunities of youth, which I have since lived to regret.

Yet I have learned how to cope with my regret by understanding, accepting, and even embracing the fact that I cannot judge myself accurately in hindsight. What was lived out at the time had to be experienced first; each lived moment of our lives is finite and cannot be reversed. We can only understand and learn the best we can as we go along.

It is perhaps ironic that in my attempt not to love and lose, I turned my back on important life lessons my mother taught me about remaining open not only to the joyful experiences of life, but to its disruptive and frightening visage as well. I opened my last book with an anecdote that I will repeat here, because it was emblematic of the values of my childhood, which, in turn, have influenced my attitudes toward life and my clinical values.

When I was about five years old, I had a nightmare after seeing the Disney film *Snow White and the Seven Dwarfs*. I was overwhelmed by the terrifying profile of the cackling witch looming very large before me and cried for help. My mother came into the room, calmed me down after

I recounted my terror, and then immediately before leaving again, said: "Now think about the witch, so you don't dream about her."

Little did I know at the time that I was being introduced into the most basic tenets of Freud's talking cure: To confront and speak toward and about what is most frightening, what one most dreads, what bothers or disturbs one the most, so it does not ambush one later on when one least suspects it to do so.

Since my mother died in 2015, I have been most grateful to her for encouraging me to express myself openly in my joy and excitement, as well as in my upset and my anger. She taught me to be open and true to my desires rather than to cover them over, regardless of whether they were fulfilled in the real world or not. Indeed, already as a child, I began to notice stark differences between my friends as to whether they acknowledged what they wanted more openly or whether they tried to pretend to themselves that they did not want what they thought would not come true in the outside world. In my own mind at the time, I referred to this difference as people who prioritize happiness because they retained clear access to what they want versus people who prioritize the cover-up of their pride by "bracing for disappointment." In my clinical work to this day, I still hold to a firm conviction in the healing components of the talking cure to dissolve the power of the inner demons that haunt all of us, and to help my patients open up the vulnerability of their hearts to life rather than to close it down.

My struggle to love and lose and then attempting not to love so much again in many ways continues a primary theme that I explored in my first book, *Despair and the Return of Hope: Echoes of Mourning in Psychotherapy* (Shabad, 2001), which was published more than 20 years ago. In that volume, I explored a parallel concern of how hope and disillusionment lead to a defensive attempt not to hope so much again. More specifically, I examined how traumatic and significant disillusioning experiences suffered in relationship to one's parents lead to constricting defenses that are designed to prevent further injury but instead hinder the expression of our life force.

In the more than 20 years since that book's publication, I have given myself ample time to let those themes further percolate. From both my clinical and life experiences, I became aware of the self-paralyzing havoc that shame wreaks in people's lives. Whereas in the first book, I mainly explored defenses against wishing and desiring, in this volume I examine how those defenses are actually reflexive, automatic reactions of shame and self-consciousness to significant ruptures in early relationships. In the attempt to cover over one's sense of rejected vulnerability and prevent further injury, shame increasingly entraps a person within an enclosed prison of self-enclosed isolation.

Moreover, within that prison, the individual tragically believes there is something wrong or sinful or off in the very essence of her being, when actually there is nothing wrong at all. Yet that misapprehension and doubt about one's basic goodness leads to a slew of life problems: self-inhibition, anxiety about going forward in life, self-pity in retreating from life, envy of all the others who are more fortunate, resentment at the powers that be, and entitlement to some recompense from life. Ultimately, one incurs much despair and regret because of retreating from the anxieties of imagining and anticipating the losses and disillusionments that await one in the future. In the meantime, the preciously irreversible opportunities and experiences of life pass one by.

It is not a coincidence at all, then, that I have titled this book: *Passion, Shame, and The Freedom To Become: Seizing The Vital Moment in Psychoanalysis.* In the use of that title, I am not only referring to the importance of grabbing and fulfilling each passing moment of life, but also thinking of the entirety of one's uniquely different individual life as a significant moment in the history and evolution of time on earth. The significance of our individual lives is grounded simultaneously in its all-too-painful finiteness and the precious, even eternal meaning of its passing moment in the sun. Yet what is special about the gift of life we have received is the uniqueness of our individuality; no one just like us has ever been before, and no one just like us will ever live again. In this sense, we have an existential responsibility to "seize the moment" afforded us by this gift of unique life and fulfill our individuality in love, work, and play before we die.

Isn't the problem of loving and losing from which I was retreating only a dramatic extension of the fundamental human dilemma of accepting the ongoing passing of life itself? Yes, the traumatic disruption of my "continuity of being" (Winnicott, 1956a, 1956b) rudely ushered in an awareness of the inevitable; nevertheless, I was not going to be able to stay *that age at that place at that time* in any case. It was all going to pass, and it is that unrelenting change and impermanence with which we all must struggle. How then do we truly live before dying?

Sometimes when we are confronted with an amalgam of wants and shoulds in the midst of making a life decision, we can gain access to our conscience by simply inquiring of ourselves:

> Imagine that you are on your deathbed and looking back at this moment in time, how would you have liked to have lived out this moment? What choice would you like to make? Which decision are you least likely to regret?

This projection of oneself to the time immediately preceding one's death may thus be used as a mirror reflecting back to each evolving moment how we can best live according to the authority of our conscience. Paul Tillich (1952) has said:

> Man's being is not only given to him but also demanded of him. He is responsible for it; literally, he is required to answer, if he is asked, *what he has made of himself.* He who asks him is his judge, namely he himself.
>
> (p. 52)

Perhaps, however, we don't even always have to go so far off into the future to uncover who we are today. If each new day were to be viewed as a metaphor for one's conduct in life, then the reverie state of unbidden thoughts that often visits us at the end of each day and before we dissolve into sleep may be used as a daily caution to us concerning those aspects of our lives that once more we passed over unreflectively. Often, these unguarded moments of meditative reverie are sending a "warning shot across the bow" to address an aspect of our lives we have avoided before we suffer the bitter pangs of regret for a life left unconsumed by the fires of our passion. These are the stakes in the decisions to love and lose passionately or never to love at all. It is really a matter of living and dying or never having truly lived at all.

# Chapter 1

# In the Shadow of Death

## Freedom and the Passion to Become

The confrontation with death—and the reprieve from it—makes everything look so precious, so sacred, so beautiful that I feel more strongly than ever the impulse to love it, to embrace it, and to let myself be overwhelmed by it. My river has never looked so beautiful... Death, and its ever-present possibility makes love, passionate love, more possible. I wonder if we could love passionately, if ecstasy would be possible at all if we knew we'd never die.

From a letter by Abraham Maslow while recuperating from a heart attack

(In May, *Love and Will*, 1969, p. 99)

Such a caring for death, an awakening that keeps vigil over death, a conscience that looks death in the face, is another name for freedom.

(Derrida, *The Gift of Death*, 1999, p. 17)

## The Passion to Become

*How are we able* to relinquish the apparent safety of our attachment to the familiar and engage change with open hearts and minds? What enables us to grow and transform into a different person than we are today? The divide between this moment and the next is a chasm that we continually cross without thinking about it, mostly because of the taken-for-granted force of our developmental passion. When a four-year-old child spots a toy store 50 yards away and speeds toward it immediately, she is taking steps in an unfolding time and space without hesitation due to anxieties or fears about encountering novelty. It is only when we lose access to that passion and become paralyzed by passivity that we notice how difficult it is to make transitions of our lives. Our capacity to use this passionate life force is fundamental to the developmental movement from "who I am today" toward "who I will be tomorrow," and from "who I am here" toward "who you are

DOI: 10.4324/9781003559559-2

there." As Bachelard (1932) puts it: "A being that offers itself to life, in its passion for novelty, is itself inclined to welcome the present as a promise of the future" (p. 38).

The unfolding movement of passionate becoming is always intertwined with a sense of expectant hope. When my dog Andy chased a squirrel, his thinking, feeling, and imagination all were animated by the expectant hope of catching the squirrel and embedded in the purposeful action of chase.

What is this passion to become of which I am speaking? The pre-Socratic philosopher Heraclitus (500 BCE) uses a metaphor of a river to describe life in a constant state of flux: "One cannot step twice into the same river, no one can grasp any mortal substance in stable condition; but it scatters and again gathers; it forms and dissolves, and approaches and departs" (p. li). The river of passionate becoming also is forever evolving through the force of its current; a current that resembles Bergson's (1907) notion of an *élan vital* or "vital impetus" animating creative evolution. Inasmuch as the death of each moment is instantaneously replaced by the birth of new moments, the processes of creation, destruction, and re-creation are intrinsic to the continuing evolution of this passionate life force. The relentlessly moving river of passion does not stop for anything; it does not take a final "No" for an answer. It does not yield to death, defeat, or loss, but like the mythological Phoenix rising from its own ashes, passion spontaneously regenerates in the wake of loss.

Whether a mother is tilting her head down toward her baby's smile, a dog is chasing a rabbit, or a bee is pollinating a flower, there are many ways in which each living being expresses the directedness of its own passionate life force. Maslow (1962) states:

> Man demonstrates in his own nature a pressure toward fuller and fuller Being, more and more perfect actualization of his humanness in exactly the same naturalistic, scientific way that an acorn may be said to be "pressing toward" being an oak tree, or that a tiger may be observed to "push toward" to being tigerish or a horse toward being equine....
>
> (p. 160)

These different forms of spontaneous expression constitute a subjective freedom of intentionality or will with which each organism shapes its passion. Spinoza (1677), in considering natural organisms, says: "Each thing, as far as it is in itself, endeavors to persevere in its being" (III, Prop 6). He thus considers virtue to be "the unfolding of the specific potentialities of every organism" (IV, Prop 24).

Nietzsche (1887) refers to this force of life as having an "instinct for freedom" (p. 87). In *Beyond the Pleasure Principle*, Freud (1920), too, describes self-preservation, self-assertion, and mastery as "component instincts whose function is to assure that the organism shall follow its own path to death ... the organism wishes to die only in its own fashion" (p. 39). I view this freedom of each being to live and die "in its own fashion" as fundamental to the subjective dignity of each organism.

Farber (1966) referred to this spontaneous, unconscious intentionality as the "will of the first realm," in contrast to a more consciously purposive will of the second realm. According to Farber, the unconscious will of the first realm moves in a general direction, not toward a specific thing, and its predominant experience is freedom. Significantly, he continues, this direction is a "way whose end cannot be known—a way open to possibilities including the possibility of failure" (p. 9).

Farber's view of freedom of will as an unfolding process into a world of multiple possibilities decoupled from any particular outcome has important implications. When the process of freely willing is tethered to the aim of attaining a particular love from a particular person or wedded to a certain number of people coming to one's birthday party, one's freedom is constrained by the need to reach that preconceived end. To the extent that moral weightings of good and bad are then further attached to whether one has reached one's goals, a moralistic pressure dictated by outcome will be imposed on the process of willing, which corrupts the integrity of its unfolding freedom.

Otto Rank (1936), who made the notion of creative will a centerpiece of his "will psychology," suggested that the artistic process of creativity was intrinsic to the daily self-creation and re-creation of one's own personality. In emphasizing the notion of intentionality and will, I am also very much emphasizing the active, continually dynamic quality of our minds. Our experiences do not just impress themselves on us as if we were empty, blank slate beings; rather, we are always superimposing meaning upon our experiences and creatively transforming them into something quite different than they may look to the outside observer. In this sense, the active intentionality of our passionate life force lends each person a dignity of subjectivity by creating an ongoing narrative in which our minds transform the events of our lives into meaningful personal experiences.

## The Challenge of Mortality: Becoming a Singular Individual

The mortal limitations to our lives, always present in the fact that we exist in one body at one time and one place, are a major challenge to our passionate sense of organismic freedom. It is humbling to consider, for example, that the whole of a person's life is but a droplet in the evolutionary river of the cosmos. Pascal (1670) speaks eloquently about this fundamental limitation of our human condition:

> When I consider the brief span of my life, swallowed up in the eternity before and behind it, the small space that I fill, or even see, engulfed in the infinite immensity of spaces which I know not, and which know not me, I am afraid, and wonder to see myself here rather than there, now rather than then.
>
> (p. 36)

Through loss and limitation, Becker (1973) suggests that death seems to remind us daily that we are not only the lordly creators of our destiny, but also creaturely pawns of forces beyond our control. The randomness with which death cuts short young lives and deprives us of our most cherished relationships seems to strip life of all meaning. The limits to the reach of our powers are everywhere; other people seem stubbornly not to bend to our wishes, or worse, they interfere with our own private path; the mysteries of the future abide only by the unfathomable laws of its unwinding path. We descend into despair about being subjected to the mercies of an impassive fate, which will not heed our plaintive cries for justice. More than a few teenagers and young adults, while pondering questions regarding meaning and purpose, have wondered about the seeming absurdity of being born into a world of passionate attachments only to have to give them up at a later date.

The limits that mortality imposes on the passing of the life we inhabit only as guests seem to intrude into the spontaneous unfolding of the passionate freedom to become. Yet precisely because we do not have all the time in the world to do whatever our heart desires, the time we have allotted to us takes on great value. In contrast to Plato's (360 BCE) thinking and the teachings of many religions, in which meaning derives from the eternal "forms" or the everlasting "soul," Freud (1916) suggests that it is precisely life's brevity that enhances its value. It is precisely because of the shortness of this life that we must set a hierarchy of priorities of how to make best use of that time.

In this sense, Hoffman (1998) notes that our mortality makes it necessary to create meaning in our lives. The ultimate limits on our life necessitate that we set priorities on how we spend the precious moments of an oh-so-briefly illuminated life. Since having but one life in one body constrains our possibilities of being in more than one place at one time, our mortality infuses the freedom of our passion with a deadly seriousness such that our unconscious intentions are necessarily transformed into committed choices. Our deaths belong to each one of us as an inextricable aspect of our lives, adding a tragic depth of personal necessity and form to the spontaneous unfolding of our life force. Derrida (1999) declares:

> Now to have the experience of responsibility on the basis of the law that is given, to have the experience of one's own absolute singularity and apprehend one's own death, amounts to the same thing. Death is very much that which nobody else can undergo or confront in my place. My irreplaceability is therefore conferred, delivered, "given," one can say, by death.
>
> (p. 47)

The "gift of death" that is conferred on and belongs to each one of us is the irreducible, unprecedented, and unrepeatable essence of our unique individuality, as well as the freedom of choice and responsibility that comes with that gift. In the epigraph to this chapter, Derrida (1999) illuminates how our answerability for our life and death, as mediated by our conscience, is rooted in our fundamental freedom as unique individuals. No one just like us has ever existed before, and no one just like us will ever be born again. Derrida continues: "It is from the perspective of death as the place of my irreplaceability, that is, of my singularity, that I feel called to responsibility" (p. 470).

The choices we make in carving out our own path in life may weigh us down as a burden, but our freedom to choose for ourselves is a great gift and privilege that life has bestowed upon us. Nietzsche (1873) speaks to this great sense of responsibility:

> No one can build thee the bridge over which you must cross the river of life—save thyself alone. There are paths and bridges and demi-gods

without number, that will gladly carry thee over, but only at the price of thine own self: thy self wouldst thou have to give in pawn, and then lose it. There is in the world one road whereon none may go, except thou: ask not whither it leads, but go forward…

(p. 3)

Perhaps this necessary aspect of mortal limitation or "lack" is built into the passionate quest of desire itself already (Lacan, 1966). After all, desire often attaches itself to particular outcomes, to personally chosen spouses, friends, and careers. If it were not so, we would resemble impersonal abstractions of "universal man" rather than flesh-and-blood individuals who actively create concretely personal experiences, make choices, and renew commitments. The tenacity with which we attach and hold on to love relationships implied by Freud's (1905) term "adhesiveness of the libido" infuses personal meaning into our lives. As Kierkegaard (1849) has suggested, it is important to strike a balance between possibility and necessity, between the spontaneously unfolding freedom of passion and the personalized shaping of choices to which we commit our signature in order to find meaning.

Our mortality then holds a paradoxical but fundamental place in all of our lives. Insofar as our deaths signify an end or rupture to our "continuity of being" (Winnicott, 1949), our death may be experienced as an unfeelingly impenetrable wall that abruptly halts any ambitions or purposes we may have hoped to achieve. By the very fact that death delimits our passions, however, it also enables us to know where our familiar inner worlds end and a "real" world out there begins. Without containing limits, we would not be able to anchor ourselves in the sanity of discerning between what are extensions of our imaginations and what reality endures independently of the wishful or fearful constructions of our minds. I imagine a limitless world would be akin to landing on the moon and encountering the desolation of an unending empty landscape. That would be a meaningless life indeed! In the most profound sense, our limitations, by circumscribing the contours around our individual lives, provide us, at least, with the potentiality of transcendent meaning, if only we did not become demoralized by a despairing sense of helplessness.

It is precisely because our deaths are automatically built into our genetic hourglasses—that is, from conception onwards as we are living we also are dying—we seem to be constituted in such a way psychologically and spiritually so as to be on a quest for transcendent meaning in which we realize the *quality* of our lives. The shadows of our mortality exist within each change or transition, whether it be the end of childhood or high school or the empty nest experience of parenthood, or perhaps more mundanely, the end of an evening out on the town. Each of our experiences is different and unique and will not duplicate itself ever again. Each one of us is charged with the responsibility of "seizing the moment" of our brief lives.

Yet whether it is because we are simply limited by the organismic constraints of being imperfectly human, or because our defenses rigidly shield us not only from threat but also from opportunity, we seem unable to distill the preciousness of life as we are living it. Indeed, we may observe that whenever we do not pass through a stage of life as successfully as we would have liked, we get stuck; we delay our leave-taking indefinitely and attempt to relive and redress what went wrong, as if begging the powers that be for one more chance to get it right. In this sense, I have wondered at times whether the inability to seize the moment with regard to the *quality* of our lives leads to a desperate urgency to extend the *quantity* of our lives.

Perhaps, then, rather than reducing the urge for transcendence to a consolation prize as compared with the immortality that we cannot ever attain, the concept of transcendence may be viewed as having primary significance in and of itself. In fact, it may be worth asking if our constant craving for more time, our need for immortality itself, derives from our inability to realize our lives and relationships while we are living them.

When we become too overwhelmed by and fearfully retreat from limitations that seem like insurmountable barriers to any creation of meaning by denying death, we may become locked into an endless cycle of indefinite procrastination, despair, and regret over the missed opportunities of an unlived life. It is thus an existential and spiritual human imperative to "befriend" the alien, Other quality of our own death and its continual shadow of limitation, change, and transition as an intrinsic aspect of our lives. Only then can we transcend its challenges.

## Self-Realization and the Necessary Element of Otherness

While our personal journeys may be shaped by creative passion, that passion alone is not enough to create meaning. Our mortal limitations in time and place require that we find meaning outside the isolation of our individual existence. We cannot live meaningfully only in and of ourselves as self-creating individuals.

Levinas (1969) suggests that there is an abyss between the subjective me and the "Otherness" of mystery, whether that mystery be the otherness of death, of God, or the essential difference of another person. I would add that the unknown ambiguities of the future, as opposed to the familiarities of the here-and-now, also could be included as an important aspect of this multi-faceted visage of Otherness. For Levinas, the ethical responsibility of each human being is shaped by coming "face-to-face" with this uncontrollable mystery of the Other. Miller (1995), too, states that the movement toward the embrace of the stranger involves a crisis in which one opens up with all of one's wounded vulnerability to welcome the stranger in his strangeness. Welcoming the stranger in his strangeness entails an acceptance of the unfamiliar, unpredictable, and uncontrollable aspects of Otherness.

Looked at in this way, the passionate life force to create, grow, and make meaning is rooted in a drive for transcendent self-realization in which we creatively devote our lives to an Other beyond ourselves, whether that be God, our children, or the essential difference of another person. The term "transcendent" here refers then to the passionate movement toward an Other who transcends or lies beyond oneself. As Foss (1949) puts it:

> Wherever life becomes conscious of its creativity, it is faced by a living entity, the "Thou," and this Thou is to the I a revelation of its own meaning and future. It is always a Thou, as an expression of life which carries the I forward and makes it aware of its destiny.
>
> (p. 75)

This interplay with an Other is a necessary counterpoint to the provision of a sense of realization intrinsic to the attainment of meaning. Self-realization ultimately requires that a threshold be crossed from an insulated world of our own making to one that is beyond our creative control, one in which we encounter the genuine dimensions of Otherness. We arrive at some semblance of self-realization when we recognize that an Other who lies beyond our omnipotent reach has registered and recognized our presence. Foss (1949) again states:

> The I, to be sure, remains the potential, but a potential for the Thou which reveals and expresses the I in its movement upward and beyond. In the process of life, *expression always means communication* with a

Thou which is never fully realized but remains an inexhaustible power, leading on into a meaningful future.

(p. 75, italics added)

The realization-derealization dimension of human experience has been somewhat underappreciated in psychoanalysis, and yet it is precisely a sense of the real through which we all derive a modicum of sanity. Whereas realization refers to a sense of one's experience as grounded and real, a sense of derealization characterizes the subjective experience of one's life as hallucinatory and dreamlike. Freud (1936) described derealization when he first glimpsed the wonder of the Pyramids and declared, "What I see here is not real" (p. 244).

We could say that realization of experience occurs when we are able to internalize the meaning of our experiences into our emotional bloodstream, to really allow the import of our experiences to "sink in." Even though we may remind ourselves that our loved ones could die tomorrow, we may get angry or hold grudges about petty matters that would evaporate instantly if we heard that the loved one had 24 hours to live. By not fully internalizing the otherness of the mortality of loved ones—or our own, for that matter— we are hindered in our ability to fully realize experience. A wife may hear her husband's insistent words "But I *do* love you" and somehow know that the husband is conveying his sincere feelings, but it is a quite different matter for her to actually believe his words and let their meaning penetrate her emotional bloodstream.

We seem to be inherently limited in allowing ourselves the open-heartedness to completely realize the mortal import of our experiences; there often seems to be something ever-elusive about the actuality of our experiences that is difficult to fully take in. Perhaps this limitation derives from the constancy of the defenses that we have that are necessary for our survival. Along these lines, whenever we experience something traumatic, we automatically protect ourselves by defensively dissociating from the experience. In so doing, we are attempting to keep the experience of traumatic threat at a safe distance from our psychic core, to disown rather than to internalize. It is because these disowned experiences do not get taken in and dissolve into our unfolding emotional bloodstream, and instead become "stuck in the craw," that our lives may become stuck and governed by a fixed preoccupation on the unaccepted, uninternalized, and ultimately unrealized.

Winnicott's (1960b) concept of an "area of omnipotence" is of great relevance to the dimensions of realization-derealization. The denial and obliteration of the boundaries of otherness in one's omnipotent self-extension in time and space lends itself to a sense of derealization very quickly. When through our mind's eye we believe that we entirely create the good or bad fortunes that we encounter, it becomes difficult to differentiate between the world as a dreamlike hallucination of our own making and a reality that exists beyond any powers we may possess. Our minds are so creatively dynamic and imaginative that we continually superimpose our own constructed meanings on our experiences as soon as they occur, at which point we no longer may be able to discern the "event" of actual experience apart from the meanings, which we have superimposed upon that event.

Indeed, since we are inherently creative beings, we cannot help but perceive others through a creative "transference" filter, in which the new we find is reframed in terms of what is familiar, at least to some extent. Human beings are inherently limited in the extent to which they can discover others independent of their own omnipotent minds. There is a way in which because of the creative aspects of our passion, we are not able to recognize the other who lies beyond our mind's eye. In our omnipotence, we creatively swalllow up or "totalize" other persons as incorporated object representations in our own minds. (Levinas, 1969). Perhaps in a strange way, the human capacity to realize experiences with a different Other is delimited by an element in all relationships that is self-created and therefore ultimately circular. Perhaps that is as it must be.

Our re-creation of new experiences in terms that are at least somewhat familiar enables us to anchor ourselves in the experiential continuity of what Winnicott (1956a) refers to as "going on being." At the same time that we are opening ourselves up and welcoming in new experiences, we are simultaneously remaking and metabolizing them as a part of an ongoing pattern of experience that we recognize as ourselves. Our perceptual transference filters provide us with a recognizable kinship between our past and future, and between ourselves and the radically alien quality of Otherness.

Without the orienting compass of this self-recognizing lens, we would feel as if our minds were on an attentional and attachment swivel when experiencing anything new. In a peculiar way, perhaps our transferences, by reducing the risk of being overstimulated by novelty and change, serve the same delimiting function for our minds that inhibitory neurons serve with regard to excitatory neurons in the sensory-perceptual systems of the body, such as the eye. Through the complementary balancing of excitatory and inhibiting neurons, we are able to perceive where an object begins and where it ends, thereby allowing us to make out its form.

The human tendency to infuse ourselves as prime mover of our experiences, or put differently, our mind's tendency to project our inner life and re-create the world of external events in the image of our mind's eye, also may lend itself to a sense of derealization, which is at the core of paranoid experience. Encountering something that is clearly externally "real" that is bad, such as a physical illness, is often preferable to the crazy-making ambiguity of not being able to discern whether we are imagining our illness or there is actually something "wrong" with us. We may struggle against the enemy, opponent, or antagonist that hits us straight in the face, but at least we do not lose our grounding of the real that is characteristic of paranoia.

To the extent that we can never fully relinquish our re-creative tendency to insert our minds into the new people we meet, the capacity to fully realize the intersubjective quality of human relationships ultimately is limited. Winnicott (1951) reminds us: "It is assumed here that the task of reality acceptance is never completed, that no human being is free from the strain of relating inner and outer reality" (p. 240).

The passionate striving toward the Other may then be viewed as a lifelong process of creating and finding the Other. In the beginning of life, the Other is not recognized as such but as primarily a mirror of one's own creation. Benjamin (1988) says:

> The need of the self is paradoxical, because the self is trying to establish itself as an absolute, an independent entity, yet he must recognize the other as like himself in order to be recognized by him. He must be able to find himself in the other.

> (p. 32)

The transitions and growth of human development proceed through the self-affirmative suffering of passion, in which we strive to relinquish our omnipotent creative control in order to find Otherness through which we can realize our lives. Winnicott (1968) describes this process of letting go eloquently:

> We have to say that the baby created the breast, but could not have done so had not the mother come along with the breast just at that moment.

The communication to the baby is: "Come at the world, creatively, create the world. It is only what you create that has meaning for you." Next comes: "The world is in your control." From this initial *experience of omnipotence* the baby is able to begin to experience frustration and even to arrive one date at the other extreme from omnipotence, that is to say, having a sense of being a mere speck in a universe, in a universe that was there before the baby was conceived by two parents who were enjoying each other. Is it not from *being God* that human beings arrive at the humility proper to human individuality?

(p. 101)

## Suffering Passion: The Arduous Journey from Self to Other

Winnicott (1969) and Benjamin (1988) have suggested that in order to achieve a realization of experience, we must be able to recognize others not only as fantasied objects of our omnipotent making, but also as their own persons who are independent of our omnipotence.

When we deny the deaths of loved ones and take for granted that they will be with us forever, we lose a sense of their Otherness, as mortal subjects in their own right rather than possessed objects of our indefinitely extending omnipotence. Without the capacity to imagine the deaths of loved ones, we also cannot renew the relationship through its imagined rebirth. When the process of birth, death, and rebirth is thus stymied, and we take for granted that the other person will live on indefinitely, passion may become dammed up and the relationship will grow stale. Indeed, in the epigraph to this chapter, Maslow touchingly and vividly articulates this intimate link between confronting death and the capacity to love. (May, 1969)

The implicit acceptance of the tragic limitations to one's individuality inherent in giving oneself to an Other requires us to "suffer our passion" with intact courage. The word "passion" derives from the Latin *passionem*, or suffering, enduring. Perhaps it is in this sense of passion as endured suffering that we can understand also the overlapping meanings of suffering in our *patients* and the meaning of enduring suffering in *patience*. To "suffer" passion is to be disciplined and patient enough to negotiate the transitions and way stations along the way toward our desired aims. Instead of adhering to the magical thinking of our own minds in which we are able to move from a conceived wish to its imagined gratification instantaneously, suffering passion involves the process of relinquishing the time-traveling magic of our minds and patiently enduring the unfolding of life in a time frame beyond our control. Such endurance may involve the need to wait for the responsive receptivity of others on whom we depend, or we may have to negotiate our way patiently through the discipline of hard work and various frustrations in order to persevere in an active quest to reach our passionate heart's desire, our own unique Holy Grail.

To the extent that the changes required to engage the unfolding of our own unpredictable growth then parallel the shifts in perspective necessary to reach out to the inscrutable mystery of strangers, the "suffering" of our passion is centrally implicated in our evolution as ethical individuals. When I use the term "suffering passion," I am referring to the capacity and willingness to use our passion to help see us through the numerous transitions that occur in life that often are experienced as losses. Letting go of a preoccupation with who one has been to engage the future possibilities of who one could be differently implies also an emergent movement from a "loyalty to oneself and one's own kind," whether that is one's own family, nation, religion, tribe, race, or species, to an embrace of the "stranger" in our midst.

The experience of pleasure or joy from what we frequently refer to as "happiness" is very different than the "self-fulfillment" that derives from the experience of embracing the transitions of our lives. Aristotle's (332 BCE) concept of *eudaimonia*, literally translated as "good spirit" from the Greek, corresponds to this notion of self-fulfillment. Maslow (1962) describes this bittersweet aspect of life:

> Growth has not only rewards and pleasures but also many intrinsic pains... Each step forward is a step into the unfamiliar and possibly dangerous. It frequently means a parting and a separation, even a kind of death prior to rebirth, with consequent nostalgia, fear, loneliness, and mourning.
>
> (p. 190)

When we make creative use of our passion and are at one with the internal necessity of surrendering to the future, these losses or changes may be imperceptible. For example, unbeknownst to themselves, children may be learning the notion of respect for the right of others to their own self-determining choices without knowing it by engaging in the pleasures and endured patience of "taking turns" in board games. As adults too, we may voluntarily make way for a better life for our children than what we may have had ourselves.

As human agents, we are charged with the responsibility of fulfilling ourselves before we die, of continually "choosing ourselves in action" in Kierkegaard's (1843c) words. Hoffman (1998) declares: "To choose is to absorb sacrifice, loss, and the relentless loss of time" (p. 25). The choices we make and the transitions we move through are constituted by the creative self-dying and the construction of reborn meanings through realized relationship. Perhaps paradoxically, then, human agency may be viewed as the individualized form through which we suffer our passion by shaping ourselves as creative vessels to be surrendered to someone other than ourselves. A receptive response from an Other mirrors back the special contribution that we are making, providing us at once with both a sense of belonging and significance as individuals who have something of unique value to offer, thereby infusing our labors of passion with meaning.

On the other hand, when we lose access to our passion, we also tend to desperately hold on to the way things have always been, because we lose a confidence that we can overcome the anticipatory anxieties of making transitions into an unknown future, in fear of becoming the unknown person who we will become. The dread of enduring the exposed vulnerability of reaching out to others may be so daunting that many individuals retreat from their anxieties entirely. They struggle mightily with the question of whether it is better to love and lose or to never love at all, or to hope and be disillusioned again or never hope at all. This dilemma is very much also intertwined with the choice between the bittersweetness of passionate living, changing, creating, and dying, or the emptiness of a more inert existence in which we attempt to dilute the sting of loss and death. Becker (1973) thus declares: "The irony of man's condition is that the deepest need is to be free of the anxiety of death and annihilation; but it is life itself, which awakens it, and so we must shrink from being fully alive" (pp. 181–182).

Indeed, Rank (1936) emphasizes how neurotics attempt to scale back on their investment in life through the little death of not living passionately, thereby hoping to avoid the full impact of actual death: "He (the neurotic) refuses the loan of life in order thus to avoid paying the debt (death)" (p. 126). This retreat from a full engagement with life and death is evident whenever we forsake the creative passion in the change and growth of *becoming* for the apparent security of holding on tenaciously to the inertia of just *being*.

With the loss of passion, the "death" of the self in life's transitions becomes delinked from the continuing "rebirths" of the self; one is left only to cling to the life raft of an indefinitely extending self-sameness to withstand the annihilating tides of change. In this sense, our fear of death at the end of our lives may be viewed as a temporal displacement for the continual self-dying that is implicated in the metamorphoses of growth; it is a means of quarantining the otherness of death from the life process and segregating the endings implicit in change from self-sameness.

For such individuals, the *transitional spaces* separating two different persons and the *transitional times* separating who I am in the present from who I will be in the future —that is, change itself—takes on the antagonistically monstrous appearance of Otherness. Such persons continue to put off always for another day the necessity of reckoning with their particular "dragons" of change and deny the necessity of making committed choices to their own life. The transitional processes of life—manifest in the metaphors of birth, death, and rebirth—are postponed indefinitely, and in the end, one discovers that if one is not willing to face one's metaphorical "deaths," one is not able to reap the rewards of their accompanying "rebirths."

For such individuals, however, holding back what Dylan Thomas referred to as the "dying of the light" is only the semblance of a comfort zone because, in retreating from the existential mandate to live and create passionately, what once was a fortified sanctuary against the constant onslaught of the dying and dawning of new life begins to turn into a boxed-in prison of gnawing regret. The self-immobilizing attempt to "play dead" to magically evade life and the death that inevitably follows ultimately backfires because one has to die anyhow, but now more despairingly because of not fulfilling one's destiny.

Such persons find to their great distress that it is not possible to disentangle life and death so easily. Hanging on for dear life to oneself and all that is familiar and avoiding the concrete action choices implicated in one's own unfolding changes may lead to a different kind of death, a "spiritual" death of meaninglessness and despair. Lives that are lived in quiet desperation are often reflective of a great hesitancy to endure the movement of passion inherent in each choice and transition and letting go to the unfolding changes of self-dying. Perhaps it is in this sense of a spiritual death of despairing inertia that we can understand Shakespeare's (1599) declaration in *Julius Caesar*: "Cowards die many times before their deaths; the valiant never taste of death but once" (p. 64).

In writing about these matters, I think back to my experience as a parent. I remember holding my son in his first day of life and whispering down to him that I wish him a "perfect" life free of suffering. For 15 years, I did my best to fulfill my promise and attempted to shield him from various difficulties and disappointments of life. However, in that avoidance, I had mystified and aggrandized the very thing from which I was attempting to protect him, and consequently, he, too, became fearful of the very suffering that I was attempting to help him evade. Now, in retrospect, I realize that I was well intentioned but misguided in the life lessons that I was intending to impart. Perhaps the greatest gift that we can impart to our children is not to shield them from suffering at all costs, but to teach them how to fall and get up again, to teach the resilience of overcoming adversity by setting a parental example of persevering.

The tensions mediating the times and spaces between two persons, or between who we are in the present and the different "Other" person who we will be in the future, in which we come face-to-face with all of our exposed vulnerability, is suffused with both the risk of annihilating shame and the redemptive possibilities of meaningful self-realization. The decisions we make to love and lose or not love at all, or to live and die or not really live at all, cannot be disentangled from a relational/developmental ethics as to how we engage the "strange" of the stranger in our midst.

Perhaps the most important legacy Freud himself has left us, however, is the profoundly paradoxical notion that we can never make a beeline escape from any part of ourselves just because it is not practical or does not conform to the propaganda of shoulds or should-nots in our heads. For any automatic compliance with the "politically correct" rules or prohibitions that are used to tyrannize oneself, there is also in us always a dissident voice of resentment and rebelliousness standing up for the oppressed freedom of self-determination that does not trudge gently into the night with its tail between its legs. The more we attempt to exclude frustrating parts of ourselves, the more we guarantee that we will return to those exiled aspects of ourselves like bees to honey. Our access to a usable passion to traverse those tensions mediating time and space depends on accepting the dark underbelly of life and ourselves—our mortality, our limits, and the necessity of loss and suffering—as intrinsic aspects of the human condition. As Farber (1966) emphasized, we must retain an access to our intrinsic freedom, regardless of the "possibilities of failure."

Kierkegaard's critique of Christianity very much rested on the idea that Christians all too often bypass the crucible of human suffering and despair inherent in the difficulties of maintaining faith in God; in so doing, they lose the true meaning of Christianity. If one evades the tragic dimensions of existence such as loss, despair, and death, how can one experience the corresponding redemptive experiences of compassion and love? The affirmation of one's passion to love, lose, grow, and die is linked with accepting the inevitability of suffering and the concomitant necessity of compassion. Kierkegaard thus suggests the ethical self emerges only after accepting the despair of limitations.

Ultimately, if we recognized that our passionate life was both self-interested and self-surrendering, we would be less fearful of the spontaneity of our passion. Human development depends on the affirmation rather than negation of that passion.

Chapter 2

# Planting Seeds of Belonging
## Giving of Oneself and Being Received

> To give something is to give a part of oneself a part of one's nature and substance, while to receive something is to receive part of someone's spiritual essence.
>
> (Mauss, *The Gift*, 1924, p. 10)

## The Communion of Giving and Receiving

There were many cold winter nights in Chicago when I dreaded trudging through the snow to walk my beloved dog, Andy. I would briefly race through my thoughts, searching for an escape hatch from the arduous task lying before me, but then I became aware there was none because Andy was counting on me, and that helped me accept my responsibility. Somehow then during the walk itself, as is often the case in the anticipation of dread, I realized this was not as onerous a burden as I thought it would be. Suddenly, in fact, it all became eminently worthwhile. On the last leg of the 20-minute walk, Andy would stop and look up at me with what I imagined to be gratitude and communal solidarity for the time he and I had just spent together in the frigid cold. In that moment, I, too, felt the warm glow of a fulfilling kinship and my own gratitude to Andy for just being who he is. I fully understood then that my seemingly selfless sacrifice of walking Andy in the cold had not been so selfless, because it had been at least as much for me as it was for him. It was for us.

There was almost something magically surreal in the effortlessness with which Andy and I were able to bridge the gap between our two different species. In our unconditional mutual respect, Andy could do no wrong in my eyes, and it seemed that he felt the same way toward me. In our passionate mutual devotion, we formed a sense of communion. The word *communion* derives from the Latin *communia* or mutual participation, and more specifically from the root *munia* or shared gifts.

DOI: 10.4324/9781003559559-3

In order for Andy and me to have constructed a bridge of shared giving traversing our differences, both of us also had to genuinely receive each other's offerings of love. At the very same time that Andy happily soaked up my head massages out of what seemed to be mere self-interest, he was also implicitly entrusting himself to me and accepting my benevolent entreaties without guile. In whatever creative ways I shaped my petting of him, Andy received my offerings with infinite gratitude. Any shared giving implies then the open-hearted reception of an Other's creations as its own kind of humble offering of goodwill. Perhaps Andy's implicit trust in my goodness, his unself-conscious placing of his well-being in my hands, inspired me to respond to him by giving of myself with my own passionate openness and trust of him.

Is it then really "more blessed" to give than to receive? If everyone followed the Biblical maxim in the narrowest sense of the term, then who would be there to receive those gifts? How would we all help each other reach the transcendent ethical status of making a contribution to others if the would-be givers of the world were to meet with a closed door to their offerings?

Indeed, for us human beings, fraught as we are with conflict bubbling within and clashing agendas putting us at odds with each other, the second-guessing and cover-ups of self-consciousness make the communion of shared giving far more complicated, and the trust and openness required for receiving an Other then becomes a difficult task.

In actual practice, giving and receiving are not easy to disentangle, especially when they are occurring simultaneously. If two people embrace each other, who is giving and who is receiving? It is only when relationships break down that individuals who feel deprived, resentful, and entitled begin to scrutinize an imaginary scoreboard and keep close track of how much they are giving out and how much they are getting in return. Elsewhere (Shabad, 2017), I have written that when children are not *received* as cherished gifts in and of themselves, they often feel unworthy of *receiving* something good. Instead, they may exhibit a greedy "taking" from others to cover up a despair of emptiness that derives from a sense of being "unwanted" and "unreceived."

If we were to believe in the economics of giving and receiving in this way, we would think that receiving or getting something for ourselves is the first priority for many of us. Indeed, traditionally, giving and receiving between the therapist and patient has been based on the model of the parent-child relationship. Like the parent, the therapist is viewed as the one who gives, and the patient, like the child, is the one who needs and receives emotional sustenance. This view of the baby as a receptacle is primarily based on the evolutionary view that the child is an essentially biological being who must internalize material and emotional supplies in order to properly mature, adapt, and survive. Taking in mother's milk is then viewed as the prototype for this metaphor of incorporating needed maternal sustenance, one that then is also applied to emotional life.

In this chapter, I will be viewing the process of giving and receiving within the parent and child relationship through a different prism. I will specifically outline how children have an inherent need to give of themselves and to be received by an Other. More specifically, the rhythms of the child giving, the parent receiving, and the child then receiving back the gift of the parent's receptivity form the heartbeat of the relational/ethical process of human development.

## In Search of an Other: The Passion to Give of Oneself

When psychoanalytic theory has included the notion of children giving of themselves to parents, it is often seen as reparation *after the fact* of separation. To the extent that losses and separations are inherent in the transition from one generation to the next, the tensions between the guilt of children who are emerging as authors of their own lives and the envy of declining parents who are left behind are woven into the fabric of our lives. Indeed, in my clinical work, I have seen many young people hesitate about the prospect of becoming parents because of fears of acting out their resentments on their children. They seem to be struggling with anxiety in reaction to anticipatory fantasies of enviously begrudging their children a better life because of feeling cheated out of their own happier childhood. Such young people also often fear advancing to the second generation and closing the curtain on the first generation because they are still stuck on what could have or should have gone better in their own lost childhood. Ironically, it is often not these young people, who are so concerned about their own destructiveness and hurting the well-being of their prospective children, who become problematic parents. It is when individuals are not at all aware of their potentiality for envy and do not struggle so mightily with their parental consciences that their fantasies can become enacted on their children in destructive forms of displaced revenge and envy.

Elsewhere (Shabad, 2001), I have emphasized how such parental envy always hovers in the background of children's lives and is manifested often in parental possessiveness. Such parents may exact a heavy toll of "separation guilt" from their children for moving on with lives that are independent of their parents. Rank (1936) suggests that there is a fundamental human struggle between affirming one's creative will to separate and individuate, and a countervailing force of guilt that works to inhibit that will. Looked at this way, separation itself becomes a primary pathway through which the child's destructiveness toward the parent is manifested.

Inasmuch as the child's separation or letting go of the mother is intertwined with the sense of injuring her, from the beginning of life the child must sacrificially atone for the "sin" of separating. It is worth noting here that the word *sacrifice* derives from the Latin *sacer facere*, "to make whole or sacred." The mythologists Baring and Cornford (1991) stated that sacrifice has to do with "restoring to the whole something that has been lost in order to allow life to continue" (p. 161). As Klein (1937) pointed out long ago, reparative processes for imagined or real acts of infantile destructiveness are also a commonly observed developmental and clinical phenomenon.

Very early in my clinical career, I did child therapy as part of my work in an outpatient services center. One of the children I saw, John, a six-year-old boy, still stands out in my memory. Over the course of a number of sessions, John would repeatedly create a particular scenario in which the interplay between destructiveness and reparation was dramatized quite vividly. First, John would shoot me dead. I enjoyed this part because I could try out my acting chops in the melodrama of my dying scene. After I finally lay prone in the middle of the playroom, John quickly went over to the sandbox and filled a pale with sand, which he called his "soup." I then would slowly crawl over to the sandbox and beg for the soup,, where he would offer me a spoonful of his magical elixir. After "sipping" it, I slowly began to revive and looked searchingly around the room and asked: "Who made this so good?" As my eyes finally focused on him, I am still touched to this day when I remember his huge smile as he beamed with pride and pounded his chest and simply said "me."

When a mother accepts the "sacrificial" offerings of her children and the transgression of separating is redeemed, those children are able to work through the destructiveness of relinquishing the omnipotently held mother, thus earning themselves the right to continual rebirth as self-creating human beings. Winnicott (1954–1955) states that "the small child must go on

having a chance to give in relation to guilt belonging to instinctual experience, because this is the way of growth" (p. 271). As Loewald (1980) noted
astutely, "The self, in its autonomy, is an atonement structure, a structure of
reconciliation, and as such a supreme achievement" (p. 394).

In a way, we might say that one of the primary ways children give of
themselves to their parents is by allowing their parents sufficient access to
deposit themselves in their children. Children are viewed as repositories of
their parents' gifts of love and the indoctrinations of influence and values
that often accompany that love. When parents "recognize" their children,
they are then better able to re-find a part of themselves with which they can
identify and participate vicariously, thereby neutralizing their envy of the
budding life leaving them behind.

In light of the intergenerational tensions of parental envy and children's
separation guilt, it is tempting to reduce the inherent need to give to guilt
and reparative motives. If we did so entirely, however, we would be adhering to an individualistic view of passion in which the enhancement of
self-actualization is the goal of life, for which one must therefore atone
after the fact. This view of development would mean one begins with and
ends with oneself, like a circle that culminates back at "square one".

In contrast, I would suggest that the developmental trajectory of passion moves toward an Other who is increasingly viewed as a differentiated
subject rather than as a possessed object. In this view, the separation of
growth means the generous letting go of one's possessing of others to their
own personhood with which one continually reconnects throughout one's
lifetime. This pathway of the passionate life force toward giving and then
receiving the subjectivity of the Other culminates in the realized fulfillment
of a human life.

Fairbairn's (1941) view of libido as object-seeking rather than pleasure-
seeking hints at a passion that not only seeks to manipulate objects toward
our narcissistic ends, but one that needs others to be human subjects as
ends in and of themselves. Winnicott (1969) greatly extended and refined
Fairbairn's notion of libido when he described the crucial shift of object
relating to object usage. This shift involves a process by which a child
moves from relating to a mother as his omnipotently held object to a view
of her as her own subjective person who he can now use to benefit himself.
More recently, Benjamin (1988), too, has explicitly highlighted the developmental importance of the child's recognition of the mother as somebody
who has her own subjectivity.

Each person is on a quest that is at once spiritual, ethical, and relational to belong to and contribute to an Other who both contains and transcends his or her existence. Although this transcendent quest inherent in passion overlaps somewhat with Freud's (1920) notion of Eros—especially with regard to sexuality, reproduction, and the devotional care of children—the drive for self-realization is not reducible only to the biological dimensions of human experience.

## Self-Expression: The Creative Gesture as a Gift of Oneself

When we consider the term *unconditional acceptance*, we often think of it as something that children seek to receive from their parents. Yet when we consider the meaning of acceptance in this context, we are speaking about the parental capacity to receive their child with appreciatively open arms. When patients complain that no matter what they do, they cannot gain their parents' approval, that nothing seems to be good enough to please them, they are conveying how difficult it is to be received by their parents as a cherished gift.

Each expressive gesture of the newborn—every movement of her limbs, every plaintive cry emerging from her mouth, each bowel movement—is a created gesture, whether voluntary or involuntary. These created gestures are not expressed merely into a void. Gusdorf (1965) states: "Expression is the act of man establishing himself in the world, in other words adding himself to the world" (p. 71).

These expressive gestures are thus generated and relinquished as communicative offerings, which are meant to be received and heeded by an Other. Winnicott (1954–1955) hints that the "spontaneous gesture" of the infant also is a "gift gesture." It is interesting to note here that "create" and "generous" derive from the same Latin root *genera* or "to produce, beget." The infant's spontaneous gesture that is created and expressed as a gift offering reflects the generosity inherent in the infant's passionate life force.

When a baby reaches out toward its mother with outstretched arms, the gesture is not expressing only a need for an object to relieve its physical tensions, but also a means of giving herself over to the receptive care of an Other. Eigen (1981) thus states: "The infant lives through a faith that is prior to a clear registration of self and other differences" (p. 413). This giving of oneself also corresponds to Ghent's (1990) description of a universal longing for surrender.

Such longings do not convey so much the need of "I want" as they do the need to "be wanted." The verb *belong* derives from the Middle English *longen* or "to long after." Such longings may be viewed then as communicative gestures, or what Hyde (1979) describes as "threshold gifts" (p. 40), seeking entry into a state of communion with a receptive, accepting Other.

Angyal (1965), in speaking of homonomy (in contrast to autonomy), says: "To be, to exist on this level is to mean something to someone else" (p. 18). The fundamental human passion, as expressed through the infant's first vocalizations and gestures, is to creatively participate in and contribute to a transcendent Other to which it belongs. The creations that are offered and received by others reassure us that we are not all alone, that we have not merely conjured up the world in which we live. Just as Peter Pan eventually left behind the eternal childhood of endless possibilities to retrieve the containing, delimiting stability of his inescapable shadow, we, too, yearn for some sort of confirming response from outside of ourselves to feel sane and complete.

The birth of a child is the first gift to the parents. From the beginning, the newborn's expressiveness reflects the need to be a desired object, an unconditionally accepted gift in and of himself. Children must feel themselves to be wanted gifts who are of primary value to their parents. For Winnicott, the gift gesture of self-surrender can easily become susceptible to parental exploitation. In this context, parents may exploit the child's gift gesture by extracting a conformity from the child to match the parent's conceptions, while casting out the child as his or her own unique creation. Since the infant, in a helpless, dependent state, is a "beggar" who is desperately seeking to belong and therefore cannot afford to be a "chooser," he is forced to construct a False Self (Winnicott, (1960a))that slavishly submits to the parents' conceptualizations.

The child's two parents, as well as their relationship with each other, the primal scene in the broadest sense of the term, are the first to welcome the newborn into life. The quality of the parents' relationship to each other, the source from which the child was conceived, reflects the reaffirmation of their original intention to make love and conceive in the first place. Part of what is so important about the relationship of parents with each other is that it is the one side of the triadic relationship in which the child is not directly involved. If parents are able to get along well on their own merits, their relationship can serve as a prototype for a life outside of the child's omnipotence that can go well. This template of parental togetherness provides a source for the courage to let go of his mental control on a life-long journey toward accepting differentiation, difference, and otherness.

Already at an early age, the child's intuition that the parent's relationship with each other is a good, affectionate one, which is eagerly awaiting his arrival, helps fuel a sense of his life as "meant-to-be." This feeling of meant-to-be helps launch the unfolding and shaping of a destiny that has purpose. That sense of purposefulness to one's life contrasts sharply with the sarcastic comments that some patients make about the lack of physical intimacy between their parents: "I think they had sex twice in their marriage, when my brother and I were conceived." In such circumstances, individuals may feel that they were "accidents" or "errors" who are plagued with doubt about the righteousness and purpose of their very existence. This is especially true if they feel that the error of their conception and birth disrupted a much better relationship between the parents that existed prior to their arrival.

A mother's welcoming hospitality to her child's spontaneous offerings becomes an implicit gift of recognition back to him. The grace with which parents receive their children's gift gestures greatly influences the goodness with which children are able to view their passion and consequent ability to creatively affirm themselves toward further development. When a mother accepts the spontaneous gestures of her baby, her receptivity reverberates back that his passion will bear fruit, thereby providing him with the initial sense of having something good inside that is worthwhile to someone else. That sense of goodness and usefulness, in turn, enables children to feel worthy enough to receive sustenance, affirm their passion, and generate an offering of themselves once again.

In saying this, I very much want to emphasize the extent to which an ethical sense of rightness about our passion and capacity to further development depends on the reception we receive in early relationships. Simply put, when we feel our passion bears fruit in someone else and is therefore good, we are able to affirm it in order to further growth, and when we feel it is inadequate or destructive, we are more likely to become stuck in our lives. Growth, in large part, entails mobilizing a sufficient generosity of spirit to continually relinquish the familiar and move toward the unknown.

Winnicott (1954–1955) refers to the mother's unconditional acceptance this way:

The infant has good and bad to offer. The mother takes the good and the bad, and she is supposed to know what is offered as good and what is offered as bad. This is the first giving, and without this giving there is no receiving.

(p. 269)

## Parental Responsibility: The Challenge of Generosity and Openness of Receptivity

Genuine receiving is a challenging process. In order to open up and let in a new experience, a new person, we must welcome the difference of a change that disturbs the equilibrium of whom we had been previously. We must mobilize sufficient faith in a life outside the familiarities to which we have become accustomed and relinquish ourselves to something new. Receiving thus requires the receiver to surrender a mental dominion over time and space and acknowledge the need of what is alien and new, what is Other to himself. Implicit in this process is the greater value one places, at least momentarily, in welcoming what is different than one's habitual patterns of thinking, feeling, and doing.

This openness entails an implicit acknowledgment of a hole or flaw in our individual make-up and owning up to a profound dependence on the lifeblood of relationships with others. In this sense, receiving a gift from another exposes us to what Becker (1973) refers to as the "vital lie" of a self-contained, self-sufficient narcissism. That tacit acknowledgment of a hole or lack in oneself also creates a niche that can be made hospitable as a potential home for a newborn, the infant, and later in life, one's beloved. Derrida (1995 suggests it is because of this acknowledgment of a lack in our individuality, that accepting a gift also signifies a form of implicit consent to our mortal limitations as individuals.

Ricoeur (2005) highlights the critical importance of receiving in the interchange of "give, receive, give in return." He says: "The way in which the gift is accepted determines the way in which the person who receives the gift will feel obliged to give something in return" (p. 243). He then continues:

The generosity of the first gift does not call for restitution, which would properly speaking mean annulling the first gift, but for something like a response to that offer. At the outside, we have to take the first gift for the model of the second one, and think, we could say of the second gift as a kind of first gift.

(p. 242)

Focusing on the mechanics of the ritualistic obligation to reciprocate a gift shifts the focus from the responsibility to genuinely receive and let a gift penetrate our interior. If that is true, then perhaps the second gift that is modeled on the first gift is none other than the humble gift of welcoming receptivity itself. Moreover, this second gift of receptivity is modeled also on the unilateral, unconditional basis of the first gift, in which no payback is possible. Derrida (1995) says:

> The moment the gift, however generous it be, is touched by the slightest hint of calculation, the moment it takes account of knowledge (*connaisance*) or recognition (*reconnaisance*), it allows itself to be caught in transacting ... the alteration of the gift into a form of calculation immediately destroys, as if from the inside, the very thing that is given.
>
> (p. 113)

For Derrida (2000), a genuine hospitality means that a guest be treated in such a way that he could be mistaken for the host. This is one way that we can make sense of a host's expression of hospitality: "Make yourself at home." Only then can the guest know that his yearning to belong has been realized.

Without the deterministic mechanics of "what must I most appropriately give back to equal the original gift?" to distract the receiver, the receiver is challenged to mobilize a humility of gratitude toward the strange, new given itself. A simple silence, in which one is "overcome" with emotion, demonstrates the profound gratitude of receiving a gift. More ordinarily perhaps, a heartfelt "thank you" also reflects the self-surrendering humility of gratitude, in which one does not *have to do* anything in return but simply be open to receive what is given.

I am reminded of a memory in which a friend and I were vying to control the ethical privilege of treating the other person to lunch. After a few exchanges of mutual protestation, he finally exclaimed: "Why don't you just shut up and say, 'Thank you'?" The humility of open-hearted receptivity has never been better illustrated for me.

Each incoming new moment, as a new moment in and of itself independent of previous moments, may be viewed as a "given" of a person's life. Similarly, the birth of a newborn may be viewed as a "given" without any known giver. The inaugural appearance of a child can be likened, in Derrida's (1995) words, to a gift of "infinite goodness" from an unknown source. The child is therefore a unilateral gift that has no origin or explanation that adequately accounts for the birth itself. Parents may understand the science of impregnation, pregnancy, and childbirth, but they nevertheless are often awestruck by the "miracle" of the newborn's head popping out of the mother's body. Just as the abrupt transition from life to death, from "there you are" to then "you are not" is incomprehensibly surreal, so, too, the transition from non-life to life, from nothing to something, eludes realizable grasp.

This new arrival of a child as a given without a known source becomes a metaphor for what Levinas (1969) calls the "face of the Other" who parents are challenged to recognize. In this sense, all newborns, regardless of a biological or non-biological relationship to parents, are like "foundlings" who have been mysteriously deposited at our doors, strangers from we know not where. They are foundlings in search of being found, a home to which they can belong and claim as their own. Since their children are gifts that can neither be matched nor reciprocated adequately, parents are presented with the choice of either welcoming or turning away the new being in their midst without preconditions.

The inexplicable, indeterminate, and unrequitable goodness in the "miracle" birth of a child's life presents parents with a challenge to gratefully receive their gift with unconditional acceptance. Ricoeur (2005) states: "Gratitude lightens the weight of obligation to give in return and reorients this toward a generosity equal to the one that led to the first gift" (p. 243). The "debt" for the original gift of the child can never be repaid to an unknown benefactor but can only be met with the unconditional reception of the new life itself *without payback* required as a precondition. However, the twists and turns of life's currents have come to deposit the newborn at the doorstep of the parents, it is now their responsibility to embrace that foundling close to their bosom.

The child's two parents, as individuals and in their relationship with each other, therefore are the first gatekeepers to welcome the newborn into the human endeavor. They claim the children as their own and take them into a "home" and thereby enable their children to plant initial seeds of belonging within the passionate procession of life.

Parents display this unconditional acceptance repeatedly. Stillborn infants and newborns, who have but a few days to live, are welcomed into the world with infinite gratitude and provided with the recognized dignity of a name and identity. On the surface of it, such children seem to bring nothing but the torment of endless heartache. Yet parents who have endured the profound grief of intensely loving and losing their stillborn child all too soon are forever grateful for the privilege of knowing their child and providing it with the dignity of belonging to the family.

## Do I Exist? Recognition as Re-Finding and Finding as if for the First Time

The child's need to be wanted reflects a fundamental question that begins at birth and is always central to the lifelong quest for self-realization: "Do I exist?" When the answer to this question is a resounding receptivity of recognition—"Yes! We have a special niche in our home awaiting *your* arrival, not just *any* baby"—the infant is able to achieve an all-important sense of uniqueness and belonging at the same time. Erikson (1964) emphasizes the all-important role of the mother's eyes and face in the first recognition of the infant.

Indeed, Winnicott (1967b) says:

> What does the baby see when he or she looks at the mother's face? I am suggesting that ordinarily, what the baby sees is himself or herself. In other words, the mother is looking at the baby, and what she looks like is related to what she sees there.

He continues: "Of course, the baby does see the mother's smiling face, but this, which is in reality her response to his smiles, reflects back to him his own aliveness" (p. 112).

Winnicott's emphasis on the receptivity of being recognized by the mother's eyes is closely linked to a confirmation of the baby's existence. In describing the infant mind, he says: "When I look, I am seen, so I exist" (p. 114). The faces of infants light up with excitement whenever an adult plays peek-a-boo with them. As both the adult and infant play with presence and absence, we see the infant take great delight in being re-found and found as if for the first time in the parent's recognition. These pleasures of being re-found and found are then extended into later childhood in the classic game of hide-and-seek.

The primary means by which parents convey their receptivity is through their recognition of their children. The term *recognition* derives from the French *reconnaissance* or re-knowing, re-discovering, as in "Oh, I know you. I've seen you before." This definition parallels Freud's (1905a) statement that "Each finding of an object is in fact a re-finding of it" (p. 222). For Freud, the recognition of the new dissolves into incestuous transferences in which the newly discovered object is re-created through one's mind's eye in terms of a primary template. Freud thus says that the baby sucking at its mother's breast is the prototype by which human beings love one another. In this sense, the discovery of the new and strange is reduced to a repetition of the same.

It is true that when we fall in love, we often feel that in some sense we have known the loved one as someone very familiar to us from long ago. It is also true, however, that when we fall in love, we *really* are becoming acquainted and discovering someone who had previously been a stranger to us. Recognition may then be viewed as a paradoxical process in which we both re-find an old object and find an Other *as if for the first time*.

Since a shift from absence to manifest presence is always implied in recognition, re-finding and finding an object as if for the first time involve two parallel ways of addressing the experience of absence. When we re-find someone familiar after an absence, we are re-discovering them always through the creative prism of our mind's eye as someone we have already conceived or remembered. The recognition of the child who seemingly appeared out of nowhere as a preconceived memory allows the child eventually to feel "held" as a mental belonging in the parent's mind.

On the other hand, there is also a dimension of recognition in which there is the discovery of something new, such that the re-emergence from absence is experienced as a rebirth, as if for the first time. Whereas re-finding a familiar person refers to the repetition of cyclical time and helps establish a sense of sameness or continuity through time, the finding of a new object as if for the first time implies a linear trajectory in the passage of time in which change rules. The future is never then viewed as a repetition of the past. The recognition of a birthday thus is simultaneously the repeated celebration of the original date of a person's birth and the acknowledgment of the passing of time in the celebration of an age the person had never been before.

In speaking of the child being received through recognition then, I am describing a process in which parents both re-find and find their newborn as if for the first time. Benjamin (1988) vividly describes this paradox in the mother's recognition of her child: "Perhaps never will she feel more strongly, then in the first days of her baby's life, the intense mixture of his being part of herself, utterly familiar and yet utterly new, unknown and other" (p. 14).

On one hand, parents conceive their baby, both mentally and biologically, as an arrival they await with eager anticipation. They provide a name and identity for the new being before it officially makes its appearance, and who they then will refer to with the proprietary "my baby." When their child is finally born, they "re-find" a child of whom they have already conceived, this sense of close kinship with their child enables parents to claim ownership of their belonging, which then complements well the baby's need to belong to someone larger than himself.

For Benjamin (1988), this sense of kinship is a necessary aspect of recognition. She describes the mother's recognition of a child with whom she somehow is already familiar: "As she cradles her newborn child and looks into its eyes, the first-time mother says: 'I believe she knows me. You do know me, don't you?' Yes, you do" (p. 13).

Yet she is not so sure. Benjamin thus says: "Hey, stranger, are you really the one I carried around inside of me? Do you know me?" (p. 13). This question allows for the possibility that this child is a stranger who is different than the mother's preconceptions. This alien aspect of the newborn delimits the mother's recognition of the newborn as not only being an extension of her imagination, but as somebody wholly Other.

The parental recognition of the new being as if for the first time ultimately protects the child from being taken for granted as only an extension of the parent's imagination. It is a forerunner of the child being its own independent being with its own subjectivity and freedom of self-determination. This strange aspect of the newborn enriches the lives of parents with the infusion of its otherness, her very difference from what they expected.

The child's developmental process of moving toward her future is facilitated by a continual interplay between creatively giving of herself and being received through the repeated experiences of being recognized: re-found and found as if for the first time. This sense of being recognized, in turn, continually inspires a renewed passion of gratitude and generosity to let go, create, and give of herself again.

From Winnicott's (1969) perspective, the separation from the mother necessary to the process of becoming an individual entails the destructiveness of relinquishing the mother as an omnipotently held object and the mother's repeated survival as her own person. If the mother can survive the infant's omnipotent destructiveness, the child can then make use of the mother's personhood who "contributes-in to the subject according to its own properties" (p. 90). As Benjamin (1995) noted, human beings need the recognition of persons who are not in our control, but who have their own subjectivity. The child's creation and discovery of the Other through the destruction/letting go of his omnipotence is an enormously important and generous developmental step in the passionate journey toward self-realization.

It is important to add, however, that the "surviving" mother does not qualify for continuing survival only if she retains her own subjective being; she also must be someone who is still recognizable to the child who relinquished her as a mental possession in the first place. The child must be able to find a self-created thread of continuity through change, between the mother object that had been a part of her omnipotence and who she is now relinquishing and the separate person of the mother that she is now newly discovering.

The mutual interpenetration of giving and receiving between parent and child provides an opportunity for the child to find a sense of continuity through otherness. The mutual recognition of being internalized and internalizing allows children to progressively relinquish the mother with the trust that she won't just survive but will survive intact with some fruitful part of themselves inside of her. The continual re-finding of oneself in the loving resonances of the mother's receptive recognition thus inspires the trust necessary to break up an intact self-sameness for the transcendent sake of surrendering offerings to otherness.

The mother's receptive recognition of the child's spontaneous offerings inspires her passion to give of herself and be received again. Here is a brief illustration of this sort of interchange: A three-year-old child draws a stick figure and says to the mother, "Mommy, look what I did!" and the mother responds by saying, "That's great! Who is that?" The child says, "It's a man!" and the mother responds by saying, "That's the greatest man that I ever saw!" The child, feeling like no one else has ever done a picture quite like that before, smiles with great pleasure and then offers the picture to her and says, "This is for you, Mommy!" When she concludes this interchange by saying, "Thank you so much!" the child's passion, inspired by gratitude for the mother's gracious reception, moves to creatively generate another stick figure and present it to her again.

When all flows smoothly in this way, the child derives much pleasure from affirming the passion of letting go of herself in creatively generating offerings. With a ready accessibility to one's passion to help make transitions feel more fluid, growth may not at all be experienced as a tragic, angst-driven process. When the child receives back acknowledgment that her gifts have been received and recognizes, in turn, how the effects of her gift have moved the mother to be different from whom the mother had been previously, as transformed through her subjectivity.

The meeting place of offerings surrendered and offerings received provides the child with an initial sense of self-realization—that she has a special contribution to make to an Other beyond herself. Inasmuch as the child receives some sense of continuous sense of herself back through the "change" of letting go and being received by a mother who is increasingly seen as someone who is her own person, mutual recognition serves as a "transformative mirror" for the child's development. The transformative mirror of mutual recognition is different from self-object mirroring precisely because the mother's mirror of recognition of her child has been transformed by her own subjectivity.

Although Ghent (1990) notes that the self-surrender is usually "in the presence of another" and that surrendering oneself "to another" is actually more akin to submission, it is precisely children's faith that they will receive a resonant response—and not lose themselves in the infinite difference of another—that prevents surrender from degenerating into masochistic submission. When that faith in "what goes around, comes around" is rewarded with receptive recognition, and children receive a sense of a continuous self, familiar but changed, their now-renewed passion provides the courage to let go of self-sameness again and engage the unpredictable otherness of the future. Ghent thus also states that self-surrender may express: "The centrality, despite its buried secrecy, of a *longing* for the birth, or perhaps re-birth of true self" (p. 120). In this sense, the ritualistic process of letting go, being received and recognized, and giving again is inextricably intertwined with the continual transitions of the birth, death, and rebirth of the self.

Mircea Eliade (1954) has described how these repetitive cyclical processes become a way of touching base with a prototype of time and space: "Through the paradox of rite, every consecrated space coincides with the center of the world, just as the time of any ritual coincides with the mythical time of the 'beginning'" (p. 20). This repeated touchstone with the "center" and the "beginning" becomes a means then of acquiring a sense of reality: "The reality and the enduringness of a construction are assured not only by the transformation of profane space into a transcendent space (the center) but also by the transformation of concrete time into mythical time" (pp. 20–21).

If we were to apply Eliade's concept of the prototypical "center" to the ritualistic process of giving and receiving, the transformative mirror of mutual recognition may be viewed as a relational center of self-realization that consecrates the child's offerings in a shared time and space. Margolis (1998) says: "When we give gifts, we break down boundaries and create, instead of me and you or mine and yours, us and ours" (p. 109).

The experience of recognition or being "known again" then reverberates back both "locally" to various patterns of self-other relationships, and more generally, to a continuous but increasingly differentiated sense of self "standing in the spaces" (Bromberg, 1998) between the selves of the past and future. Looked at in this way, the boundaries of the self are not reified structures, but instead reflective of a repeated dialectical interplay between surrendering and receiving back a sense of continuous self-in-process, as mediated by mutual recognition.

## From Gratitude to Generosity: Conscience and the Ethics of Mutuality

Inasmuch as the fantasied mother is a part of the child's mental realm, there is an implicit generosity in the child acknowledging limits to his omnipotent extension of self-sameness and giving the mental possession of the mother away to the freedom of her subjectivity. The mother's appreciative reception of the child's offerings spurs a grateful impulse to respond to her with reciprocity. This gratitude inspires a passionate generosity to "let go" of the mother as a fantasy object to her own subjectivity. The transition from object relating to object usage thus requires a continually renewed ethical leap of faith inspired by a passion of gratitude and generous letting go. This generosity provides a courage to suffer his passion and transform the times and spaces separating them into creatively fashioned offerings.

In a brilliantly evocative book *The Gift*, Lewis Hyde (1979) calls this process a "labor of gratitude." He states:

> I would like to speak of gratitude as a labor undertaken by the soul to effect the transformation after a gift has been received. Between the time a gift comes to us and the time we pass it along, we suffer gratitude.

(p. 47)

Perhaps we can understand this inspired movement of gratitude more clearly with a small illustration of a young toddler just learning how to walk. As his mother calls out to him from the other side of the room and awaits him with open arms, he struggles through a few tentative steps before collapsing into her arms in a warm embrace. The toddler beams with pleasure at his newly discovered competence and his mother's appreciation of his creative feat. Now this mother walks out of the room into the hallway and calls out her son's name while out of clear sight. His memory of her pride in him inspires him with the passion to search for her over the uncertain spaces separating them and to present her with the gift of his renewed accomplishment.

Further, we might imagine that this mother, who is out of clear sight, is not only calling from the hallway, but from a future in which she is encouraging him to come toward her. Her familiar voice, emanating as if from the wilderness, now becomes internalized as his calling and becomes the embodiment of developmental hope and movement. The impassioned movement to respond to this calling propels development forward, making it possible to bear the inevitable transitions and losses of psychic growth. In this sense, when a child appears to relinquish relationship for separateness, it is a separateness that paradoxically is contained by a transformed version of that relationship awaiting the child in the future.

As a parent, I have been very alert to the importance of an appreciative receptivity in providing my children the courage to move toward the unknown. When my older son was very young and anxious that he would somehow disappear within the imminent world of sleep, I would end the bedtime ritual of saying goodnight by saying to him: "Sleep loves you, the darkness loves you." A few years ago, he reminded me that I said that and that he wants now to repeat that mantra with his own son.

This relational process of human development, bridging the abyss that separates self and other as well as present and future, provides the foundation for human conscience. The term *conscience* derives from the Latin *con-scientia*, "knowing together" or "knowing with." Conscience reflects a faith, and eventually a conviction, based on repeated experiences of mutual recognition, that if one lets go now, one will find a thread of continuity later amidst the chaos of change, of commonality through difference. From repeated experiences of giving and being received, the child derives an ethical knowledge that the "good" of creating a bridge to the Other contains the "bad" of suffering the passion that shapes the metamorphoses from self to other. Conscience, at once a developmental and ethical construct, links the continuity of an individual life through its numerous metamorphoses with its inspired participation in the human endeavor.

The passion to respond to the calling of the Other, now internalized as one's own calling, comes to concretely shape an ethic of mutuality. Through this ethic, we discern a close link between conscience and responsibility. By suffering through the passion of our own losses and transformations, we gain a sense of kinship with the subjectivity of suffering souls who are different. The "knowing together" of conscience, that relationship can and should contain the transitions of lonely sufferings, provides us with a sense of responsibility to use our knowledge to respond compassionately to the suffering of strangers. The word *compassion* derives from the Latin stem *com-pati* or "suffering with." Informed by the knowledge of conscience, our passionate life force is no longer a blindly impersonal force but harnessed by a very personal sense of responsibility and direction toward others.

To respond to the calling of our conscience is to respond to the difference of who we will be, to our own Otherness in the future. To be true or answerable to our past and future selves is to be answerable to others. In the book of the Upanishads, the universal structure of mutuality comes through clearly: "He who sees all beings in his self and his self in all beings." This knowledge of conscience, a knowledge that there is an essential dignity to the very subjective freedom of self-determination shared by all living organisms, is what links us conscientiously to what otherwise are quite disparate, separate beings.

The relational basis of conscience, of knowing that the suffering of separateness can and should be contained by the humanity we share in common, binds an individual's evolving personal truths to the universal ideals of the Golden Rule. The ethic of mutuality thus weaves together an individual life with the interdependent human fabric of which he or she is a unique part. Conscience, based as it is on the *affirmation* of our most elemental relational passions rather than their negation, is an important counterpoint to the "Thou shall nots" of Freud's concept of superego morality.

A human life may be viewed as an evolving ethical/relational medium that is both inspired by and generated toward an Other. The continual renewal of creative gifts offered and received are the meaning-making commerce through which we emerge from a sphere of omnipotence and move toward an increasingly respectful sense of others being their own persons with their own freedom of self-determination. In so doing, we are able to discover we can make a special contribution to someone beyond ourselves and thereby derive a sense of self-realization. A resonating reply from an Other consecrates our dramatic stories by completing the circle of meaning from without, thereby allowing us to realize that we are not merely conjuring up the world in which we live and reassuring us continually that we are not all alone. Very much of what is entailed in being oriented toward an Other is an open-faced, hopeful, and receptively giving attitude toward one's own future and toward other individuals. It is precisely this open-heartedness that is covered up and often reversed when people encounter too much suffering, trauma, and cumulative buildup of frustration and disappointment.

Chapter 3

# Divided Against Oneself

## The Self-Conscious Mind and the Crisis of Shame

Someone who runs the risk of being generous and is hurt as a consequence may afterward decide never again to leave himself in such a vulnerable position. Such a person does not realize when he makes this decision that only suffering makes our lives real.

(Miller, *The Way of Suffering*, 1988 (p. 43))

Then the eyes of both of them were opened, and they knew they were naked, and they sewed leaves together and made themselves coverings.

(Genesis 3:7–11 (*KJV*))

## The Crisis of Exposed Vulnerability

On more than one occasion, I have taken my dog Andy out for a walk and braced for the inevitable violent tug on his leash as I chased him chasing a squirrel up a tree. During these bursts of spontaneity, Andy did not stop abruptly in the middle of his hot pursuit to ask himself whether he had a right to pursue the frightened squirrel. He did not torment himself with doubts about the adequacy of his essential dogginess. He consciously pursued his quarry with the passion and excitement of an unself-conscious animal.

Like Andy, we humans also need access to our passionate life force to inspire us to move toward the fulfillment of our most cherished desires and the attainment of our personal goals. Unfortunately, fraught as we are with conflict, our spontaneous access to our passion is not nearly so easy to come by. More than anything else, we wish to be accepted for who we are, but we shield ourselves from genuine self-revelation because we are terrified that we will not be received well. Yet how can we be accepted if we are afraid to show ourselves and never really become known?

The passionate journey of giving our selves over to others is a daunting one. Each action choice on the journey toward otherness is suffused

DOI: 10.4324/9781003559559-4

with the limitations and vulnerabilities of our individuality. The choices we make and the transitions we move through are fueled by continually letting go and retrieving ourselves after having been transformed by the receptivity of others. As Foss (1949) puts it in his profound little book *Death, Sacrifice, and Tragedy*: "In every essential decision we are taking leave, destroying something of the past, dear and valuable to us, for the sake of a transcendent fulfillment" (p. 32). These losses inherent in human development occur whenever we make the transitions from who I am today to who I will be tomorrow and from who I am here to who you are there. Openness to one's growth entails a willingness to suffer through a continual "stranger anxiety" and painful self-exposure as we navigate through these "rites of passage" (Van Gennep, 1908).

Van Gennep (1908) described three phases in transitional rites of passage: a beginning phase, a middle "liminal" phase, and an end phase. Whereas within the insulated sanctuary of our minds, time and space are collapsed in the magical immediacy of primary process thinking (Freud, 1911), during the liminal phase of transitions, one must relinquish these mental capabilities and give oneself over to the world of actual experience. In so doing, we must endure stretched out periods of time and space between beginnings and endings, between the need to be received and its actualization. That is, we must suffer through the exposed vulnerability of being fully dependent beings waiting to be received by an Other.

For Kierkegaard (1843a) the process of leaving behind the home comforts of our mind entails a committed "leap of faith." He uses the metaphor of "leap" precisely to highlight the radical discontinuity of action, as opposed to mere shifts in thought, and the necessity of putting ourselves at exposed risk in order to move through genuine change.

In the immediate aftermath of leaping from the ground of the familiar, we often must get through an eerie sense of self-estrangement that may follow. Whether we have been small children experiencing the separation anxiety of the first day of kindergarten, or we are young people leaving home for the first night away at college, or we have suffered the shock of losing a close family member, we often must endure the dissociative sense of floating above the ground of our own experience. Even happy transitional events, such as walking down the aisle to get married or giving birth to one's child, may lead to these feelings of surreal groundlessness. In the midst of these experiences, we may ask ourselves incredulously: "Is this *really* happening? Am I *really* going through with this?"

Perhaps in giving up the many possible life pathways of our fanciful imagination to actualize but one of them, we are getting an all-too-real whiff of the poignancy of our mortality. Such transitional actions seem to occur with far more ruthless decisiveness than our emotional lives can readily take in and register. The dread of patiently moving through this liminal phase of self-estrangement is often too intimidating to endure alone, especially when it is not sustained by the hope of reaching the Other.

Winnicott's (1967) lucid description of a baby's separation from its mother illustrates the vulnerability of waiting to be received:

> The feeling of the mother's existence lasts x minutes, then the image fades and along with the baby's capacity to use the symbol of the union... The baby is distressed, but this distress is soon mended when the mother returns in $x+y$ minutes.
>
> (p. 97)

What is the baby experiencing during the liminal phase of those extra $x + y$ minutes, during that interval when the mother's image is fading? As if entering a chasm yawning menacingly between two cliffs, the infant falls into a space in which the link between creating and finding the other is temporarily severed. With the mother's return, the baby's exposed vulnerability is contained by her renewed presence. In the meantime, the anguish of waiting and yearning has sensitized the baby to the experience of suffering. Bridging the gap to the mother instills a hope that such sufferings can be redeemed, that painful experiences can be made good again.

What occurs, however, if an infant continues his journey across this mental landscape without finding the mother he seeks, instead falling through the cracks between self and other? Here is Winnicott's (1967) description of the child's experience when the absence from a mother is prolonged: "*In $x+y$ minutes the baby has not become altered, but in $x+y+z$ minutes the baby has become traumatized*" (p. 97). In such circumstances, the baby's wish to find his mother transforms into an unbearable anxiety of never finding her. This experience is akin to the infinite desolation evident in the face of a panic-stricken, "homesick" child who is waiting to be picked up at school by a parent.

From birth onward, however, the child's quest into the unknown for a welcoming home is fraught with the peril of being turned away. With each transition, there is a risk of falling through the cracks and exposing oneself to the abyss between self and other. As Tomkins (1963) notes: "The child who is burning with excitement to explore the face of the stranger is nonetheless vulnerable to shame just because the other is perceived as strange" (p. 267).

Take the example of a three-year-old boy who painstakingly constructs an edifice of building blocks. If the whole structure were to suddenly collapse, he might break into a flood of tears and rage. In identifying himself so closely with his creation, he feels like he has collapsed into a despairing heap as well. At this juncture, if a parent were to immediately jump into the momentary crisis of catastrophic panic, put her arm around him, and soothingly say, "Don't worry, honey; we can build your castle again," his momentary exposure to the abyss is contained by her consoling response.

Even when a child suffers falls, pains, and disappointments, he may retain the conviction that his experiences of suffering can be contained, that is, made better by the responsive understanding and compassion of his parents. In this important way, the relational containment of sufferings continually embeds children back into a lived sense of their own embodied being. This vital sense of continuity, inspired by the responses of others, derives from inhabiting an interconnected mind and body in which one is on the inside looking outward toward one's future and toward other persons.

If the little boy's desperation concerning his collapsed building blocks were to go on indefinitely without a parent's comforting embrace, he may eventually have to cope with his inadequacy alone through the protective covering of self-insulating defenses. If such uncontained frustrations and disappointments were continually repeated, he may become so intent on masking the insult of exposed inadequacy that he loses the needed openness to move toward others in the future.

When a child searches for a resonating response from an Other and none is forthcoming, he may become painfully conscious of his exposed vulnerability as a helpless, flawed creature who is incomplete in and of himself. Already in infancy, as the child encounters absences that go on for too long or connections with caretaking figures that are overly frustrating, the internal compass of a hoped-for image of the mother may break down, and the guiding purposefulness of searching gives way to the aimlessness of mental disorientation. The infant's experience of absence then may become increasingly flavored by a desperate panic of *not* finding the mother rather than by the wish to find her. This state of being is so unbearable that Winnicott (1967) says: "Primitive defenses now become organized to defend against a repetition of unthinkable anxiety" (p. 97).

Even the briefest of experiences of helplessness, if intense and significant enough, may leave an indelible mark by compromising the force of passion with a dread of the unknown world beyond one's mental control. Perhaps it is because the very meaning of our lives depends so much on the welcome mat that we provide for each other, that the exposure of our most profound vulnerabilities is exquisitely sensitive to the touch of rejection.

Suffering the patience of one's search for the Other is a crisis of exposed vulnerability, which can either be contained by the receptivity of the Other or lead to a sense of traumatic desolation. As the child endures the helplessness of his exposed vulnerability, will he receive help? Alternatively, if the protracted isolation of his helplessness becomes too much to bear, will he have to find a way to cope in his own defensive fashion?

The dread of exposure may eventually lead such individuals to shrink back in fear from changes necessary for their own growth. This retreat from change, though, entails a doomed attempt to deny the fact that life is inherently an evolving process of becoming. No matter how much we might want to hold back the dying light of each moment, the ruthless passage of time takes no prisoners. These concerns about the changes that separate who we are now from who we will be in the future parallel our anxieties about the bounded differences that separate each unique individual from other individuals.

Too often, during times of stress, and often in the most intimate of our relationships, when the stakes are highest and we expect the most, we may attempt to re-make and coerce other persons to do our beckoning rather than let them heed the call of their own drummer. We shrink from recognizing their self-determining freedom of subjectivity, for they remind us of the gulf that separates each one of us and ultimately of our aloneness as unique individuals.

To collapse these distances, we seek enviously to possess other persons as objects of our desire, often without respecting the boundaries between us. Farber (1966) observes insightfully:

> Whereas true admiration keeps its distance, respecting the discrepancy between the admirer and the admired one, envy's assault upon its object with a barrage of compliments serves not only its need to assert itself in the costume of admiration, but also the lust of the envier to possess the very quality that initially incited his envy.

(p. 122)

Inasmuch as the birth and growth of one's own children are concrete, embodied reminders of life passing by all too quickly, some adults resist parenthood entirely or attempt to hold back their children's increasing differentiation as their own autonomous persons. The self-insulating defenses of some parents are not always able to remain open to what is at stake in receiving the next generation with welcoming arms.

## Parental Envy of a Child's New Beginning

While time may be thought of as an ongoing river, a human lifespan eventually runs down. As intimations of aging beckon, the illusion of an indefinitely extending future gives way to reverberating pangs of regret over unrealized opportunities. These missed "dead" opportunities of an idealized past can be revived, however, if they are imagined as "living" opportunities being realized in the now-idealized and envied lives of others. The greed for an eternal flow of passionate life, having encountered the roadblock of death, finds an alternate route to salvage the past through envious fantasies of undoing and grabbing back missed opportunities from the young and innocent. Elsewhere (Shabad, 2001), I have suggested that such envious fantasies of spoiling a child's innocence are a primary motive in child sexual abuse.

Previously (Shabad, 2001), I have used the metaphor of the evil eye to describe the envy of those individuals who have missed opportunities to take their turn at one or another time of life and crave a second chance. Like the mythological vampire who feeds off the blood of the living to sustain itself, envy attempts to ward off the constant dying of the light by seeking out the budding of passionate life. The evil eye targets the vulnerability of everything that is vital and in the process of becoming, everything that is precious yet easily harmed.

Whether it is life-giving manna, regenerative youth, or food, there is only so much life to go around. Boris (1994) thus suggests that envy has its roots in the rivalry of natural selection. If one lives, then the other dies. The idea that there is only so much good to go around, what Foster (1965) calls the "image of the limited good," forms the antagonistic zero-sum principle of envy in social life. In this zero-sum universe, when we envy an individual who is experiencing good fortune, we infer automatically that we must not be doing well. If that same person were to encounter misfortune, we may feel that lady luck is now smiling upon us.

Parents are not exempt from such envy. The human order of a shifting cycle of generations, conforming to the dictates of mortality, marks off the ascending and descending transitions of our biological clocks. As children grow and come into their own, parents often are beginning to decline in the own lives. Loewald (1980) says quite directly:

> If we do not shrink from blunt language, in our role as children of our parents, by genuine emancipation we do not kill something vital in them—not all in one blow and not in all respects, but contributing to their dying.
>
> (p. 395)

This intergenerational drama of ascending children and declining parents brings the themes of parental envy and children's separation guilt into sharp focus (Shabad, 2001). Many parents repeat the hated behavior of their own parents in their interactions with their own children far too frequently. Why would a parent call his children stupid repeatedly, knowing how it felt when it was done to him? Why would a father consistently break promises to his child, if he could not tolerate it when his own father was unreliable toward him? Perhaps we can discern a subtle intergenerational revenge and envy in these parents' perpetuation of the wrongs done unto them. Although Klein (1957) theorizes that it is the infant who envies the contents of the mother's breast, I would emphasize instead that it is parents, especially those who feel cheated out of their own childhoods and harbor unconscious fantasies of retrieving that of which they felt robbed, who envy their children for the opportunity at a new beginning.

Many parents have their own lifetime of disappointments in which their hopes for the best had long since curdled into fearing for the worst, with the consequence that they have numbed themselves to receiving anything good coming their own way, including the gift of their own child. For such parents, the resentful afterimages of being cheated out of their rightful childhood can burn bright many years later. At the very same time that such persons were evicted prematurely from their childhoods, they began to harbor unconscious yearnings to retrieve that of which they felt deprived. Such parents externalize their regret for their own lost innocence into an unconscious envy of children who they imagine are living it out.

Freud (1913) described how mothers defend against an emotional monotony in their marriages by identifying with the lives of their children:

The aging mother protects herself against this by living through the lives of her children, by identifying herself with them and making their emotional experiences her own. Parents are said to remain young with their children, and this is, in fact, one of the most valuable psychic benefits which parents derive from their children.

(p. 22)

The degree to which such parents are able to identify with the child's new beginning through the child's receptivity engenders the constructive illusion of participating in the child's burgeoning growth. The child's generosity of receptivity and openness to these parental identifications, through the sharing of joys, pains, and accomplishments with the parent, facilitates the success of these identifications. Parental identification and sense of participation in a child's growth go a long way toward neutralizing any feelings of envy.

When a child grows further away from a parent and the generational difference between parent and child becomes increasingly apparent, a parent's illusion of identification/continuity with her own childhood may become ruptured. Now, the parent, desperately grasping at the straws of eternal youth, may rear a covetous head of envy and attempt to grab, hold back, and take possession of the child's growth. In this light, it is interesting to note that the etymological root of the evil eye in Latin derives from *fascination*, to fasten one's eye on another or to bind one substance to another.

In the previous chapter, I suggested that there are two dimensions in the parental recognition of their children. One dimension entails a re-finding of one's child as someone of whom the parent already conceived; the other dimension entails the discovery of the child as a different, separate person who the parent is finding as if for the first time. When re-finding the child of one's pre-conceived image predominates, the parent, instead of acknowledging that their child has a mind and will of her own, may see her child primarily as a created extension of her own mind. By recognizing and attending only to the idealized child of whom they conceive, parents cast out, often in the most subtle of ways, the actual child who exists outside of their sphere of influence. Erikson (1977) points out: "Very early in life, there is good reason to believe that in the child's unconscious, the habitually unresponsive adult assumes the image of a dangerous, an inimical Other; the unresponsive eye becomes an evil one" (p. 58). The non-recognition of the child's unique difference may have a petrifying effect on the child's growth. Instead, the cast-out child, unseen and unheeded by the parent, is left exposed, isolated, and desperately seeks cover perhaps ironically by submitting to the authority of the rejecting parent. In this way, the parent's envious evil eye may be viewed as a metaphor for a parent's narcissistic transformation of a child from a freely willing agent into a captured object of the parent's mental domain.

What then occurs when a child's cherished hopes are dashed and dearly held expectations are ignored or rebuffed? When a mother does not return her baby's smile with her own delight? Or abruptly withdraws her affections from her previously beloved only child in favor of her new baby? Or when a father ignores his child? In other words, what happens when children are insulted, injured, and ignored in any assortment of ways without their experiences being validated or consoled?

## Merging with Threat: The Disembodied Mind as Counterphobic Defense

When parents do not accept or recognize their child's offerings, the child is stopped short in his tracks and evicted from the containing context of the relationship. He is suddenly exposed in all his naked vulnerability, like a hungry baby bird left hanging with its mouth open. The child is exposed, if even for a brief instant, to his profound helplessness as a solitary individual who is dwarfed by arbitrary, unpredictable forces beyond his control. The word *expose* thus derives from the Latin *exponere*, "to put out" or "to place out."

From an evolutionary point of view, shame then may be looked at as an emotion that signals the danger of isolation and exposure to mortal threat. When a baby or sick caribou becomes detached from the herd, for example, it becomes much easier to target as prey for the encircling, ravenous wolves waiting to pounce. The isolated animal must find a way to regain the protective embeddedness of getting lost in the midst of the other caribous.

Shame, derived from the Germanic term *skam*, can be traced back to the Indo-European *kam*, "to cover up." Wurmser (1981) has noted that hiding is intrinsic to the concept of shame.

Often, human beings use counterphobic defenses to help them cover up their sense of exposure. In sharp contrast to the phobic flight from exposure to danger, counterphobia involves a movement *toward* precisely what is most threatening or frustrating. It is a means of rendering passive into active, of defending by taking the offensive. In so far as quick, decisive action in the face of an inhospitable environment is adaptive, counterphobic defenses have led to the survival of the fittest.

In the aftermath of traumatic experiences or overwhelming frustrations, the counterphobic shift from passive to active involves the defensive movement of mental activity to cover up and ensure that unexpected experiences of exposure are never to happen again. When these disruptive experiences begin very early in life—before a baby is able to crawl, walk, or run toward any threats or dangers in the outside world—the precocious intensification and projection of mental activity outward may become a primary means by which the child meets any external or future threat of relational disruption. Through the immediacy of forethought, the future is met instantaneously. The cultivation of precocious mental activity, based on the transference fear of re-traumatization, is tinged with a mistrust of all things spontaneous and unpredictable.

As Adam Phillips (1995) says,

> In fear we assume the future will be like the past... Fear, in other words, makes us too clever or at least misleadingly knowing... In fear the wish for prediction is immediately gratified; it is as though the certainty— the future—has already happened.
>
> (pp. 58–59)

Romanyshyn (1989) calls this defensive style of thinking "the mathematical": "The projection, in advance of the appearance of things, of precisely how those things are to appear" (p. 78).

Through the masked use of imitative or sympathetic magic, the mind takes on the predatory guise of frustrating external reality in order to magically inoculate itself with the representation of threat ahead of time so as not to be overwhelmed when that threat makes its actual appearance. In ancient Greece, for example, wearing the mask of Medusa was used as a protective amulet to shield one's exposure from the petrifying effects of her evil eye. Through the imitative magic of meeting an "eye for an eye," in Egypt the eye of Horus attached to a necklace has also been used as a protective amulet against the evil eye. By identifying with and introjecting the threat of unanticipated disappointing reality, one is able to control and neutralize its unpredictability. Ferenczi (1909) says:

> The neurotic helps himself by taking into the ego as large as possible a part of the outside world ... this is a kind of diluting process by means

of which he tries to mitigate the poignancy of free-floating, unsatisfied, and unsatisfiable unconscious wishes and impulses. One might give to this process the name of Introjection.

(p. 47)

I am reminded of a young man who had been diagnosed as schizophrenic a number of years ago. He had been admitted to an inpatient psychiatric unit because he heard voices telling him to kill people. When I met him, it was immediately noticeable that he spoke in an extremely high-pitched voice and had let his fingernails grow quite long. When I asked him about his voices more specifically, he responded that they sounded like "shrieking cats." With his own high-pitched voice and long fingernails, this young man may have been trying to combat his antagonistic voices by identifying with his own form of feline power.

Early in life, we learn to curl in on ourselves in defensive self-enclosure and employ the introjection of frustration as a counterphobic defense to preempt the danger of rejection.

Many individuals often go too far in preemptively covering up their vulnerabilities by "bracing for disappointment." (Shabad and Selinger, 1995, Shabad 2001) In such circumstances, bracing for disappointment, originally meant to function as a defense mechanism, can become so entrenched as an aspect of the self that one becomes alienated from the passions that animate one's life. As a result, life then can seem to be a never-ending merry-go-round of living out the prophecies one makes about one's future. The tendency to use pessimistic predictions as to what *will happen in reality* becomes a way of using an identification with a future bad reality as a cover up to prevent any exposure of what *one would wish* to happen.

Whereas phobia may be viewed as a straightforward fear of the hopeless and the bad, counterphobic defenses reflect the fear of hope and the good because of the disillusionment that will inevitably follow. As if rejecting an offer to love and lose by not loving so much, the counterphobic individual attempts to outwit the dangers of trauma and loss by closing himself off from his desires.

This counterphobic defense may be especially evident in the person who is more comfortable with short goodbyes than long goodbyes. For example, before 9/11/2001, people who said long goodbyes would park their car at the airport and escort a loved one to the departure gate. In contrast, people who said short goodbyes would bring the process of separating to an abrupt halt by saying something like, "I have to do some errands, so I'll just drop you off here." In order to forestall the anticipatory tension of passively waiting for the departure of the loved one, they cut short the time in which they could still be with the loved one. Such individuals scale back on love so they do not have to wait for the proverbial axe to fall. Loewald (1980), too, has described this defensive dynamic as an attempt to deny loss by denying that the other person still exists or did exist.

I am reminded here of a man I saw a few years ago, which showed how even a very subtle form of "bracing for disappointment" can cost a person in situations where desire is needed instead. Joe, a 42-year-old man, was separated from his wife and had started dating other women. He had been burdened by shame for most of his life, exemplified by early memories of his father's frequent teasing, or as Joe put it, "holding a carrot just enough out of reach so I could not get it."

In the course of growing up, it became important to Joe to rescue "damsels in distress" from their unhappiness. To his great disappointment, however, he was not able to help the women of his life with their sexual needs because of a tendency toward premature ejaculation. The sexual problem, which exacerbated his early shames, contributed to his own and his wife's avoidance of much of a sex life.

At one point, Joe spoke about a date with a woman in which there was a lull in the conversation that had been going well. Joe then glanced down at his watch and said, "Well, it's getting late. I know you have a lot of work to do after this, so maybe we should go so you don't have to stay up all night." She then said, "No, I can stay a little longer." A little later, when Joe walked her back to her car, he asked for her phone number. While she was fumbling for a pen in the cold, he said: "That's all right, you can just email it to me." The next day the woman emailed him with a "Thank you for dinner, take care" and never responded to him again.

As Joe recounted the experience in his next session, he felt perplexed by his date's sudden loss of interest in him. After Joe went over the evening's events, I wondered out loud whether he had attempted to wrap up the evening during a break in the conversation before she could do that to him. Under the guise of acting chivalrously, Joe was protecting himself from being teased and shamed again.

By glancing at his watch in the middle of their conversation, he conveyed much to his date about his constriction of passion. Romantic passion is greedy; it cares not about time, nor does it necessarily consider another's needs to leave in the middle of a good conversation. In his determination to cover up his vulnerabilities of hoping and being disappointed, of loving and losing, Joe opted not to love so much.

## Self-Enclosing Consciousness: Through the Imagined Eyes of the Other

When we suffer as children, we often are not aware of what is triggering our emotional pain, let alone able to convey it in words to someone else. The experience of exposure to a broken relational connection gives way immediately to a reflexive counterphobic shift from unself-consciousness to a state of being self-conscious, in which the child dissociates his mind from his body and projects mental activity outward to fill the void between self and other. As Schneider (1977) says, "the undivided self in action gives way to the doubled self" (p. 25).

In detaching mind from body, Fairbairn (1952) says the "splitting of the ego" gives rise to schizoid phenomena. He further indicates that "intense self-consciousness" and a "sense of looking on at oneself" are characteristic of schizoid phenomena (p. 51).

When we picture someone who is self-conscious, we may think of two people who are attracted to each other and who are second-guessing themselves about the words they use in their first meeting. There is a famous scene in the film *Annie Hall* when the characters played by Diane Keaton and Woody Allen stumble through a stilted conversation in which they try to act cool, while the screen reveals little captions about their constant doubts about what they just said, such as "That was really stupid. She'll think I'm an idiot now" or "Why did I just say that? I just blew it with him."

In these situations of exposed vulnerability, perhaps we would ideally like a third person to be present who reassures us constantly not to worry about the words just uttered, to tell us that we did not make a fool of ourselves. In the absence of the reassurances of a containing other, we lose our bearings and attempt to cover up our isolation by "becoming" that third person, viewing ourselves from the outside. It is through this reflexive process of viewing ourselves as if through the Other's eyes that we form an enclosed self-conscious relationship with ourselves.

The historian Owen Barfield (1973) likened the objectifying characteristic of self-consciousness to a camera, saying "It looks always at and never into what it sees" (p. 73). Perhaps Barfield's distinction between "looking at" and "looking into" can serve as a means of distinguishing the state of being self-conscious from self-awareness. Self-awareness is characterized by an openness to an awareness of one's vulnerabilities as they are rooted in a mortal body, whereas the "looking at" aim of self-consciousness is to cover up one's exposed vulnerabilities. Broucek (1991) views the self-objectification of "looking at" to be central in understanding the experience of shame.

Sartre (1956) states: "Shame is by nature recognition. I recognize that I am as the other sees me" (p. 222). Morrison (1989) describes shame as "The eye turned inward." As we train this inward eye on ourselves, we seem to shrink in significance, for now we are nothing but an object dwarfed by the overwhelming forces around us. This disturbing consciousness of viewing oneself as an isolated, insignificant object that is incomplete in and of itself is well described in Nietzsche's (1909) statement: "The feeling of shame seems to occur when man is a tool of manifestations of will greater than he is permitted to consider himself in the isolated shape of an individual" (p. 6).

In shame, we no longer are the unself-conscious, lordly creators of our destinies. Instead, through the eyes of the Other, we catch a disorienting glimpse of ourselves as static objects who are nothing but limited, mortal creatures. Sartre (1956) draws parallels between the shameful descent in status from extraordinary individuals in our own right to fully dependent creatures, and the Biblical account of the fall in the story of Genesis:

> Shame is the feeling of an original fall, not because of the fact that I have committed this or that particular fault, but simply that I have 'fallen' into the world in the midst of things and that I need the mediation of others to be what I am.
>
> (p. 384)

He captures the humiliating aspects of the self-conscious gaze: "Our shame is not a feeling of being that or that guilty object but in general of being *an object*; that is, of *recognizing myself* in this degraded, fixed and dependent being which I am for the Other" (p. 255).

For Levinas (1969), this fall from being God-like creator in our own mind's eye is a necessary disillusionment in our continuing evolution as ethical individuals. In forcing us to question the assumptions and expectations created by our own minds, shame allows us to remove the filmy gauze of mental representations through which we view others and reveal the underlying truth that our human existence is conditioned always by each other's subjectivities. Dalton (2009), in describing Levinas's views on shame, thus says: "Shame, as the affectivity of having been open and exposed, reveals the way in which the subject is fundamentally vulnerable and available to the other and not hermetically closed in on itself" (p. 127). The humbling consciousness of our status as creatures who are fundamentally dependent on others thus alerts our consciences to care for the Other. Regarding shame, Levinas (1969) says: "Instead of offending my freedom, it calls it to responsibility and founds it" (p. 203). Indeed, in discovering oneself as a creature incomplete in and of itself, he declares that the Other is "desired in my shame." On this view, the crisis of shame opens up an ethical pathway toward coming face-to-face with the Other.

Whereas Levinas (1969) emphasizes that shame, by revealing the fundamental truth of our incompleteness as individuals, opens up "my desire for the Other" (p. 84), I would suggest that the capacity to sustain this openness depends very much on whether our experiences of suffering are contained by the receptivity of the Other.

When a little boy's building blocks collapse, the parent's consoling embrace contains the isolation of the child's lonely suffering. The child therefore does not have to cover up his sense of exposure to a relational void by using his mind defensively to form a self-enclosed relationship with himself. His mind can remain "at home" within his embodied being. Yet the experience of suffering and momentary "trace" of consciousness may have been sufficiently humbling to delimit his omnipotent world and open him up to "desire for the Other." Consciousness may thus emerge gradually as self-awareness rather than self-consciousness in the presence of such repetitive relational containment by remaining rooted in an integrated psyche-soma. In such optimal situations, there is no urgent defensive need to split one's mind from one's body.

In my experience, however, the exposure in traumatic experiences to being insulted, injured, and ignored, when experienced in the absence of a containing Other, does not lead to more of an opening toward others. Rather than viewing the revelatory exposure of their limitations as a wake-up call to openness and "desire for the Other," many individuals cover up by forming a self-conscious relationship with themselves rather than with the Other. If that same little boy's panicky tantrum continues indefinitely without receiving solace, his glimpse of himself from the outside may become fixed as a petrifying gaze of self-consciousness.

## Dissociation and the Derealization of Subjective Experience

The state of being self-conscious may be viewed not only as a defensive attempt to foreclose further vulnerability and rejection, but also as an automatic reflex to a relational connection that was sought but never found. In this sense, self-consciousness is a means of filling a relational vacuum by forming a relationship with oneself. If at birth, we resemble half-open circles who are searching to be completed by an Other, in the state of being self-conscious, we, like Narcissus, close the relational circle upon ourselves. Any relationship, even a bad one with ourselves, is better than nothing. As Winnicott (1949b) declares:

> In the overgrowth of the mental function reactive to erratic mothering, we can see that there can develop an opposition between mind and the psyche-soma, since in reaction to the abnormal environment the thinking of the individual begins to take over and organize the caring for the psyche-soma, whereas in health it is the function of the environment to do this.
>
> (p. 246)

When no one is there to offer comfort and validate a child's experience, she is forced into the involuted position of bearing witness to her own experience. This places the child suffering alone in a similar position to the proverbial falling tree: "If there is no one to hear a tree falling in the forest, then did it make a noise?"

Unlike trees, however, we human beings enlist our minds as a home-grown witness to our experience. Yet there are problems in this makeshift attempt to bear witness to our own experience. At the same time that we take dissociative flight from the experience of trauma endured passively from within our bodies, our now-detached minds work endlessly in the repetitive attempt to realize what just happened to us.

Russell (1993) uses the metaphor of a camera attempting to photograph its own injury to describe a person's attempt to bear witness to his own experience. He states that because: "The photographic perceiving and recording apparatus itself is damaged while it is being built ... a camera cannot photograph its own injury" (p. 518).

Self-consciousness, born of dissociative defense, is not grounded in the substantive reality of the body. To the extent that we do not inhabit ourselves and life is not being lived from within, we do not have a corpus of lived experience to fall back on for a sense of certainty.

Our aim of objectifying our experience is made difficult by the fact that we have placed our own narrative stamp of omnipotence upon our suffering as soon as it occurs. Romanyshyn (1989) speaks of psychological life deepening the empirical world so profoundly that what is, is inseparable from how it is perceived. The multitude of meanings that can be imposed on experiences is so dependent on the shifting actions, moods, purposes, and the will of a person that it is easy to second-guess the real existence of one's experience.

When we suffer alone, we both know and do not know we have actually experienced a trauma. Corresponding to this fundamental uncertainty regarding one's traumatic injury—"Did I create my own suffering, or did I find it?"—is a dark cloud of recriminating doubt of who is to blame: "Do I blame myself for my suffering, or do I blame the other person for doing this to me?"

In forming a homegrown mirror of self-consciousness from the outside looking at oneself, the child attempts to find himself in a mental self-embrace of self-recognition. But this is a faulty mirror, since the child cannot recognize his own subjectivity from the outside. Instead, the child is introduced to an uncannily strange image of himself, a fixed object, which never really captures the impassioned subjectivity of his own lived essence. Perhaps then it would be more accurate to say that the self-conscious child *does not* recognize his own lived sense of subjective being, and thus must keep staring indefinitely in the repetitive search of his own essence. Merleau-Ponty (1964) says that the look of others tells me that "I am the visible stand-in (*doublure*) in whom I would recognize only with difficulty the lived me" (p. 153).

## The Immobilizing Effects of Self-Consciousness

In Ovid's (8 A.D.) *Metamorphosis*, Narcissus is transfixed to the spot by gazing at his own image in a pool of water precisely because he is searching unsuccessfully and unremittingly for his own essence from within his own mind. Here, we can see how the myths of Narcissus and Hypnosis, the god of sleep, are closely intertwined. By draining the body of its animating passion, the narcissism of self-preoccupied consciousness has a hypnotic-like effect of casting a paralyzing spell on one's growth. The self-conscious eye, like the evil eye, threatens to extract the passionate life force from its victims and transform that flow of life into a lifeless fixed object.

This objectifying gaze of self-consciousness alienates us from a lived, subjective sense of "going-on being." Consciousness tends to freeze the movement of any living process in the failed attempt to capture its essence. In spoken language, for example, consciousness attempts to catch the elusiveness of time passing, but never can fully do that. As immediately as we can utter the word "now" to refer to the current moment, the moment has already passed.

It is interesting to note here that the gaze of Medusa's shining eye has the petrifying capacity to transform life into stone. When the evil eye of a significant other is introjected, it now takes the form of the self-conscious eye one casts on oneself. During periods of exposure, when one is in the midst of making changes and during transitions, one is most vulnerable to the immobilizing effects of self-consciousness. In ancient Greece, for example, mirrors were removed from women at the time of childbirth to protect against the evil eye. In Romania years ago, it was considered dangerous for children to glance at themselves in mirrors before their first birthday for fear of casting the evil eye on themselves, and thus mirrors were removed from the baby's room or covered up (Murgoci, 1923).

The introjection of the envious evil eye becomes transformed into the self-petrifying eye of shame. Self-consciousness, born of disruption, will be necessarily tinged with the tendency to disrupt. The problem is that, as Phillips (1995) writes,

> Because the mind comes in afterward—after the trauma—it always runs the risk of being a preemptive presence. The mind object, that is to say, has always unconsciously identified with the traumatic agent (or rather, event) that first prompted its existence. The mind that attempted to repair—to compensate for—the trauma becomes the trauma itself.
>
> (p. 238)

Rank (1936) has emphasized how self-consciousness is a primary inhibiting factor working against willed action. Nietzsche (1887) describes bad conscience as "The instinct for freedom forcibly made latent against oneself" (pp. 87–88).

If a graduate student ruminates too much about what the teacher will think of her term paper, she will not be able to write fluently. When coming in a door to a party of strangers, a person is often so preoccupied about being the object of scrutiny for others that he cannot remember the names of people to whom he has been introduced. The basketball player who focuses on the basket has a much better chance of making a shot than the player who concentrates too much on himself aiming the ball at the basket. When human beings self-consciously think about thinking about their goal, the dynamism of continuous movement gives way to the halting, stuttering steps punctuated by stasis. As Lewis (1971) says: "The divided activity of the self, which is in two places at once, and acutely self-conscious at the same time, makes it difficult for that self to function effectively" (p. 32).

Perhaps most damagingly, the closed mental system of self-consciousness perpetuates a lonely desolation. To the extent that a central feature of self-consciousness is to immobilize an inner dynamism of passion and analyze that now immobilized passion into its constituent parts, self-consciousness has a deconstructive effect on the constructed holism of our creations. The created products of our self-revelations, both verbal and nonverbal, that provide us with a sense of kinship to other persons become subject to the nihilistic doubts cast by the second-guessing of self-consciousness. When our creative animus is thus paralyzed, it is difficult to construct a bridge of generalizability from our unique experiences to the lives of others. Caught in an internal web of our own making, we become locked in an involutional prism of wondering whether our experience is nothing but our experience. In this most isolated of worlds, we lose a sense of belonging to something real beyond our self-preoccupations.

Sometimes we are too smart for our own good, as the laser of self-consciousness penetrates our illusions with annihilating skepticism, leaving the machinery of our creativity exposed in its deadened parts. We may then question the usefulness or accuracy of our perceptions to such an extent that our creations are shadowed constantly by an anxiety of collapsing into the duplications of the trivial (reinventing the wheel) or the idiosyncratic (ideas as reflective of only one's own experience). This either/or choice of being just one of many or of being relegated to the isolation of one's unique experience itself reflects the traumatic rupture in the relationship connecting self and other.

It is disheartening too to hear psychoanalytic trainees, inundated with the double-takes of self-consciousness, preface their contributory remarks at case conferences and seminars with the disclaimer, "This may just be my fantasy, but...." When the generalizing relational glue of creative insight is undone and reduced to the individual psychopathology of hallucinatory fantasy, it is difficult to find one's place within the common fabric of human experience. Self-consciousness thus leaves each of us with our own set of unique experiences in a lonely internment of self-doubt.

## Paul: The Exile of Self-Consciousness

Paul is a 25-year-old man who came for psychotherapy because of recurring anxiety, social phobia, and vague feelings of depression. He is a quite cerebral, soft-spoken young man living with his girlfriend. Paul is a graduate student in the humanities at a prestigious university. He comes from an academic family; his father is a college professor, and his two sisters are also graduate students. His mother is nearing retirement after 25 years of teaching in high school.

Paul is far more comfortable speaking about himself in generalizations and abstractions, as if he were a detached self-observer, rather than from within an embodied subjectivity. This exile of self-consciousness alienates Paul from his emotional life, and he often is frustrated by his inhibitions in expressing himself at meetings with peers and faculty at school. Perhaps this emergent problem of self-consciousness is not surprising, considering that Paul's upbringing was characterized by an emphasis on intellectualism and learning the high culture of adults at the expense of childhood play and overt displays of emotion.

Under the tutelage and pressure of his father, Paul learned how to play the violin at an early age despite Paul's protestations. He read advanced books avidly. In general, discussion of all things intellectual took precedence over any emotional communications, culminating in a kind of intellectual snobbery. This emphasis on rationality at the expense of the emotional had an ironic accompaniment to it: Paul vaguely remembers having frequent temper tantrums during his early childhood. I suggested to Paul that perhaps he was dragged "kicking and screaming" into a grown-up life that came upon him too quickly. I began to suspect also that Paul's interpersonal anxieties derived, in part, from guilt for prematurely separating from a put-upon mother who never seemed to be very happy. As it turned out, this was only part of the story.

Indeed, Paul's mother was noticeably absent from the narrative of his childhood. As I probed a little, he vaguely remembered how on a number of occasions when he was "very young," he asked his mother to marry him. Given how conspicuous a non-presence she now was in Paul's memory, I wondered about the changes he had gone through in the interim between then and now. He said he had often felt she treated him impersonally, like one of the students she taught, and that her depressive silences and emotional absence in his life became even more palpable after she was in a bad car accident when he was six years old. In Paul's mind, after that trauma, she seemed especially to cede control of much of his upbringing to his father.

Whereas Paul's mother receded into the background as his childhood evolved, his father dominated the foreground. He cooked, cleaned, and took over conversations in the family with his strongly held opinions, often insulting those who disagreed with him. Paul recalls that his father would bully him to play the violin and practice. His father had no patience for Paul's tantrums and frequently scooped him up and forcibly carried him to his room whenever he acted up. At other times, his father would mock and laugh at Paul in the midst of the tantrums. Eventually, Paul shifted allegiances from himself to that of the aggressors; he became increasingly ashamed of his infantilism and replaced it with a detached, self-conscious intellectualism, which alienated him from his emotional life.

A few months after treatment began Paul's father sent some home videos of Paul's childhood to him. While Paul's girlfriend watched the videos, Paul avoided them, saying that he found them quite disturbing. He resisted his girlfriend's entreaties to join her by saying things like "Who cares?" or "I don't care about them." In session, he confessed to much trepidation in watching himself as a three-year-old, always with great foreboding of what was to happen to himself in his personal horror movie. It was as if he was still that little three-year-old and did not want to watch and discover what he knew was about to befall him. After we discussed it, he did watch one of the videos, and when he saw himself fall and begin crying, his father remained the ever-objective film director from his observer's perch rather than the consoling father who dropped the camera in order to console his son's wound. I reacted with genuine disbelief and outrage at his father's indifference to his fall. In so doing, I was availing myself as a witness to the deeper emotional wound that Paul had suffered from neglect, one from which he subsequently dissociated and de-realized. Paul began to acquire courage to face and thaw out the emotional losses he had numbed through rationality and intellectual devaluations.

In the next session, Paul said that he forced himself to watch another video of himself as a toddler. Again, he was filled with foreboding of what was to occur to the little boy in the movie, as if it were him but not someone he recognized at the same time. He spoke of how the little three-year-old wandered around alone, always alone. Even as he began to run down the block, crying "Mama, mama" in search of a mother he could not find, his father continued only to film him. Only when he finally reached the house where she was visiting (four houses down the street) and knocked desperately on the door, crying for his mother, did his father finally drop his budding career as film director and begin to intervene. Paul said after he and his girlfriend finished watching the video, he broke down into sobs. We came to understand that his tantrums, too, were a protest against the pain and upset of a chronically absent mother. In watching the videos of a forgotten period of his life, Paul was finally able to reconnect with a yearning to be with a mother he loved and had wanted to marry but lost, leaving him in the middle of nowhere.

Paul has begun to become aware how he has used the cover-up of intellectualizing defenses to obscure and devalue his painful yearnings for an absent mother. Indeed, he came to realize how he had identified with the emotional remove of his father filming him. In his dissociative flight from the shame of his infantile temper tantrums, he, on the outside looking at himself, viewed himself as an interesting specimen to be observed under a microscope.

Soon after Paul's mother was discussed in our sessions, he called her up and attempted to reconnect with her on the phone, without any interference from his father. These attempts were only partly successful, since she was unable to sustain any length of conversation on her end. As the treatment has evolved, Paul has come to view his mother less through an idealized lens as someone from whom he was forcibly removed, and more as a person who has her own significant limitations as a mother. Indeed, she has not been able to recognize Paul's emergence as an independent young man. Her short conversations with him are always punctuated by questions of "When are you coming to visit?" or "Why are you visiting for such a short time?" She seems to have no realistic sense of his separate life. Indeed, when his girlfriend and he became engaged, she came to visit and sat silently with a vacant, even baleful, stare at his new fiancée. Simultaneously, Paul has also come to appreciate his father more as the parent who was present and responsible for his care, and whose narcissism was intertwined also with a gregariousness and warmth. And so, as often happens in psychotherapy, childhood mythologies about one's parents become altered and rewritten.

Soon after watching the home video early in therapy, Paul continued to demonstrate a willingness to explore an uncultivated emotional side of himself through his tentative but affectionate approaches to the pet guinea pig he and his girlfriend recently acquired. Not surprisingly, his parents, looking down on the "lower" animal species of the world, questioned why he would adopt an animal. As it turns out, whether by happenstance or not, one of my own passions is my love of animals. I vocally defended Paul's choice and its therapeutic value and rebutted the arguments of his parents in a playful manner, such as "Maybe, your father's condescension toward animals would have merit if and when he can refrain from relieving his own animal needs in the bathroom." Paul laughed heartily at my attempt at humor and generally has enjoyed a certain earthy directness in my manner. Sensing that this aspect of my personality could help ground Paul from his disembodied thinking, I have not held back on playing with or teasing Paul. He seems to consistently enjoy my humor, and I suspect it is because we are including and thereby neutralizing a fear of aggression, both from others and his own, by couching it in a good-natured relationship of interpersonal play.

Such playfulness has seemed to ease the life-and-death stakes with which he viewed his aggression, as it was manifested in his own temper tantrums, as well as the quality of his father's narcissistic expansiveness and bullying. Through play and humor, he has been able to diffuse his shame regarding his tantrums and take a chance on reintegrating his own "animal" aggression.

Gradually, Paul began to find his way back to his embodied subjectivity rather than a self-objectifying self-consciosuness. He spent three months of the past summer working as a field hand on an organic farm. When he returned to therapy after the summer, he reported that, rather than feeling worn down by the physical difficulty of the labor, he thrived from the sense of liberation he derived in the physical exertion and movement of his limbs.

He has followed up on this experience by taking up basketball in the past number of months. Over the course of a number of sessions, he and I have used his experience in basketball as a metaphor to better understand his conflicts and self-conscious inhibitions regarding aggression. More specifically, he has been increasingly irritated by a very large, muscular player on the opposing team, who "doesn't care whether he runs over people" whenever he drives to the basket, which he does frequently. We have spoken about his resentment of this player for his size and bullying and Paul's perception of himself as very small (he actually is over 6 feet). Perhaps not coincidentally, this resentment is quite congruent with Paul's interest in "playing good defense." Interestingly, resentment is often manifested in the passive-aggressive reactivity of preventing another person from reaching his goals rather than in assertively pursuing one's own.

Perhaps not coincidentally, then, Paul likes to remain "on the periphery" on offense, preferring to take outside shots. He is afraid himself of driving to the basket in an assertively determined way. As we analyzed Paul's approach to basketball in relation to his more general inhibitions, especially with regard to his fear of the aggression of others as well as his own, he has gradually applied our discussions to his expanding basketball playing repertoire and physically asserted himself more and more. As his treatment has continued to evolve, and Paul continues to reclaim his own aggression without fear of intemperate consequences, he has been able to find his way back to thinking, feeling, and acting from an embodied home again.

Chapter 4

# After the Fact

## The Retroactive Transformation of Suffering into Shame

> What a blank space I seemed, which everybody overlooked, and yet was in everybody's way.
>
> (Dickens, *David Copperfield*, 1850, p. 132)

### The Genesis of Shame: The Sudden Rupture of Mutuality

Early in my career, while doing a postdoctoral fellowship in psychoanalytic psychotherapy, I first became clued in to how quickly the self-doubts of shame can take hold of a person's mind. At the time, I was inundated by the recommendations of five different supervisors who believed in the virtues of strictly adhering to the psychoanalytic frame. When I was with my patients, instead of listening to my own instincts about how to be a helpfully insightful human being in a clinical setting, I attempted half-heartedly to comply with my supervisors' instructions to hold to "proper" technique.

One patient in particular, Linda, a 28-year-old woman, stands out in my memory as someone who inadvertently became a guinea pig for my ill-fated experiment in closely following authority. She came to psychotherapy because she was unsuccessful in the affairs of love, as she often became involved with men who would not commit to her more seriously. As a child, she had been repeatedly hurt by her divorced father's unavailability and unreliability.

When she was seven years old, her parents got divorced, and her father moved to another city, after which she saw him infrequently. One memory after his moving away stood out for her quite painfully. On one occasion, her father came back to visit for the weekend, and she was to meet him at an appointed time at his hotel. She was dropped off at the hotel, but he never showed up.

DOI: 10.4324/9781003559559-5

Early on in therapy with me, Linda and I had an exchange, which I have come to regret, because it did not represent my personal or clinical values before then or since that time. This interaction has helped reinforce a belief I have to trust my instincts in the living context of the clinical moment rather than obey the dictates of abstract technical principles.

Linda simply asked me: "Are you married?" With the corrective words of my supervisors echoing in my head to be a more reflective blank screen than I had ever been previously, I responded to the question with a return question: "Why do you think you asked that?" She, now immediately thrown back on the "inappropriateness" of asking her therapist a personal question, said: "I should have known better. I know you are not going to answer questions like that."

In this quite brief exchange, we can see how the experience of shame emerges reflexively in her self-consciously retroactive statement of "I should have known better." Linda's expectation of normal human reciprocity in receiving an answer to her question was rebuffed by my responding to her question with a return question. That frustration boomeranged back on her immediately as a doubt whether she had done something wrong or inappropriate. Although seedlings of shame and self-consciousness emerged in the wake of her feeling disregarded by my not addressing her question directly, she had not actually done anything wrong at all.

What further occurred to me after this exchange is that Linda never would have thought she had done anything inappropriate or wrong, had I simply answered her question "Yes" or "No." In other words, her shame and self-conscious sense of wrongness only emerged *after the fact* of hearing my non-response. What, then, might we learn more generally about how the genesis and dynamics of shame emerge in Linda's self-consciousness from her exposed vulnerability to relational disruption concerning her unanswered question?

When we are self-conscious, we attempt to view ourselves as if from the vantage point of the Other without of course being able to fully get beyond our projections. These projections of what we imagine the Other is thinking about us, *as if* we are viewing ourselves from the outside, are always informed by the experiences of sudden disruption that gave rise to shame in the first place. One of the more salient characteristics of being self-conscious thus is its self-derogatory quality; it is difficult to imagine Woody Allen and Diane Keaton's self-conscious characters in *Annie Hall* playing out their same scene full of compliments for themselves. Self-consciousness is thus infused with negative introjects that emerge from unanticipated experiences of relational disruption that are then projected into the *imagined* vantage point of the Other.

Tomkins (1963) describes how breakdowns of mutuality in relationships are implicated in shame:

> If I wish to touch you but you do not wish to be touched, I may feel ashamed. If I wish to look at you but you do not wish me to, I may feel ashamed… If I wish to be close to you, but you move away, I am ashamed.
>
> (p. 192)

Rank (1927), too, in attempting to describe the disowning or denial of feelings in neurotics, says: "One is ashamed of having feelings at all if they are not reciprocated, the unpleasant feeling of shame again being an emotional reaction to realization of difference, of separation" (p. 156). In this sense, Hyde (1979) emphasizes:

> The gift is lost in self-consciousness. To count, measure, reckon value, or seek the cause of a thing, is to step outside the circle, to cease being 'all of a piece' with the flow of gifts, and become, instead, one part of the whole reflecting upon another part.
>
> (p. 15)

Moreover, because often we are not anticipating this disruption to the continuity of our being, the experience of shame involves the element of surprise. In her pioneering study of the phenomenology of shame, Lynd (1958) says: "We are taken by surprise, caught off guard, off base, caught unaware, made a fool of" (p. 32). She continues further to characterize shame as: "Sudden exposure of a violation of expectations, of incongruity of trust in oneself, even in one's own body and skill and identity, and in the trusted boundaries or framework of the world one has known" (p. 46).

Perhaps it is because expectant hopes always spring eternally, human beings often are taken by surprise by breakdowns in the reciprocity of relationships. Since these hopes are often based on an unconscious adhesiveness to wish-fulfilling fantasies, the sense of surprise reflects how individuals often do not deeply internalize the rebuff of a final "No" for an answer. As a result, such persons often manifest a repetitious masochism of knocking their head against the wall of unbendable realities, such as who the other person actually is. I have noticed that even after long years of marriage, some patients have remarked how surprised they were when their spouses reacted in the same disappointing fashion that they always have, as if they had only just become acquainted with him or her.

## Chronic Shame: Cycles of Hope and Disappointment

When children offer themselves for acceptance to their parents, they are particularly vulnerable to shame. Elsewhere (Shabad, 1989, 2001), I have emphasized how this dynamic of expectant hope and unanticipated rejection is central to children's chronic experiences of shame.

If, for example, a father sits silently one night in his armchair and ignores his six-year-old son, most likely his son will not be traumatized after one incident. But if night after night, year after year, this son can do nothing to inspire his father's attention, the repeated experience of being ignored eventually takes on the cumulative meaning of a trauma.

Each day his father goes to work, hope springs eternal in the boy that perhaps today will be different: A wished-for father would return that night and have some kind words to offer or questions to ask that convey his fatherly concern. Instead, the boy's hopes are deflated, and his vulnerabilities are exposed by the reappearance of the same frustratingly unchanging figure of his father again.

Elsewhere (Shabad, 2001), I have used the term "traumatic themes" to describe interactions in which parents repeatedly enact their unmourned character faults on to their children. Traumatic themes are patterned configurations of rejection that emerge from chronic parent-child interactions. Angry vindictive silences, breaking small promises, petty criticisms, persistent intrusiveness, or calling a child stupid or ugly may all constitute traumatic themes of varying severity. For each individual, the traumatic themes emergent from these parent-child configurations form a blueprint of developmental helplessness.

The psychic loss of a physically present parent, based on these traumatic themes, derives specifically from the repeated disappointments of the child's continued hopes to change the frustratingly real parent into a wished-for parent. Most importantly, the child is not able to find closure easily and mourn psychic loss precisely because during the periodic absences from the real parent (child is at school; parent is at work), the child's hope forever springs eternal that the real parent will finally change into the wished-for ideal parent. The dragged-out endlessness of psychic loss is directly traceable to the relentless persistence of wishing in the face of a contradictory reality. The child wants what he wants and continues unconsciously to knock his wishful head against the immutable wall of the parent not changing.

These repeated experiences of hope and disappointment can have a profoundly demoralizing effect on children. Miller (1985) describes the emotional state of such a child:

> The core of the feeling experience is distress concerning a state of the self as no good or not good enough. To capture the state, one can think of a young boy standing before an admired parent who berates the child as stupid, thoughtless, or clumsy … he wants to disappear or hide, not to fight, because the self is experienced as not strong enough or valuable enough to proceed into the world.
>
> (p. 32)

More recently, Crastnopol (2015) has referred to these chronic traumatic experiences as "micro-traumas." She describes micro-traumatic experiences as "subtler occurrences … that are hard to notice, and harder to minister to, with the consequence that they accumulate invisibly." (p.2). Eventually, she continues, "such injuries can distort a person's character, undermine his or her sense of self-worth, and compromise his or her relatedness to others." (p. 2).

When a child has been repeatedly evicted or excluded from a parent's good graces, those cumulative experiences of rejected vulnerability may weave their way slowly into a chronic sense of shame. Chronic shame, caused by a person's inability to secure a sense of rootedness and belonging to his parents, is characterized by a perpetual feeling of unmoored isolation. Without that sense of belonging, one lives in dread of being exposed and found out for one's irreconcilable difference, weirdness, or defectiveness, and of thereby being excommunicated forever from the human community. It is precisely because one strives to hide these feelings of inferiority from others and oneself at all costs that the problem of chronic shame often remains unresolved indefinitely.

Wurmser (1981) suggests that many of these chronic experiences of rejection may be viewed as forms of "soul blindness," and results in the child's sense of feeling unlovable and unwanted. He states: "To be unlovable means not to see a responsive eye and not to hear a responding voice, no matter how much they are sought" (p. 97).

The term *mortification* expresses a close link between shame and the experience of psychic dying. Inasmuch as we all need human connections to transcend our mortality, when the bridge of human interdependence is broken, our shame threatens to leave us exposed to our frailty as isolated creatures. In this more global sense, our existential helplessness to alter the fact of our death is reflected concretely in our shame-inducing experiences of rejected vulnerability to make ourselves more acceptable to parents, who seem impossible to move or touch or change into the parents we would wish for.

If we have to endure trials and tribulations for what may seem like an interminable duration at the hands of parents whom we don't choose, it may well feel like our lives have been handed over to the cruel whims of a fate beyond our control. Very few of us are able to integrate and mourn these patterns of rejected vulnerability as they are being experienced during our growing up years. Instead, such patterns often become encoded as personal templates of helplessness that we attempt to escape and cover up, which then form the dark underbelly of our adult characters.

Over the past 40 years, I have conducted informal exploratory research to discern parallels between the specific ways in which we most fear dying and our "traumatic themes" (Shabad, 1989). I have hypothesized that our particular fears of death are metaphorical ways in which we reveal personal templates of helplessness that were shaped by our traumatic themes. For example, the fear of being stabbed to death may correspond to the repeated experience of being intruded upon by a parent, and the fear of drowning may correspond to fears of remaining still-born, of never emerging as an individual from an enmeshed relationship with one's mother. Here is a brief vignette to illustrate the clinical utility of fleshing out the underlying connection between particular fears of death and traumatic themes.

A number of years ago, I treated a 42-year-old man who had suffered from lifelong symptoms of anxiety, depression, and fears of death. Mike disclosed that often his fears of death intensified when he was less depressed, as if he were "bracing for impact." Significantly, he said that the worst way he could imagine dying was to be run over by a car without forewarning. He said he could not stand the idea of being unaware of when he was going to die.

Mike's history was replete with experiences of physical abuse at the hands of his father. On a number of occasions, Mike's father, without warning, would slap him across the face. He said that this arbitrary doling out of violence at a moment's notice often occurred at the dinner table. His father's malignant envy of Mike's creativity was particularly evident in a memory Mike recounted. Once Mike proudly displayed a model ship to his father that he had worked on for two months, saying, "Look, this is the *Santa Maria*." His father responded by smashing the boat and saying, "Now it's junk."

I suggested that perhaps his particular fears of death had to do with a fear of being re-exposed to the impact of his father's fits of violence. To counter his lack of preparedness for his father's unpredictability, Mike braces for impact through the self-deadening symptom of depression. It is only when he entertains the possibility of a better life that he is filled with the intense death anxiety of vulnerability and re-exposure to his father's envy and sadistic violence.

## The Transformation of Human Limitation into Shame

In exploring how experiences of trauma, loss, and disappointment are transformed after they have occurred into a sense of shame, it is important to understand that for children in particular, frustrations, disappointments, and even random misfortunes do not occur by accident. Instead, they reflexively take on the burden of responsibility for the bad things that happen to them. As Winnicott (1960b) pointed out, "In psychoanalysis, there is no trauma outside of the individual's omnipotence" (p. 37). A little later, he elaborates further on this point: "Impingements may be gathered by the ego organization into the infant's omnipotence and sensed as projections" (p. 47). When a child embraces his mother and expects her to reciprocate with a smile and a hug, but instead she remains tight-lipped, sad, and oblivious to him, his sense of being rejected automatically boomerangs as a sense of having done something wrong to make her unhappy.

Whereas the omnipotence of wish magic consisting in wishes leading directly to their manifest actions in the external world might be called positive superstition, such omnipotence becomes especially problematic when things go wrong in our lives. We react to relational disappointments *not by admitting the limitations of our powers*, but as a punitive sign reflecting back to us some wrongness or sinfulness about our wishes. The omnipotent burden of responsibility for what occurs in the outside world inherent in wish magic backfires, because now when bad things happen to us, we are at fault for the disappointments and failures that we ourselves suffer. The misfortunes we encounter reverberate back reflexively on our passionate life force as a punishment for our lack or failure, sowing doubts on our fundamental sense of worthiness.

On the surface of it, this automatic reactivity to a rejecting parent resembles guilt ("I must have done something wrong"), but it does not at all resemble the remorsefulness of a guilt in which one suffers the pangs of one's own conscience. As an immediate response to a parent's lack of reciprocity and what the child imagines to be the parent's disapproval, I am describing a process of self-doubt that is set in motion by a lack of expected reciprocity or responsiveness. One immediately has the sense of having done something wrong but does not know what. It is that sense of wrongness for one knows not what that suggests the reactive automaticity of this process culminates in something much more like shame rather than guilt. Reflexive guilt is a sense of wrongness, which is based primarily on an automatic reaction to the discontent of a more powerful Other without having *actually committed wrong*.

Both Nietzsche (1887) and Freud (1917) clearly differentiate between reflexive guilt and remorse. Perhaps most relevantly to the contrast between shame and guilt, the self-attack of Nietzsche's "bad conscience" and Freud's melancholia are not characterized by remorse, but by a reflexive sadism against oneself. Nietzsche (1887) vividly describes the merciless self-torment of bad conscience as "This uncanny, dreadfully joyous labor of a soul voluntarily at odds with itself that makes itself suffer out of joy in making suffer" (p. 87). Here is Freud's (1917) description of the melancholic patient:

> The patient represents his ego to us as worthless, incapable of any achievement and morally despicable, he reproaches himself, vilifies himself and expects to be cast out and punished. He abases himself before everyone and commiserates with his own relatives for being connected with anyone so unworthy. He extends his self-criticism back over the past; he declares that he never was any better.
>
> (p. 246)

Significantly, Freud (1917) emphasizes then that the melancholic's self-contempt is not based on a remorse over a substantive misdeed: "The melancholic does not behave in the same way as a person who is crushed by remorse and self-reproach" (p. 246).

Here is a brief snippet to illustrate how the second-guessing self-doubts of shame emerge in the aftermath of disappointments in relationships. Patricia, a 35-year-old woman, recently was having "what if" fantasies about Jason, a man who she had dated three years earlier. When Jason went on a short trip out of the country at the time, she began dating another man. Patricia expressed misgivings about her decision to turn her back on a then-promising relationship with Jason, who seemed to her to be a "nice guy," in favor of another man with whom she mostly had a tumultuous relationship that did not end well. After Jason returned from his trip at the time, he made it clear that Patricia had to decide between him and the other man.

Patricia's curiosity about Jason led her to track down his phone number to another state. She wanted to call him up, she said, so that at least she could gain some closure on the past. At the next session, Patricia reported that she phoned Jason earlier in the day and that he was quite reserved and cool, even somewhat rude, on the phone. He seemed annoyed at her phone call and said it was a bad time for him to talk. He then reluctantly agreed to talk the next day.

Patricia said her immediate response to the phone call was to think that she had done something wrong, and she scolded herself for calling him in the first place. She thought about not calling Jason back the next day but then determined that she would call to inform him, in no uncertain terms, who did not need whom. With a show of pride, Patricia then called to tell him she no longer had to speak with him because she had already gotten closure on their relationship.

It is significant that Patricia automatically turned on herself with such intense condemnation for having called in the first place *only because her conversation did not go in the good way that she had expected.* Although the morality of making the phone call is the same, regardless of whether Jason was happy to hear from her or not, Patricia felt as if she had erred because she was disappointed in the way he had responded to her.

In this example, Patricia uses a counter-phobic defense to cover up her sense of exposed vulnerability through an instantaneous mental shift to an imaginary omniscient future of 20/20 hindsight. By leaping to an all-knowing vantage point, she attempts to double back on her experience of not knowing how he would react and subject the helplessness of sudden disappointment to the omniscience of mental control. If only she had been clever enough to accurately predict what was going to happen ahead of time, she could have avoided the shock of disappointment. She is thereby able to use her mind to co-opt the power of unexpected suffering by rewriting the narrative meaning of her experiences only after seeing how all her efforts to win back Jason did not succeed.

Although Patricia attempted desperately to adapt to the harsh "reality" of Jason's response, the experiences of disappointment inevitably pervaded her thinking, which was anything but an autonomous ego function. Just as Freud (1917) pointed out that in the aftermath of loss: "The shadow of the object falls upon the ego" (p. 251), so, too, in shame the shadows of unexpected relational disruption infuse the retroactively transformed narrative of one's experience with the harsh judgment derived from the omniscience of 20/20 hindsight.

It is unfortunate that human beings turn on themselves with self-loathing of their "badness"—as if they had done something terribly malicious when they have just been exposed to the human frailties and limitations we all share with one another. When the various layers of memory are peeled away, the moral basis for the self-contempt of shame is frequently elusive because it was not one's malice that was coded as evil, but only one's own experience of being victimized by parental fate and random misfortune. In this reflexive, non-rational fashion, children transform the inevitably tragic elements of their experiences that lie outside of their control, such as deaths, losses, or even a mother's chronic depression, into a shame they believe could have been avoided. There is a heavy cost to pay in sacrificing a sense of one's own self-image as good when taking on one's misfortunes as one's own burden of shame. The victimizing powers that be, such as God, fate, or one's parents, are not at fault; the enemy now lies within.

## Shame Morality: Blaming the Victim in Oneself

The tendency to attribute evil to oneself on the basis of outcome rather than prospective intentions is manifested in the ancient but still widespread belief that if one is victorious in war, it means that God or "goodness" is on one's side. Although the morality of the war in Vietnam did not change fundamentally from its inception when the United States still had high hopes of a quick victory, it was only as American casualties began to mount and the war effort bogged down that there was an ever-increasing outcry about its immorality. On a less deadly scale, when a professional sports team wins an athletic event, a coach is often thankful that God answered his prayers for victory. One wonders, however, what consideration God gave to the players and coach on the losing team.

Similarly, during the Middle Ages, trials by endurance were used to prove the innocence or guilt of a person accused of a crime. If the accused person endured the particular torture and did not show any lasting ill effects, it meant he was innocent. Success or failure at "running the gauntlet," was used as a trial by fire to decide whether to set a prisoner free. Such trials by fire are still used in the initiation rites of various college fraternities to arbitrate whether an initiate may be included in the group.

Catastrophic natural disasters throughout history, such as the Lisbon earthquake in the 18th century, have been attributed to God's punishment for human sin rather than viewed as accidents beyond human control. In a desperate attempt to be rid of the Black Death in the 13th century, bands of self-flagellants traveled from town to town in their attempt to repent and expiate human sin by flagellating themselves in public squares.

When a person wins a good amount of money at gambling, he may become giddy, not just because of the practical uses to which he can put his new winnings, but because his good fortune signifies that God or fate has smiled upon his life for a brief moment. On the other hand, when we lose or fail, or in any way exhibit the fallibility of human weakness as when we suffer, it is as if God is frowning down on us. As Ricoeur (1967) says: "Punishment falls on man in the guise of misfortune and transforms all possible sufferings, all diseases, all death, all failure into a sign of defilement" (p. 27). He continues: "If you suffer, if you are ill, if you die, it is because you have sinned." (p. 31).

*Defilement* here means being stained with impurity, "a 'something' that infects" (p. 33), in Ricoeur's (1967) words. The meaning of *fault* as a traumatic break in one's "continuity of being" now overlaps with a self-attribution of moral fault for demonstrating the fatal flaw in the armor of omnipotence. The evil of suffering as a harbinger of one's helplessness in the face of death is a mortal stain that defiles the perfection of everlasting eternity and is linked with fault in ourselves. Ricoeur states: "Man asks himself: Since I experience this failure, this sickness, this evil, what sin have I committed?" (p. 41). He notes insightfully: "Evil and misfortune have not been dissociated, in which the ethical order of doing ill has not been distinguished from the cosmo-biological order of faring ill: suffering, sickness, death, failure" (p. 27).

Lest we become too taken with our post-Enlightenment 21st-century rationalisms and rationalizations, our own shames may be viewed as the newest psychologized edition of sin. The sense of defilement and stain in sin has now been transformed into what Pattison (2000) terms the "internalized pollution" of shame. To gain control over the randomness of suffering, human beings have attempted to identify with and introject the overwhelming powers of fate and locate the cause of suffering in the "sin" of their fundamental helplessness as human creatures.

Human beings punish themselves through self-shaming in order to inhibit and forestall the dangers of exposure to external dangers. In transforming the shadows of suffering into God's retribution, individuals identify with the power of that retributive power in their own personalized superegos.

Elias (1939) also has described the historical cultural process by which fear of external punishment has become introjected as fear of one's own superego authority:

> Inner fear grew in proportion to the decrease of outer ones, now a major part of the person. In a sense, the danger zone passes through the self of every individual. The direct fear inspired by men has diminished and the inner fear mediated through the eye and through the superego is rising proportionately.
>
> (p. 497)

Blaming the victim in ourselves after our choices turn out badly ultimately derives from encountering the limits to our omnipotence, our sense of failure in being unable to make our desires come true in and of ourselves alone. Pagels (1988) thus says: "Were it not for the fact that people would rather feel guilty than helpless… I suspect the idea of original sin would not have survived the fifth century" (p. 146).

Freud (1930) says of the superego:

> Ill-luck—that is, external frustration—so greatly enhances the power of the conscience in the super-ego. As long as things go well with a man, his conscience is lenient and lets the ego do all sorts of things; but when misfortune befalls him, he searches his soul, acknowledges

his sinfulness, heightens the demands of his conscience, imposes abstinences on himself with penances... If a man is unfortunate, he is no longer loved by the highest power, and threatened by such a loss of love, he once more bows to the parental representative in his super-ego... The severity of the super-ego ... is simply a continuation of the severity of the external authority, to which it has succeeded and which it has in part replaced.

(pp. 126–127)

The mortifying experience of shame and the dread of re-exposure thus inform one of the primary functions of introjecting threat—the constant vigil of watching over oneself to make sure that one does not make a fool of oneself again. In this sense, we might think of the superego not so much as a structural entity per se, but as a repetitious process of hypervigilance that is always bracing for the dangers of traumatic exposure to rejection and attack from the external world. Ricoeur (1967) states:

The interdict anticipates in itself the chastisement of suffering, and the moral constraint of the interdict bears in itself the emotion-laden effigy of the punishment. A taboo is nothing else: a punishment anticipated and forestalled emotionally is an interdiction. This the power of the interdict, in anticipatory fear, is a deadly power.

(p. 33)

This determination to sidestep the exposure of shame may then shape one's moral rules, standards, ideals, and values with the intensity of a life-and-death struggle, thereby forming a "morality of survival." In this fear-based world of kill or be killed, success is measured by the degree to which shame-inducing experiences are avoided. The all-or-none standard of perfection is required, because any errors mean falling into a relational abyss between self and other. The ruthlessness of natural selection takes no prisoners. Only the fittest survive, and failure is punishable by death, or worse, the dreaded mortification of exposed vulnerability. There is no middle ground between life and death, between the perfection of surviving psychically intact on one hand, and the shame of rejected vulnerability and forgotten oblivion of isolation on the other.

These life-and-death stakes now spill over into the either–or moral designations of good or bad that are attributed to strength versus weakness and success versus failure. The strong win the ultimate battle for survival over the weak, who die out as extinct losers, and the struggle for power, exemplified by the maxim "might makes right," guides a desperate quest for survival and significance. If one can no longer trust that one can secure one's unique place of belonging in the world through one's offerings and gifts, one must combat the dangers of ignominy and isolation by guaranteeing one's impact through the exertion of power and force. Wurmser (1981) says: "The sense of shame is characterized by weakness, dirtiness, and defectiveness" (p. 189). Fascism, as the prototypical morality of power, specifically targets the vulnerability of shame, which Wurmser refers to as an evil to be covered up and even eradicated. For example, Adolf Hitler, interpreting acts of mercy only through the lens of a shame-based morality, viewed such kindnesses as weakness.

Unlike guilt, the shame-based morality of power is not based on the right and wrong of intentions, but on the success or failure of outcome. Whereas guilt reflects a remorseful sense of wrongdoing for transgressing universal standards of the Golden Rule, shame is based on attributions of right and wrong that are made retroactively, depending on whether one has won or lost, succeeded or failed.

Through the constructed prism of the rationalized rules and standards of our harsh superegos—our own very personal tyrannical Gods—we "blame the victim" in ourselves retroactively for being victims of an unfortunate fate. Whether we have big elephant ears, a large protruding nose, uncontrollable zits, parents who never stop bickering, or an abusively alcoholic father, we hound ourselves mercilessly for our all-too-human flaws and weaknesses, as if we had committed the worst of transgressions.

When a person is raped or sexually abused or called an ethnic slur, the victim incurs a shame, in which she blames herself rather than the abuser for bringing on her experience of victimization. Fritz Perls (1969) says: "I have called shame and embarrassment Quislings of the organism... As Quislings identify themselves with the enemy and not their own people, so shame, embarrassment, self-consciousness, and fear restrict the individual's expression" (p. 178). The self-cruelty of shame is like a tragic misunderstanding in which the police have apprehended the wrong person for a crime he did not commit. To the extent that one has not done anything really wrong but feels as if one had, the source for the sense of badness that undergirds shame is like an elusive phantom that is difficult to catch.

Even the more educated, liberal-minded among us who pride ourselves on our enlightened ethics of tolerance are not immune to circumscribed rigidities and harshness when our hidden Achilles heels of disillusionments—turned into shames—are pricked. For example, in our white American culture that glorifies very slim figures for women, a normally open-minded woman may tolerate plus sizes in other women, but she will attack herself viciously if she were to gain a few pounds.

## Carl: Shame in the Shadow of Perfect Hindsight

One of the most common ways that individuals transform their human limitations into shame is through the omniscience of 20/20 hindsight. I have sat with many patients as they have talked through the choice between two life pathways, such as taking a job in a different city or whether to marry or get divorced. After finally committing themselves to one pathway that did not turn out the way they would have liked, such patients often scold themselves by saying "I should have taken the other job" or "I shouldn't have left my wife." I often remind such patients that I was present as a witness when they painstakingly went through their decision-making process without knowing how it would turn out. I often remind them that they made their choice with the best of intentions and good faith while projecting themselves into a future *that could not be predicted.*

Here, shame derives from a morality that is based on the omniscient perfectionism of looking back after seeing the outcome of a choice, and then attempting to rewrite the actuality of past experience in order to match the outcome. Punishing oneself for having "spilled the milk" or making the "cookie crumble" or not "striking when the iron was hot" reflect a backward-looking retroactive aspect of shame. On the other hand, when one truly experiences pangs of guilt that have been filtered through one's conscience, one takes responsibility for one's mistakes with a future-oriented perspective in which one takes reparative actions moving forward.

Rather than acknowledging our limitations, however, we resort to a form of magic in looking back at ourselves after the fact of our lived experience in order to manipulate what could have been done differently. From this bird's eye view in the future, and knowing what we know now, there is a kind of plea in shame for a second chance at a do-over in order to avoid life's sufferings.

Carl, a 54-year-old bear of a man, is afraid of his own shadow. He cannot take a step forward in life without second-guessing himself. Every time he decides to move in one direction instead of another, he doubles back and doubts the wisdom of his own choice.

Carl is divorced and has two children of college age. He has his own business and dabbles in real estate in his free time. Quite recently, he has decided to invest more money to enhance the infrastructure of a building he owns because it had not been attracting renters. He had been advised by an uncle to sell the property, but other family members recommended that he make the extra outlay of cash for the building. Carl frets constantly about whether he should have poured more money into the project, always wondering whether he made "the wrong decision." A wrong decision for Carl means an unsuccessful outcome. Carl is terrified of making any decisions because each failed outcome reflects shamefully on his sense of inadequacy.

Carl has also been involved with a divorced woman in an on-again, off-again relationship for the past three years. They have agreed to get married on three separate occasions, but he backed out each time for fear that he will become trapped in a future that he does not want. The woman finally decided to break up with Carl and move on with her life. Carl felt sad because he says he loves her, but he is also relieved to be free of the pressure of pleasing her.

Although Carl retreats from his anxieties, which occur at the crossroads of any changes, he is also not happy to find himself always relegated to the drudgery of his same routines. He complains about his lack of hobbies or interests in doing anything that would be culturally elevating, such as going to the symphony, the opera, or an art museum. He has very much enjoyed being with his children, but they are now away at college. Carl finds himself in a boring life of quiet desperation and emptiness.

Life had gone downhill for Carl after his strong-willed father died 10 years earlier. His father had started the real estate business and brought Carl in as his junior partner. To Carl, his father seemed invariably to make sound financial decisions. Even though his father could also be arrogant and overbearing, Carl depended heavily on his father's force of will for guidance in life.

Carl is caught in a catch-22 between encountering the inevitable anxieties that surround the uncertainties of change and inability to commit himself to a life pathway, and the despair that results in constantly shying away from his fears. In the aftermath of living on the ghostly outskirts of his own life, he continually struggles with the regret of missed opportunities. Since he had not mourned the death of his father, Carl had never deposed him from his idealized perch. His contempt for himself in comparison to a father who could do no wrong has perpetuated a cycle of self-shaming and dependency on stronger others to show him the way.

When Carl comes for a therapy session, he trudges into my office with his hands in his pocket, as if to say: "I need help. I cannot do anything for myself." In part, Carl would like me to be the second coming of a father who will tell him what to do with his life. I instead ask Carl about his fears of making "wrong decisions." I wondered whether he feared making actual decisions in his life because he dreaded the cruelty of his own self-berating hindsight.. When Carl speaks about "wrong" decisions, to Carl's surprise, I responded that for Carl in particular, there were no wrong choices. For him, any decision and commitment that he makes is the "right" choice because it is better than his indecision. I add that no one really knows what the future will bring and that we all do the best we can with the information at our disposal at the time we make our decisions.

Carl has not been fully satisfied with this appeal to human imperfection, since for him there are objective "right" and "wrong" decisions, and the proof is in the successful or failed outcome of the decision. In his mind, the competent adult knows how to make good decisions that lead to successful outcomes. Despite my pointing out to him that he is always judging himself *after the fact* with the perfectionism of 20/20 hindsight, Carl has tenaciously held on to his self-imposed perfectionism. In a sense, Carl has introjected his idealized father's own denial of limitations and made that his own ego ideal. Through the prism of that perfectionistic ideal, he can never do anything right.

I have confided to Carl my own temptation to retreat from the anxieties and pressures that surround the transitions of life. I have spoken of being conscious of a wish to stay in bed in the morning rather than encounter the pressures of the day, but that I then jump into the shower with the knowledge that I will feel better afterwards. This disclosure has resonated somewhat with Carl since he, too, struggles most in the beginning of the day.

More recently, Carl has begun to let go of the paternal ideal to which he has always compared himself for the worse. With both the help of pop psychology books and my appeal to the human imperfections we all hold in common, including my own, Carl has begun to realize that everyone has some anxiety about encountering change and making difficult choices. This normalizing of what Carl thought was only his inadequacy in conquering his fears has made a significant difference in his feeling of wellbeing. As Carl puts it: "I realize I'm not the only one who has anxiety."

From Carl's experience, we can see how self-doubt leads him to lean on the authority of stronger others to make key decisions for him. Whether he was trying to decide to get married or not, or to invest money in his real estate properties or not, Carl solicited the opinions of many family members to help guide him in one particular direction or other. He sought to be without the harsh self-recriminations that had infiltrated and burdened his consciousness with anxiety.

Piers and Singer (1953) describe shame as a "tension between ego and the ego ideal" (p. 24). By erasing or denying one's shamed actual self in favor of the ideal self one should have been, one still harbors hopes of undoing and cleansing oneself of the moral stain of internalized pollution in the aftermath of traumatic disruption. If our desires have led only to endless disappointment, then it is better to be rid of the sinfulness of hope that only leads to suffering. In this sense, the superego constraints of ascetic self-control are a form of eradicating desire, cleansing oneself of the impurities of sin and ultimately to avoid suffering.

It is as if we must satisfy a blood lust when we experience the unfortunate vagaries of fate, by either shaming ourselves or externalizing that shame and scapegoating others. *Someone*, though, must always pay for misfortune. This search for a scapegoat to "take the fall" for the comedown we have experienced in suffering reflects a non-acceptance of the tragic aspects of life, such as chronic disappointments, losses, and death, on their own terms. It is a means of splitting good from bad so as to defensively shield the tidy perfection of eternity from the existential stain of death.

Such splitting means that we are always looking to displace the "hot potato" of fault somewhere else in order to cleanse our souls of stain. When individuals do locate the problematic source of their shame in floppy elephant ears or a protruding nose or a receding hairline or in the mere fact that their parents are getting divorced, they may harbor a fantasy of sacrificially eliminating this "bad" aspect of themselves in order to purify and make themselves whole again and thus embark on a perfect new beginning.

This fantasy of sacrifice and targeted elimination of flawed aspects of oneself that taint the whole organism can become dangerous when we project the same thinking into the body politic of the culture. In such cases, by killing off the Other, we may kill off the stain of death/sin to purify the larger cultural body and attain a perfect future.

Instead of humbly acknowledging our fundamental limitations as individuals and ethical responsibility toward the Other, in our shame, we adhere to a self-oppressive omnipotence and omniscience in which we imagine that we have created our own victimizations. As a result, many persons interpret traumatic experiences superstitiously, as a divinely-inspired retributive comeuppance for the hubris of overstepping their limits. In the wake of shame experiences recast as punishments, the consciousness of one's fall from creator to creature then is reinforced by too much of one's own self-degradation.

Chapter 5

# Exile and Self-doubt

## The Inversion of Passion into Passivity

> He fell in love with an empty hope, a shadow mistaken for substance ... he plunges his arms in the water to clasp that ivory neck and finds himself clutching to no one.
>
> (Ovid, *Metamorphoses*, 8 A.D., pp. 112–113)

### "I Should Have Known Better": Self-Doubt and the Reversal of Passion

Perhaps more than anything else, we all wish to be accepted for who we are, for who we feel ourselves to be as unique individuals. We seek to be cherished as "objects of primary value" (Becker, 1973), not so much in spite of our idiosyncrasies and eccentricities, but because of them. Through this receptive welcome of our expressive offerings as individuals who have never lived before and will never live again, we gain an indispensable sense of belonging to the ongoing human enterprise. Without the embedded feeling of participating in a larger community to inspire hope and meaning, we are like floundering fish, desperately flapping for the cover of our watery home. "Home" here does not refer only to a sense of belonging engendered by human relationships, but also the "home" of one's own psyche-soma from which the self-conscious mind is alienated.

In the wake of our injured vulnerabilities, we defensively preempt further injury by using our minds to fill the vacuum of a relationship with an absent Other and form an enclosed relationship with ourselves. With this shift of identifications in one's center of gravity from inside our lived experience to our disembodied mind, we construct an enclosed but alienated consciousness of our embodied vulnerabilities.

Moreover, this enclosed relationship with oneself is constituted by an introjection of self-shaming, in which one is both the shamer and the one

DOI: 10.4324/9781003559559-6

who is shamed. In the previous chapter, I emphasized that when children suffer through traumatic experiences, they do not believe that they suffered by random accident or happenstance. Winnicott (1960b) emphasizes that such bad experiences are automatically incorporated into an "area of omnipotence," in which individuals take on an excessive burden of responsibility for having caused their own trauma.

Children thus don't view parental non-responsiveness neutrally but infuse those experiences of rejected vulnerability with the intentionality of an antagonistic power. The frustration of expectant hope and desire in a child's experiences of injury and hurt are interpreted as a punishment for simply desiring, and the child then constructs meaning of "deserving" this punishment by inferring something sinful or shameful about himself.

In feeling worthless because of not being received by the parent, the child feels it is up to him to use all means necessary to earn his way into the good graces of the parent. When, for example, a depressed parent cannot enjoy her child's offerings or rebuffs his numerous attempts to lift her mood, the child may feel excluded from the inner sanctum of the parent's life; he may then fall back on fantasies of omnipotence to compensate for his actual helplessness to have a lasting effect on the depressed parent.

Trapped between the parent's continued rebuff of his offerings and his own refusal to take "no" for an answer, the child is left with a great sense of mental responsibility for the parent's well-being. As many attempts to give of himself come to a dead end in a parent who cannot or will not receive the child's offerings of help, the child is left with a fundamental helplessness of knowing about the parent's unhappiness without being able to do anything about it. This burden of mental responsibility for the parent's unhappiness continues to weigh heavily, like the unremitting pressure of a debt that never gets repaid. As a result, such individuals forfeit the deserved worthiness of a "right" to move forward with the continued process of increasing separation, individuation, and claimed autonomy from one's parents.

The frustrated wish to give back and restore a connectedness with a parental home base, now "backed up," infiltrates the child's mental spheres of imagining, knowing, and thinking. Since the parent is not accessible to the child's offerings, the child's gifts of *doing* are necessarily restricted to the mental gifts of *worrying*. Each wish to give that is frustrated in actuality, stillborn at its conception, is recycled in the incessant false starts of worrying or obsessive ruminating. Phillips (1993) thus describes a ten-year-old boy whose worries "were like gifts he kept for his mother." It is interesting to note here that the etymology of "anxiety" derives from the Latin *anxietas* or "to choke." In German, the expression *sich aengstigen* or "to feel anxious" also literally means "becoming narrow, being narrowed in." Choked off or inhibited action is relegated to the thinking sphere of anxious worrying.

Furthermore, since shame always emerges *only after* experiencing the outcome of relational disruption, the dissociative shift from a lived-in psyche-soma to disembodied mind also parallels a shift from an embodied present to a disembodied omniscient future. From this projection of one's consciousness onto the all-knowing vantage point in the future, the experiences of traumatic victimization once lived through with an unsuspecting prospective time orientation are reframed, distorted, and judged self-punitively through the omniscience of 20/20 hindsight. For example, when something goes wrong in a relationship or a life choice does not turn out as we would have liked, we may berate ourselves with constant refrains of "I should have known better." The echoes of these regretful self-accusations pervading one's mind have the oppressive effect of transforming endured sufferings into shameful feelings of failure, weakness, and ineffectiveness.

One of the hallmarks of self-enclosed shame consciousness is its focused orientation on undoing the past. Many patients scold themselves mercilessly for the failure to live up to an idealized image they have for themselves. Patients with shame often persist in punishing themselves for having made "the milk spill" long after it has already spilled. Such self-punishment implicitly reveals unconscious fantasies that it is really not too late to go back in time and erase what has occurred in order to "unspill the milk"; what's done is not really done because it can be undone.

The retroactive shadow of self-consciousness, informed by the aim of annulling the flow of lived time and perfecting one's inherent limitations, threatens to undermine all self-expressiveness and activity with its tormenting echoes of second-guessing. Those individuals who continue to look back wistfully on an idealized past before making past mistakes would do well to heed Kierkegaard's (1844) cautionary words about the self-deceit of continually wishing to return to the past: "Innocence is not a perfection, that one should wish to regain, for as soon as one wishes for it, it is lost, and then it is a new guilt to waste one's time on wishes" (p. 37). The self-objectifying inverted eye of such shame consciousness may be viewed as a magic spell that one casts on oneself; a spell in which one believes there is something fundamentally wrong about oneself when, in fact, making mistakes is just imperfectly "human, all too human," in Nietzsche's (1878) words.

Shame undermines the conviction that one can both be passionately self-assertive and ethically good at the same time. Wurmser (1981) notes:

> Since by and large shame is evoked by weakness and guilt by strength, it is evident that the person who defends against aggression by passivity is consequently more disposed to manifest shame than the one who turns his aggression into activity. That is, the primarily passive person tends to feel ashamed, the primarily active one guilty.
>
> (p. 62)

Inasmuch as shame is based on omnipotence, it does not only target one's actions, but also tyrannizes desire itself in all of its manifestations of thinking, feeling, and imagining. From within one's primary-process thinking (Freud, 1913a), human beings hold to a superstitious belief in the automatic linearity of wish magic. The premise of wish magic (a process which Freud (1913b) termed "motor hallucinations") is that, like a runaway train, there is an unbounded, straight-line fluidity between wish proceeding through thought and then eventually culminating in actions. In speaking of wish magic, Fraser (1890) writes: "Men mistook the order of their ideas for the order of nature, and hence imagined that the control which they have, or seem to have, over their thoughts permitted them to have a corresponding control over things" (p. 420).

Through the lens of shame, we can see why we would view negative outcomes as a reflection on the wrongness of our thoughts and even desires. Shame reflects the way traumatic experiences, sufferings, and losses reverberate back on our own sense of inadequacy, even when, to all rational onlookers, we do not seem to have any control over what occurs in the outside world.

The omnipotence of wish magic places a heavy burden of responsibility on our inner life for the practical consequences that must necessarily follow. We must always be on the alert for harboring nasty thoughts and hurting the persons we love; to have lust in our hearts is dangerous and judged as morally wrong because of leading inevitably to lustful actions. We must constrain our imagination and watch what we think or feel or say for fear of where it may lead. In speaking of the neurotic, Freud (1913b) says: "He refuses to believe that thoughts are free and is always afraid to express evil wishes lest they be fulfilled in consequence of their utterance" (pp. 113–114). When one does not trust the fundamental goodness of one's passion, one always feels at risk of doing something wrong without knowing how or why. Any bad lurking within must remain unimaginable, unthinkable, and unspeakable.

Since now, in the shadow of shame, the child does not trust that the free rein of his passion will lead to anything constructive, he must constrain the force of his passion at its source. Without the confidence in the "rightness" of his decisions, he becomes mired in the uncertain confusion of indecision. Filled with self-doubt, the child inverts the inherent strength of his passionate life force into a weakened moral state of passive unworthiness and finds it increasingly difficult to assert himself with confidence. Indeed, Critchley (2015) describes shame consciousness as the "inversion of intentionality" (p. 65).

With the reversal of passion into passivity, the encounter with the strange exposes the child to crippling anxiety. Whereas the process of growth is based on the intertwining developmental/relational rhythms of giving and being received by an Other, of giving oneself over to the unpredictability of change *and* re-finding a thread of continuity afterwards, now, in the wake of relational disruption and emergent shame, these rhythms are dichotomized into giving *or* receiving, either getting lost in the infinite expanses of change *or* holding on to what is familiar.

Rather than growth being experienced like a passionately willed process, the passive, self-doubting child comes to anticipate the uncertainties of separation, transition, and novelty as something that is always happening too quickly, before she is ready. Relinquishing the familiar becomes coupled with the shame of premature exposure and a sense of feeling incomplete in and of one's individual self. In the meantime, the drive of the child's passion to grow, now disowned and projected outward, is experienced as an incoming coercive pressure coming from the external world.

## Shame and Avoidance of Eye-to-Eye Contact

We can use the metaphor of eye-to-eye contact as a way of delineating this pathway from intersubjectivity to the introjection of shame self-shaming. If we follow Levinas's (1969) emphasis on the intersubjectivity of coming face-to-face with the Other, then the I-Thou meeting between two uniquely different faces is specifically centered in the mutual interpenetration of eyes, the "windows to the soul." Tomkins (1982) suggests: "The shared eye-to-eye interaction is the most intimate relationship between human beings" (p. 376).

The very intimacy of this mutual gaze between two persons is a delicate balance between mutual curiosity and vulnerability. When an individual has been exposed too long and/or too intensely to experiences of being insulted, injured, or ignored, he is not able to maintain the mutual gaze of intersubjectivity. In the aftermath of his wounded dignity and shame, the powerful eye of the Other threatens to see through his social guise to his nakedness as a humble, insignificant creature. In such situations, we feel that we are in danger of being captured by the power of the Other's gaze to objectify and totalize. Among people in many "primitive" cultures, there has thus been a widespread avoidance of being photographed for fear of being robbed of their souls. In clinical work, paranoid patients may sometimes ask accusingly: "Why are you staring at me like that?"

It is not surprising, then, that for human animals, the intersubjectivity of mutual gaze is a sensitive gauge that reflects an individual's diminished injured dignity and sense of shame. More specifically, shame is manifested in the avoidance of a flight response. Darwin (1872) observed that human beings, when embarrassed or ashamed, instinctively demonstrate a "turning away, or lowering eyes, or restlessly moving them from side to side..." (pp. 328–329). Tomkins (1963) also notes that the goal of the shame response is to reduce facial communication, and Fenichel (1945) has said:

> I feel ashamed means I do not want to be seen. Therefore, persons who feel ashamed hide themselves, at least avert their faces. However, they also close their eyes and refuse to look. This is a kind of magical gesture, arising from the magical belief that anyone who does not look cannot be looked at.

> (p. 139)

When I was a young child given to a momentary hunger, I would often ask for a much larger meal than I could ever actually eat. At such times, my mother would often say: "Your eyes are bigger than your stomach." In a sense, she was saying that the infinite reach of my hungry imagination was far greater than the limitations of my mortal body would ever allow. The eyes are the expressive vehicle of curiosity by which our imaginations go beyond our limits to roam free and seek to possess what we are lacking. Rather than accept our human limitations with humility and respect the distance that shields the mystery of each other's essence as individuals, our hungry eyes transgress the boundaries of the forbidden and seek to penetrate mystery. That transgression is often met with the punishment of shame for the limitless ambition of our exploratory desires.

Fenichel's (1945) description of "closing one's eyes" to evade being looked at closely follows Freud's (1905a) view of shame as punishment for scopophilia, the love of looking. In this view, the child's curiosity to pry into the mysteries of the parent's sex life and ultimately into the riddle of life's origins is punished with the Oedipal humiliation of being cast into exile.

Oedipus, of course, is a story of a man who sought to transcend the cycle of generations by seeking carnal knowledge with his mother and thereby become father to himself. Indeed, in both Greek and Hebrew, the verb "to know" refers to sexual intercourse. In the Latin phrase *libido sciendi*, or "lust to know," there is a direct analogy made between curiosity and sexual desire. The Oedipus story is a moral fable of transgression, of prying too much behind the veil of mystery, and thereby incorporating forbidden knowledge of how life is created. In understanding that the reproduction of life originates in sexual intercourse, the possessor of carnal knowledge threatens to usurp the role of creator that is best left to the provenance of God the Creator. Oedipus's hubris of over-weaning ambition and desire thus is punished with a blindness that teaches him the necessary humility of gaining insight into the limitations of the human creature that are manifest in accepting the transitions from one generation from the next. The Oedipus myth, including the Oedipus's self-blinding, is an apt example of how the unlimited reach of our imagination is punished severely at the locus of visual curiosity and ambition.

The punishment for the curiosity to swallow up and take in possessive knowledge with one's eyes parallels also the story of Genesis, in which the hubris of Adam and Eve eating from the Tree of Knowledge of Good and Evil culminates with the end of innocence and the onset of their shame. It is not surprising then that Augustine of Hippo (397–400) warned that *curiositas*— the desire for experience and knowledge—is an even more dangerous temptation than the temptations of the flesh. The passionately unselfconscious quest to know too much meets with punishing shameful consciousness of one's limitations as a mortal creature.

## Self-enclosure: Searching Inward and Backward for One's Essence

When an individual casts his eyes downward in shame to avoid the gaze of the Other, where is he looking instead? On what is he focusing? Perhaps his eyes are preoccupied with the attempt to recognize and find himself by endlessly searching for his own embodied essence.

The phrase "stuck on oneself" aptly characterizes this repetitious inverted breakdown or stuck-ness on a relationship with a subjective other. The narcissistic individual is stuck on a self that was never received and therefore exhibited in an endless, misguided search for recognition; misguided, because the transformative experience of self-realization cannot be found in his own self-enclosure.

As the wide-eyed gaze of curiosity closes in on itself, this person no longer welcomes the infinite times of the future or the infinite spaces of the other person with open arms. When the incoming gift of life's fleeting instants pass without actualizing his contributions to the human endeavor, the unrealized moments that were not "seized while the iron was hot" may become sentimentalized after their passing. As if begging the fates for another chance to live out missed opportunities, he may then shift his open-hearted focus from living for and toward the realization of future possibilities to an enclosed preoccupation with recapturing the actuality of moments that passed us by all too quickly.

Kierkegaard (1843b) has referred to this preoccupation with recapturing a now-abstracted past from the concrete flow of time as "recollection." In contrast, he uses the term "repetition" to describe a passionate movement of freedom to actualize oneself anew in each incoming moment received from the future: "Repetition and recollection are the same movement, just in opposite directions; because what is recollected has already been, and is thus repeated backwards; whereas genuine repetition is recollected forwards" (p. 3).

Kierkegaard emphasizes that the recollection of understanding cannot recapture the actuality of present moments that have passed one by; they can only be viewed through the abstracted prism of consciousness. As he famously declared: "It is quite true what philosophy says: that life must be understood backwards. But then one forgets the other principle: that it must be lived forwards" (p. 161).

Carlisle (2006) beautifully summarizes Kierkegaard's thinking on the subject:

> Concrete existence, unlike the necessary being with which logic deals, has reality only insofar as it continues to be actualized at every moment. Existence is always *coming into existence*, arising and passing away and arising again at unfathomable speed. So for an existing thing to endure—to be itself—it must be repeatedly renewed, for without the actualizing movement it falls into non-being.
>
> (p. 76)

The challenge to remain in synchrony with the ever-evolving actuality of lived experience is especially problematic in the wake of trauma. Without anyone to validate the child's experience, the child is forced into the impossible position of bearing witness to the reality of her own experience from the dissociated self-exile of being on the outside looking at oneself. At the very same moments that a person suffers a trauma, she is also dissociating from the embodied experience of injury that was suffered.

The passive child, not feeling confident enough to face the unpredictability of the future, turns toward the past in search of the reality of her own dissociated experience. The reversal in perspective from an embodied, prospective view of time to the retrospective lens of disembodied mind is not unlike leaping out of a bus going in one direction and hopping on another bus moving in the opposite direction. Instead of facing the future with a "progressive time orientation," the disembodied mind faces backward toward the past with a "regressive time orientation." Yet, since organismic movement moves inexorably toward the future, such individuals may feel like they are reluctantly "backing into the future."

In shifting her center of gravity from body to disembodied mind, this individual may gain an emotional sense of distance from herself that fosters the illusion that she has annulled the flow of time at the site of the disruption so that she can recapture and realize the experience of victimization from which she dissociated. From within a defensive posture of self-enclosure, such persons thus are not only using their disembodied minds to preempt further injury, but they are also attempting to reverse the flow of time and heal the rupture between mind and body prior to becoming alienated from themselves.

This attempt to recapture the actuality of traumatic experience and thereby heal the fissure of past and present from within the perspective of one's disembodied mind, is doomed to failure. Inasmuch as we take dissociative flight from our embodied experience of helpless vulnerability and shame that was endured passively from within our bodies, our lives are not being inhabited from within. Without a corpus of lived experience to fall back on for a sense of certainty, our minds work feverishly to affirm that our suffering was not just a figment of our imagination, but a real event. Since we are dissociating from the very same tail of the real that we are chasing, however, we never catch up to the actuality of our own victimization.

Kierkegaard's (1844) concept of self-enclosure is variously translated as "inclosing reserve," or "self-encapsulation," and is animated by the "demonic" element in us. He states: "The demonic does not close itself off with something, but it closes itself up within itself, and in this lies what is profound about existence, precisely that unfreedom makes itself a prisoner" (p. 124).

Self-enclosed individuals thus are continually at risk of getting caught up in repeated spirals of "thinking in" (Shabad, 2001), of undoing or "deconstructing" their memories and perceptions of their experiences, leaving their sense of what is real mired in doubt. Through the prism of the disembodied mind, doubt is sown perpetually, as we become less certain that what happened actually did happen. From this point of view, Descartes's famous dictum, "I think, therefore I am," should be amended to, "I *think* therefore I am … therefore I *think*…." Indeed, Wright (1991) says: "Consciousness … can be regarded as a form of searching for that which is missing" (p. 84).

The self-enclosed person searches fruitlessly within the insulated safety of his own being for the wellspring of self-renewal, but it is not to be found there. It is precisely because of the insistently misdirected failure to find the ground of a new beginning only from within one's defensive cover-up that this individual is caught in the demonic grip of endless repetition, not unlike a dog chasing its own tail. Kierkegaard (1849) refers to the despair of this pursuit for the essence of one's being from within one's own mind as a "consumption of the self, but "an impotent self-consumption, not capable of doing what it wants" (p. 16). It is not coincidental that Narcissus declares: "Am I the lover or the beloved… Since I am what I long for, then my riches are so great they make me poor" (Ovid 8 A.D, pp. 464–468).

Through endless attempts of thinking-in to recapture the ever-elusive embodied actuality of one's own essence from within one's own disembodied and de-realizing mind, the sense of being on the outside looking in at oneself perpetuates the repetitiveness of obsessional thinking indefinitely.

Freud (1905b) makes this connection between repetition and confirmation of the real more explicit when he suggests that the aim of reality testing is not to find an object, but "to *re-find* the object, to convince oneself that it is still there" (pp. 237–238). For the self-enclosed individual who cannot get beyond his own mind, each encounter with a new person becomes *primarily* a revisiting of one's prior object representations or transferences.

I would emphasize that the confirmation of the real cannot occur only by re-finding a self-created mental *representation* of an Other, for that would mean one is still imprisoned within the circularities of one's own making. In order to validate what is real in the world, one must find the freedom of subjectivity and self-expression of actual other persons who are independent of one's object representations. Levinas (1969) thus notes: "In representation the I precisely loses its opposition to objects; the opposition fades, bringing out the identity of the multiplicity of its objects… To remain the same is to represent to oneself" (p. 126). Through the foreclosure of otherness, loss, difference, and death, continuity is guaranteed but increasingly emptied of transformative meaning. Angyal (1965) thus says: "Life lived in isolation; it is a state of being 'narrowed in,' working one's course within narrow confines, not daring to move out into the wider areas that could be encompassed by personal life" (p. 76).

Ultimately, we can calm this frenzied chase of our own essence only through the validation of someone who lies outside the controlling reach of our minds. Kierkegaard (1844) thus says: "Inclosing reserve is precisely muteness. Language, the word, is precisely what saves, what saves the individual from the empty abstractions of inclosing reserve" (p. 124). In this view, self-enclosed individuals are searching for an enduring reality that lasts beyond their own creative and destructive powers, one that is not subject to their own making and unmaking of it.

However, the self-enclosed person is so intent on covering up his sense of shame that he is not able to open up and risk the exposed vulnerability that is intrinsic to the participatory give-and-take with an Other. Kierkegaard (1844) states that the demonic tendency toward self-enclosure is always haunted by an "anxiety about the good" (p. 123), a needed openness to relationship that is not being lived out:

The demonic is unfreedom that wants to close itself off. This, however, is and remains an impossibility. It always retains a relation, and even when this has apparently disappeared altogether, it is nevertheless there, and anxiety at once manifests itself in the moment of contact.

(p. 123)

Since in one's self-enclosure, the individual cannot gain relief from the burdens of shame consciousness through an open give-and-take of loving and being loved, the need for relationship, as manifest through the "anxiety about the good" (Kierkegaard, 1844), continues to gnaw at him, until he finally collapses into a dependent relationship with a stronger Other.

A few years ago, I treated Emily, a 44-year-old married woman who had been an actress immediately after college, but then took a prolonged break to be a mother and homemaker to her two children. With her children out of the house, she wanted to turn to acting again.

When I first began seeing Emily, she was inhibited by her self-consciousness and constantly second-guessed herself to such an extent that she could not go to auditions. Emily was ambitious about wanting to stick out from other performers but ashamed of her individualizing need to be special. She had perfectionistic standards, but then berated herself mercilessly when she did not live up to her own standards. She was extremely competitive with others and envied other actors who seemed to have more self-confidence than her.

Her father was a strong, authoritative, and charismatic presence in her growing up years, while her mother was often self-abnegating and receded into the background. Emily seemed to have contempt for her mother's weakness and attempted to distance herself from her as much as she could. Yet not surprisingly, she was quite identified with her mother's tendency to self-negate in her own self-inhibition. I emphasized to Emily that the more she attempted to take flight from being like the mother from whom she felt ashamed, the more guilt she incurred for that shame, and the more she would then have to be punished by being "visited" with precisely the same behaviors of her mother of which she had been so ashamed.

When I attempted to share these reconstructions of Emily's life with her, she often would say: "I don't know how to relate to that, Peter." Although Emily was quite bright, she was quite covered up in her self-enclosure.

Although she and I liked each other and had a good rapport, she often did not know how to use much of what I said unless I explicitly showed her how to make concrete changes to help her overcome her anxieties and fears of moving forward. I, in turn, became frustrated because I did not know exactly what she wanted from me. I suspect that she felt I owed it to her somehow to find the correct key in order to liberate her from self-imprisonment.

In spite of her frustrations with me, she made incremental but steady gains, little by little, over the course of a few years. She overcame her fear of auditions and was quite successful in a few plays. Nevertheless, she still struggled somewhat with her tendency to attack herself.

When the Covid pandemic hit, we switched to video therapy. Something about the transition in the cultural surround, and loss of face-to-face treatment with me, seemed to open Emily up more to her vulnerabilities. She began to talk about her values and her upbringing more voluntarily. We began speaking about her father and how she had been her father's favorite during childhood. This all changed when she was 12 and found out that her father was having an affair, at which point her parents were separated. Eventually, her parents came back together. As she described this period of time, she sometimes broke down in tears, and at other times she became very angry when thinking of her father.

This anger and disillusionment with her father coincided with the beginning of puberty. She would attack herself harshly, lost confidence, and receded into herself. Her father always thought she had a gift for acting and wanted her very much to pursue it as a career. Her pursuit of acting and her ambitious visions of grandeur became a perfectionistic goal that she was never able to reach, and therefore she attacked herself constantly for her failures. During the more emotionally laden sessions of video therapy, I brought up the wish to restore herself as special and great in her father's eyes, and how much it hurt to be deposed. I further suggested that she interpreted her father's affair as punishment for wanting to be special in his eyes and now continued to punish herself for her ambition to be a great actress. Something shook loose in Emily, and she broke down in sobs.

Soon after that breakthrough session, Emily terminated. About a year after she terminated, Emily sent me a link to a review of a play in which she played the leading role. She received glowing reviews.

## Incompetence: Dependence and Relieving the Burdens of Self-Enclosure

Since shame derives from the fact that the worth of one's own offerings has been rebuffed by others, the shame-ridden individual, in turn, feels unworthy or undeserving of receiving anything good for himself. His shame and defensive self-enclosure, most of all, inhibit a receptivity to receiving help or love from an Other. One may yearn deeply to be loved, but that does not mean one is able to open up sufficiently in order to receive that love so as actually to *feel loved.* Indeed, for the self-enclosed person, to consciously allow oneself to learn from and be conscious of one's need of an Other is to implicitly acknowledge a deficiency in one's own makeup, which is experienced as shame.

The self-enclosed individual's doubts about the fundamental goodness of his desires and his inhibition of receptivity closes down openness to others and inhibits curiosity. After all, since within one's sphere of omnipotence, knowledge and competence brings with it the perfectionistic responsibility of doing something about what one discovers and now knows, it is safer to take cover in the constructed ignorance of "see no evil, hear no evil." Throughout history and mythology, whether it is the sin of eating from the Tree of Knowledge of Good and Evil in the Book of Genesis or a child asking where babies come from, curiosity reflects the dangerous explorative quality of our passionate life force. The truth-seeking process of curiosity is hindered by the fear of where it may lead. As that part of our desire that pushes us toward growth, curiosity seeks out the new, pries into mysteries, goes where it is not wanted, and exposes what was previously covered up.

For this reason, it is crucial that therapists be receptive to their patient's curiosity and inquiries about their personal life, reflecting as it does the exploratory probing of the boundaries of the forbidden separating the therapist's professional and personal life. As occurred in my interaction with Linda at the beginning of Chapter 4, closing down questions by returning questions or immediately interpreting the meaning of the question without answering may shame the patient. It is not surprising that Linda responded self-consciously by saying, "I should have known better than to think you would answer."

If a person has never worked through the burdening omnipotence of wish magic—that is, not distinguishing between *wishing* to be received appreciatively by a parent and those wishes being realized in the *actual* relationship with the parent— then the dissociation from those disillusioned wishes means they cannot be modified by experience. As development into adulthood proceeds, this person may instead transfer that persistent wishing to other significant relationships as well. Yet no matter how much he wishes to change the character or behavior of another person, other individuals stubbornly just continue to be themselves. As a result such relentlessly wishing individuals thus continue to have the demoralizing experience of their desires being disappointed by the actual other person. When we encounter a despairing fatalism in a patient, it often is a result of these demoralizing encounters with the limits of one's own omnipotent wish to change another person's freedom of being. If in one's omnipotent thinking, knowing about a parent's unhappiness only leads to shame over one's inadequacy for not making a parent happy enough, then the self-recriminating pressures of that knowledge can become overwhelmingly burdensome.

Behind the mask of one's defensive self-enclosure, these self-recriminations and deep sense of inadequacy may then give rise to an intense need to be relieved of one's mental burdens. In a sense, the self-doubts of shame invert a passionate sense of I WILL into a passive incompetence and fatalistic I CAN'T. This sense of incompetence then justifies one's right to collapse in the moral authority of someone who is stronger, more decisive, and knows better. After all, if a person views himself as incompetent, there is no choice but to depend on others for guidance, whereas if he internalizes a sense of competence for himself too readily, he may be fearful to be left to his own lonely devices. Many individuals therefore contrive unconsciously to remain incompetent in order not to be ignored or left alone, which they may perceive as a form of abandonment.

Take the example of a four-year-old boy who asks his mother to help him tie his shoes. The mother says, "Come on, honey, I know you can tie your own shoes. I've seen you do it before." The little boy complains a little and says, "No, I don't know how. You show me." Although strictly speaking, the little boy may actually "know" how to tie his own shoes, he may prefer at that moment to view himself as incompetent to ensure his mother's continuing involvement in his life—perhaps because he was beginning to feel too independent and alone in taking on the lonely burdens of newly discovered competencies. This same defense against one's own competence and consequent autonomy may often prevent patients from internalizing a sense of emotional competence in psychotherapy.

For individuals who are imprisoned in the shame of their own self-enclosed consciousness, it is tempting to project the freedom of their own moral authority into an idealized other who is viewed as *extraordinarily* competent and thereby gain the relief of passing on the burdens of their omnipotent perfectionism to a stronger external authority. It is much easier to hide oneself under the moral authority of parents or conform to the dictates of the crowd than to expose the naked vulnerabilities of one's individual self.

Many individuals are all too ready to collude with the collective taboo against curiosity, for fear that once they begin subversively upending the collective masks which we all use to cover up our hidden shames, their own defects will be plain for all to see. The problem with this inhibition of one's freedom of inquiry into the unknown is that it closes down the potential for independent-mindedness and renders adults into conforming automatons or overgrown children in perennial search for moral authority. The self-perpetuating result of becoming humiliatingly conscious of one's dependence on an Other is that one may suffer a redoubled sense of shame and inferiority from the very same idealization that one seeks out.

We usually think of homesickness as a form of separation anxiety, such as when a child at sleepaway camp feels the ache of longing to return home, or when at the end of the school day she waits with a single-minded desperation for her mother to pick her up. Such children, feeling lost and alone in a sea of strangers, often cannot be consoled and distracted from the urgency to reconnect with a parent. Whereas homesickness appears to be a dis-ease of facing the unknown, it often reflects a loyalty to an unstable or disrupted attachment to a parent for which the child has taken on too much responsibility to repair.

It is perhaps not coincidental that throughout the history of world cultures, the dangers of the evil eye are most commonly attributed to the stranger or the outcast or a demonic Other. When parents caution their children to beware of strangers, their words often carry the weight of a prohibiting command against the betrayal of venturing too far from home. At the same time that parents warn their children against the dangers of the outside world under the guise of providing a protective shield, they are also laying claim to their children as their possessions. In these parental cautions and warnings to their children, we see an implicit but powerful demand for loyalty: "You are either with me or against me. If you are with me, then stay by my side. If you are leaving me, then go already and don't assume there will be an open door welcoming you back home."

This unspoken ultimatum has a powerfully inhibiting effect on the child's growth, because he, now dreading the obliterating experience of being cut off, uprooted, and isolated, feels he has no choice but to re-find the secure grounding of the familiar. The homesick child, who suffers through fear and trembling in the anticipation of life transitions, is not crippled so much by an inherent failure of courage, but by a self-weakening uncertainty about his right to move forward and sustain his ongoing life.

In losing access to passion and desire, the now-passive individual may experience an internal vacuum that he may refer to as a feeling of "boredom." Camus's anti-hero Merseault in *The Stranger* (1942) exemplifies the *ennui* or boredom that results from detaching from one's passionate life force. Perhaps most importantly, this alienation from one's own desires and the resulting boredom leads to a feeling of being disoriented and lost, and ultimately to a profound dependence on other secure guideposts of how to live. Fenichel (1954) states:

> A person who is 'bored' in the strict sense of the word, is searching for an object, not in order to act upon it with his instinctual impulses, but rather to be helped by it to find an instinctual aim which he lacks.
>
> (p. 293)

The self-shaming child, in fear and trembling, and doubting that he can move on with his life as a unique individual and retain a touchstone of continuity of belonging to significant others at the same time, attempts to sell himself into the good graces of parents. Such children instead take cover in the idealized moral authority of parents, which they infuse with the disowned strength of their passionate life force. Without that sense of rightness, the child's compromises his ability to freely use his passion and becomes fearful of his own growth. The self-enclosed individual, who is preoccupied with the cover-up of shame and doubting his worthiness to move on with life, is left with no choice but to look outward for rules to live by.

## Masks of Blind Loyalty: Shame and the Cover-Up of Individual Difference

When our attempts to love and be loved fail, and we become preoccupied with defensively covering up our rejected vulnerability, our shame and self-doubts may invert the openness of our passion into a self-enclosed passivity. Blind loyalty to one's own kind thus becomes encoded as a moral good against the shame of exposing oneself to the antagonistic threat of infinite difference and separateness. Encapsulated within ourselves, we hang on to the life raft of our automatic loyalties to provide us with the safety of ongoing sameness, so as not to be buffeted to and fro by the monstrous winds of change and otherness. As the child clings to all surrogates of sameness who become associated with a familiarized "us," the passion to change and grow is disowned and projected on to "them," the strangers who embody the threat of indefinite exile and isolation. As Kearney (2003) states: "The figure of the stranger ... frequently operates as a limit experience for humans trying to identify themselves over and against others" (p. 3).

The relational ruptures and developmental discontinuities resulting from the failed attempts to give of oneself and be received by a significant become displaced on to the group discontinuities between "us" and "them." The group narcissism of loyalty to one's own family, ethnicity, religion, nation, or species is set against the different Other who takes on the monstrous visage of the sinful and feared freedom of one's own growth. Bakan (1966) thus points out that the self-assertive, agentic aspects of ourselves are projected onto the prototypical Other and representative of separateness and exile, the image of Satan.

The blindly automatic adherence to the abstract principle of a loyalty oath attempts to reduce time's ongoing flow to a static sameness rather than synchronize with its movement through its changes and the continually renewable choices of a free human being. When holding to commitments becomes entrenched as a *rule* of moral virtue that people follow just because it has taken on a life of its own as an abstract norm, then the mechanical aspects of blind loyalty rob our freedom of conscience of its heart and soul. Dewey (1980) pointedly states: "If one stops to consider the matter, is there not something strange in the fact that men should consider loyalty to 'laws,' principles, standards, ideals to be an inherent virtue, accounted unto them for righteousness?" (p. 278).

Inasmuch as love itself is based on the freedom of choice to love or not to love, the unconditional aspects of automatic loyalty preempts the passion of love from entering into our commitments. It is the very possibility of *not* renewing a commitment to another person that both engenders an anxiety of freedom and meaningful depth to that commitment.

In her excellent study of Kierkegaard's thinking, Carlisle (2006) states:

*The constancy of fidelity is grounded not on sameness, but difference…*
Because existence is temporal and therefore changing, something can
"stay the same" only if it becomes new. Whether the fidelity in question
is truthfulness to another person, to God, or to oneself. This is the kind
of truth that needs to be actualized repeatedly, rather than a necessary
static truth that merely "is."

(p. 86)

In this sense, a heartfelt, meaningful loyalty can only be constructed organi-
cally on the basis of renewable choice and the freedom to love from one
moment to the next.

Freud (1913b) delineates different ways in which early human civilization paid homage to ancestral animal totems. Various tribes coped with the
survivor guilt of separating and moving ahead with life while leaving the
dead behind through the atonement of elevating ancestors into tribal totems
and gods. Interestingly, Freud further points out that the form in which a
member of a clan emphasizes his relationship to the totem: "He imitates an
exterior similarity by dressing himself in the skin of the totem animal, by
having the picture of it tattooed upon himself, and in other ways" (p. 136).
In a similar way, is wearing the mask of the superego a form of tattoo-
ing parental indoctrinations and values on ourselves in order to assuge our
separation guilt and earn more individual life?

Children, too, often feel that they should pay homage to parents who
they are declining or will be left behind in the wake of their increasing
separateness. A child's sharing with a parent adventures and activities from
her own evolving development such as sports, hobbies, and passions, especially those that follow a parent's footsteps, are a natural way that children
give back to their parents in order to earn ever-greater individuated life.
What occurs, though, when parents block those offerings because of their
own melancholia or sense of unworthiness?

For example, an unquestioning loyalty to parents is accentuated when
parents recognize their children only as created extensions of themselves
while not acknowledging the self-creating child who has a mind and will of
her own. The threat of being "cast out" without being able to link up with
home again has a blackmailing effect on the child's development. In such
situations, when a parent does not appear to appreciate or benefit from her

child's offerings of love in any lasting way, the child may feel an increasing paradoxical pressure to give up more of himself in order to separate from the parent's unhappy state with good conscience. Such children may then introject parental indoctrinations and imitate parental values without evaluating them to such an extent that the uniqueness of their own emerging individuality begins to disappear.

In a broader sense, the loyal maintenance of tradition and ritual in adhering to parental values and traditions becomes a means of paying sacrificial dues to previous generations—of giving away a semblance of oneself in order to gain a family pride and moral sense of righteousness. The ritualistic aspects of character, reflecting different pathways of loyally reconciling with various ancestral traditions, enable us to maintain defensive integrity in the face of threat. In the mortifying aftermath of shame, by taking cover under the cloak of parental traditions and appropriation of parental values, children are able to cover their sense of individual inadequacy and give themselves a reborn sense of moral right to move forward with life again. By infusing himself with a pride gained from incorporating the power of one's traditions, the solitary individual can represent himself to the world again with a new "persona" or the masked face of a reborn personhood. As Wurmser (1981) says:

> In shame one wants to change into another being or hide, not to be seen anymore. The mask changes the shamefully exposed into the shameless exhibitionist, one who fears to be seen as weak into one who is now feared as strong.
>
> (p. 306)

This obligatory submission to parental authority is frequently described as "love" by patients ("of course, I love my parents") but bears much more of a resemblance to compulsive loyalty. For love to be meaningful, it must be based on the freedom to love or not to love. Love can never win by forfeit, coercion, or blackmail. Just as faith only makes sense as a complement to doubt, so too love becomes more robust only when it is chosen in contradistinction to the real potentiality of its absence.

By taking cover under loyalty to parental authority, children secure a sense of reconciliation and belonging, but at the cost of sacrificing their developmental soul to parental appetites and whims. The price paid for subsuming oneself loyally under the umbrella of parental traditions and authority is that one does what one should do and gives up on one's individuated freedom. This compliance with parental authority may continue indefinitely, since any attempt on the child's part to emerge from her bondage leads to the anxious sense of premature exposure. Such attempts to give creative birth to one's own life path are like so many false starts, as the child scurries back to the parental sphere of influence in retreat from an overwhelming freedom burdened with separation guilt, shame, and anxiety.

Parents now become larger-than-life authority figures whose desires become their children's commands. Eventually, these children grow up to feel their lives are not their own but the playthings of powers far greater than themselves. They perceive themselves to have no freedom to say yes or no, nor to love or hate, nor the freedom of developmental movement to come and go as they please. With nowhere to go, and without any real hope of improving their lot, these persons are left with the fatalistic sense of being imprisoned indefinitely. As the active initiative of living their own lives gives way to the despair of a reactive passivity, such persons are unable to liberate themselves from the bondage on which they felt their survival depends. For such children, parental will and authority may come to embody the dictates of fate itself, and the loyal adhesiveness to the introjection of those parental dictates may evolve into a sense of despairing fatedness or fatalism in adult life.

## Don: Penetrating Shame and the Restoration of Hope

Don is a tall, thin young man in his late 20s who came in for psychotherapy. In his first session, he seemed a little fidgety, and his eyes conveyed a vague sense of fearfulness. Don was quite soft-spoken, often silent, and sometimes stammered when he did speak. He was in the midst of doing a general residency in medicine and lived alone. He had grown up on the West Coast, where his parents still lived, and was the oldest of four children.

Don came in for help because he was frequently anxious and "too hard on himself." He spoke often of becoming tongue-tied whenever an attending doctor asked him a question, let alone scolded him. In the aftermath of these embarrassing moments, Don would viciously hurl silent insults at himself for his stupidity. As Don unfolded his life story, he described how "rough" his father was on him as a child. He recounted almost daily inquisitions his father put him through about chores and homework, in which he would alternately quiz, scream, and humiliate Don.

Perhaps not coincidentally, Don's experience of being dressed down by his father also had parallels at school among his peers. Since puberty arrived for Don quite late in adolescence, he was thin and small for most of his boyhood. He often was teased mercilessly and bullied throughout much of elementary school.

During our initial sessions, Don and I linked his difficult interactions with the attending doctors to the repetitive trauma of humiliation he had endured from his father's verbal abuse. Together, we walked through an understanding of the process of introjection, in which he became his abusive father constantly shaming himself. Often during these sessions, a melancholy pall would come over Don's face. Yet he also seemed to derive comfort from the seriousness with which I took his father's abusiveness. At times, I would ask him to imagine what he would say if he had a chance to counterattack. Once in a while, I would even model these counterattacks for him by saying things like "Get off my back!" or "Pick on someone your own size!" At these junctures, I was aware of the potentially "emotionally corrective" effects I was hoping to induce, in that I, also a father figure for Don, was actively countering what Don had experienced with his own father.

After these first months of treatment, Don and I began addressing his dating life, which had been shrouded in mystery up to that point because Don had been tremendously ashamed about the fact that he never had a girlfriend nor dated much. Despite losing his virginity in a few alcohol-aided sexual encounters, he had never been able to sustain an emotional and romantic relationship with a woman. His shame and resignation to an expectant fate of lonely celibacy now became the focus of treatment.

Don's despair about ever finding a partner ran deep; so deep, in fact, that his hopelessness, and perhaps his ambivalence, of coming upon a remedy made him hesitant to probe more deeply into the sources of his fatalism. It seemed that I sometimes worked too hard to penetrate his defenses and provide him with some hope, but eventually my efforts may well have borne fruit. I frequently reminded him that, despite the fact that his fate had not yet been set in stone, he was putting a ceiling on his possibility of success.

Gradually, Don became increasingly expressive and confident. He began taking risks and made overtures to a number of young women. During those months of treatment, his trust and ease of relating to me had grown. This increased comfort derived, in part, from the fact that sometimes at beginnings and ends of our sessions, we would discuss sports. At these junctures, his mood would perk up, and he seemed to enjoy our banter greatly. Unlike his father, who strictly and sadistically enforced rigid standards of seriousness, perhaps Don viewed me as a "father figure" who lightened the burden of his melancholy.

Four months before Don's departure for an out-of-town residency in nephrology on the West Coast, we had what I consider to be a pivotal session. During the previous session, I had asked forthrightly whether he went on pornographic sites, and he said yes. I probed further about his specific tastes, and he responded that he enjoyed seeing two women together and that the presence of a man distracted him too much. We linked his feelings of an intrusive male disturbance both to his father and to the inhibiting effects of his introjecting his father.

When he came into the next session, Don, unlike many times previously, seemed eager to be there and to speak. He told me about an episode when he was about 11 years old in which another boy, his best friend, had made sexual overtures toward him. Even though they kissed very briefly and nothing happened subsequently, Don ever since that time had harbored doubts about his sexuality. As we explored his desires and fantasies in detail, it became obvious to Don that he had no romantic interests in men but had inhibited himself from approaching women because of his nagging self-doubts. He said that revealing his secret out loud had relieved him of a shame that had haunted him for many years.

Three months before he left for residency, Don met and began dating a woman in the hospital where he worked. This relationship has worked out well, and she has since moved to be with him.

Chapter 6

# Licking One's Own Wounds
## Passivity and the Fatalism of Self-pity

Love isn't safe when pity is prowling around.
  (Graham Greene, 2006, p. 124, while interviewed about *The Ministry of Fear*)

No hope allures her, no future moves her, no prospect tempts her, no hope
excites her—hopeless she stands, petrified in memory … the world changes,
but she knows no change, and time flows on, but for her there is no future time.
  (Kierkegaard, (1843c, p. 205, recalling the legend of Niobe in *Either/Or I*)

### Robert: Feeling Pathetic and the Pathos of Self-pity

When I first glimpsed Robert in my waiting room, I was struck by the
degree to which he seemed drawn into himself. His head was bent down,
and his legs were pulled under the chair on which he was sitting, with his
hands laying on his thighs. As he walked into my office, his shoulders were
slumped as he continued to stare down at the ground, as if he wished to dissolve into it as quickly as possible.

Robert is a 20-year-old college student who came for therapy, but at
first sight he appeared to be much younger than his actual age. His hair
was immaculately combed, and he was extremely polite and respectful to a
fault. In general, he came across as a well-behaved "good boy."

For the year preceding coming to therapy, Robert said he had been
isolated, lonely, and desperate to find a girlfriend. He declared that he
wanted to have more friends but walked around campus, closed in on
himself, as if to discourage anyone from approaching him. On Friday
nights, for example, he recounted how he would go to the campus library,
ostensibly to study, but the whole time he was there, he would fantasize
about being approached by the girl of his dreams. But it never happened,
and instead, he described himself as "so pathetic" for being relegated to
studying on a weekend night.

DOI: 10.4324/9781003559559-7

Robert then told me that he had been feeling suicidal. He said he had been very isolated and depressed. He said that he had been thinking about cutting his wrists in the bathtub and letting himself bleed to death. I asked Robert who would be most like likely to discover his dead body if he followed through with his plans, and he replied that his brother would be the one, with whom he was sharing an apartment. He fell silent for a moment and then said that he would feel "rotten" at the thought of that happening.

As Robert then continued to unfold his story, he revealed that his mother was a controlling "neat freak." I wondered aloud then whether it was not his brother but his mother who was meant to find her son in a "bloody mess" of a bathtub. Was this, I asked Robert, a means of using his suicide to send a parting "fuck you" message to her?

Robert then began to speak of how his mother had "babied" him his whole life. She slept in the same room as he and his older brother for the first few years of Robert's life, while his father slept in a separate room. Worse, between the ages of 4 and 6, she would occasionally get into bed with him for the duration of the night. As he got older, he said that on numerous occasions he was not permitted to play with his friends after school because of his mother's overprotectiveness. In middle school, he recounted how he was not allowed to join his friends on sleepovers and recalled his embarrassment when he often had to return home in the evening, while all his friends were able to remain with each other overnight. For much of his childhood, Robert felt as if he was imprisoned in his own home.

Most significantly, during Robert's early teenage years, Robert's mother spoke disapprovingly of a girl in whom Robert showed much interest. Even though Robert had a more benign view of his father, his father was away at work much of the time and not much help in providing a buffer between Robert and his mother's controlling reach. On those occasions, when Robert did complain about his mother or get upset because of arguing with her, his father asked Robert just to "deal with it," because otherwise he, the father, would never hear the end of the mother's frustrations.

After the first year of treatment, Robert made gradual progress in reaching out to others and separating himself from his mother, who he said he "hated." Despite the distance that Robert placed between himself and his mother in his conscious declarations of independence, he still took pride in being the morally upright, well-behaved boy that his mother had carefully molded in her desired image.

On one occasion, as Robert and I were in the midst of discussing his transition into puberty, he revealed, with much embarrassed hesitancy, how he himself had not wanted to grow up. Significantly, Robert acknowledged that it was not only his mother who wanted to baby him, but he, too, sometimes wished to remain his "mama's boy" and imagined himself on her lap and looking up at her. He recounted somewhat sheepishly how when he was five years old, he indulged in much "baby-talk" with his mother. Later, when he turned 12, he remembered distinctly how much he did not want to grow up and wished that he could remain a very young child forever.

I responded to these revelations by saying it sounded like his fantasies of remaining a very young child had caused him much distress and shame, but that it was not unusual for many children to have much ambivalence about growing up. I then told him that when I was 12 or 13 years old, I also wondered why my peers seemed to be so much in a rush to become teenagers while I wanted still to remain a child.

I further suggested to Robert that his mother may well have been a very nice "mommy" to him as long as he remained a "baby" or little boy who filled her maternal need to be needed, thus making it all the more difficult for him to wrench himself away from her. In addition, since Robert had seen through to the needy fragility underlying her desperate possessiveness, he had not been able to mobilize the necessary ruthlessness to separate from her and save his own life for fear of causing her irrevocable injury.

It was challenging for Robert to speak about, let alone accept, his yearning to go back in time and stay by his mother's side. He viewed these longings as "pathetic" and attempted to distance himself from his mother's infantilizations. In order to gain a foothold in young adulthood, he consciously strove to conform to what he believed were the appropriate norms of his age group and desperately sought out a girlfriend who would save him from the temptations of his infantile longings.

Paradoxically, by disowning a homesickness of which he was greatly ashamed, he unconsciously shaped a fate for himself that he felt unable to alter. By not being as open to the entreaties of peers and remaining enclosed within himself as a disciplined "good boy," Robert continued to shape himself to be someone his mother would be proud to call her own to a far greater extent than many women his own age would find appealing. In this sense, he inverted the passion of a grown-up sexuality that would betray his mother into a self-enclosed passivity, in which he remained steadfastly loyal by his mother's side. Although Robert often referred to himself as "pathetic" for being incapable of having a girlfriend, he was most ashamed of his dirty little secret to remain forever pre-pubescent.

In regarding himself as pathetic, he ironically also felt sorry for himself for precisely being pathetic. Robert hated himself for feeling unable to be anyone different than who he was, but at the same time, he also felt pity for himself for being trapped in that same "pathetically" miserable state from which he felt helpless to emerge. Unable to liberate himself from the invisible chains that bind, Robert remained imprisoned in a despairing cycle of shame and self-pity.

No matter how much Robert gave of himself to his mother, it was never enough to solicit her recognition for his burgeoning growth as his own person. She saw only the "kept" child of her conceptions and had always required that Robert conform to those conceptions. Since she was not open to him as a separate person in his own subjective right, Robert had no choice but to sell his developmental soul in exchange for her approval, lest he be cast out into the oblivion of invisibility.

## Who Caused My Injury? The Uncertainty of Trauma

How are we to make sense of Robert's paradoxical experience of shame, "I am pathetic," but also someone who felt he deserved pity for being such a pathetic victim of fate in the first place? In order to understand this paradox of shame and self-pity, it is important to again delve into what occurs in the immediate aftermath of trauma.

Winnicott (1951) emphasized how babies do not make a clear distinction between what is objectively perceived and what is subjectively conceived when the mother attunes herself closely to the infant's needs. He suggests that the mother's placing of "the actual breast just where the infant is ready to create, and at the right moment" (p. 239) is inextricably intertwined with the infant's wish-fulfilling fantasy of the mother's breast:

> The mother's adaptation to the infant's needs, when good enough, gives the illusion that there is an external reality that corresponds to the infant's own capacity to create. In other words, there is an overlap between what the mother supplies and what the child might conceive of.

(p. 239)

This illusory link between what is objective on the one hand and what is subjective on the other hand is facilitated by transitional objects and transitional phenomena in an area of intermediate experience. Winnicott adds:

> Of the transitional object it can be said that it is a matter of agreement between us and the baby that we will never ask the question, "Did you conceive of this or was it presented to you from without?" The important point is that no decision on this point is expected. The question is not to be formulated.

(pp. 239–240)

As development proceeds forward, the child must learn to tolerate the disillusionment of *created* elaborations of desire and increasingly accept a *found* world that has not been conceived. Yet, even as adults, we experience a residual conflation between a subjectively conceived world and finding an objective perceived world, because to a great degree, we are always finding what we create and creating what we find through the filter of our own minds.

This same ambiguity becomes more problematic in the aftermath of trauma in resolving our doubts as to whether we subjectively conceived and thus "created" our traumatic experience or whether the trauma was an objectively perceivable event that we "found." Through the uncertain filter of his mind's eye, the child's capacity to create and destroy, and to construct or deconstruct, casts endless doubt on the certainty of his perception and memory. Russell (1993) thus extends Winnicott's paradox of creating and finding to questions one puts to oneself in the aftermath of trauma: "The residues of trauma include a fundamental indeterminacy of act: 'Did I do this, or was it done to me?'" (p. 519).

Mitchell (2000) has emphasized that when people retell stories of their prior sufferings, they invariably include the question: "Why did this happen?" For Mitchell, the answers to this question of "Why?" gravitate toward two contrasting poles: "I brought this damage on myself and on others" (p. 714) (which he refers to as guilt), and "The damage was inflicted on me through no fault of my own" (p. 714) (which he refers to as self-pity).

Whereas Mitchell refers to the conviction that one has brought trauma on oneself as a form of guilt, I have emphasized that believing that one has caused one's own suffering to oneself is more accurately viewed as shame. Whereas guilt is more concerned with making reparative good toward another person whom one has injured, shame often leads to a preoccupying self-punishment for injuring the other person in the first place. Shame involves browbeating oneself for a past mistake rather than a sense of remorseful making amends in the future. Whereas self-shaming shame leads to self-pity, self-pity is absent when there is genuine remorse and guilt.

## Responsibility and Punishment: The Contrasting Ethics of Shame and Guilt

In a classic paper "*Guilt and Guilt feelings*," Buber (1965) eloquently describes the emotionally arduous process of remaining open to one's guilt and sense of remorse. For him, the process of coming to terms with one's conscience requires self-illumination, perseverance, and reconciliation. It is this stamina of openness to the self-reflection necessary for experiencing genuine guilt and sense of responsibility that the person prone to self-shaming cannot muster. As Buber states: "The vulgar conscience that knows admirably well how to torment and harass, but cannot arrive at the ground and abyss of guilt, is incapable, to be sure, of summoning to such responsibility" (p. 125).

The ethical implications of shame, of blaming the victim in oneself for being a victim, are very different, even antithetical, than the sense of responsibility engendered by genuine guilt and remorse. From a psychological point of view, the notion of responsibility has very little to do with ideological attributions of right and wrong but is much more concerned with the inner freedom of opening up to one's desires, thoughts, feelings, and most especially, accepting the consequences for one's actions. As Loewald (1980) states: "Responsibility is owning up to one's needs or impulses as one's own" (p. 392). When one has achieved some degree of self-accepting understanding for the reasons that have contributed to one's unwanted actions, it becomes more difficult to look oneself in the mirror and repeat those actions. One now must answer to oneself.

One of the key characteristics of shame, reflective as it is of weakness, failure, and defect, is that human beings tend to dissociate and emotionally disown any relationship they may have with whoever or whatever becomes associated with their own shame. Just as one may feel tempted to walk as far away as possible from one's child having a temper tantrum in the middle of the grocery store, we do whatever we can to keep away, hide from, and obliterate shame exposure.

Due to this phobic tendency to avoid their shame at all costs, individuals may disavow a new discovery about themselves if they immediately condemn it. The shame of self-contempt leads toward exiling from one's consciousness what is too painful to know. Loewald (1980) speaks eloquently to this dilemma:

> When I speak of appropriating our desires and impulses, active forces themselves, I do not mean repressing or overpowering them. I mean allowing or granting them actively that existence that they have in any event with or without our permission. Following the lead of the word responsibility, one may say that appropriation consists in being responsive to their urgings, acknowledging that they are ours. A harsh unyielding superego is unresponsive, and in that sense irresponsible.
>
> (p. 392)

Nietzsche (1887), too, declared: "By and large, punishment hardens and freezes; it concentrates; it strengthens resistance ... we may say with some assurance that it is precisely punishment that has most effectively retarded the development of guilt feeling" (p. 214).

It is worth pausing here to consider the radical implications that Nietzsche's insight holds for the normal conventions of childrearing. Innumerable parents throughout the world employ punishment as an instrument to discipline and socialize children. Such parents also believe that punishment promotes a sense of responsibility in their children. If we follow through with a concrete example more closely, however, we can see more specifically how punishment actually inhibits a child developing a sense of responsibility.

Imagine an older brother, who, after being provoked continually by his much smaller younger brother's teasing, finally loses his temper and beats up his younger brother to the point of tears. Perhaps in the first few moments after seeing his brother cry uncontrollably, he feels the first stirrings of transgression and remorse emerging from his conscience. He is able then to reflect on his actions and begin to take responsibility for perhaps going overboard in hurting his smaller brother.

Instead, after the sobbing younger boy runs to his mother in search of comfort, she harshly scolds the older boy, and then punctuates the punishment by exiling him to his room, all without hearing him out first. Perhaps the mother might even say, "You should be ashamed of yourself for picking on your much smaller brother."

In his need to defend against his mother's accusations, the older brother has become diverted from the echoes of his own conscience, one in which the seeds of remorse could have grown into a reparative generosity. Rather than reflecting on any sense of himself as a remorseful victimizer who did wrong, he, now feeling like a victim, mobilizes a defensive self-righteousness to ward off her attack. The necessity to defend against his parent's dismissive rejection prevents him from having the reflective space to open up to his conscience and genuine remorse. Loewald (1980) says: "Punishment, whether inflicted by others or by oneself, is too much in the service of repression of the sense of guilt" (p. 391).

What if, instead, the mother were to calmly approach her older son, listen to his side of the argument, and then explain that because he is older and wiser, he must find other than violent means to stop his brother's provocations? The older boy, feeling that his mother respected him, would be able then to reflect on his actions and begin to take responsibility for perhaps going overboard in hurting his smaller brother. He might even suggest that they resume their video game again.

Genuine guilt entails an acceptance of one's limitations and the inevitability of suffering and death as intrinsic to the human condition. Such acceptance of our finiteness paradoxically enables an individual to move beyond the magical thinking and denial of our limitations with more tolerance of our imperfections. This inclusion of our errors as part and parcel of our human makeup frees individuals from a preoccupying fixation on their past failures and instead envisions a future in which it is possible to rectify the wrongs one has committed.

When committing a mistake, the individual with excessive shame is more likely to browbeat himself mercilessly even after the fact of the "milk already having spilled" for being an "idiot" or too cowardly for not having changed the course of his life as he would have liked. This preoccupation with what is past, as is manifested in the compulsion to condemn oneself mercilessly for one's prior mistakes, contrasts sharply with a guilty individual's willingness to learn from his mistakes and do better next time in a reparative and potentially redemptive future.

Shame, contrastingly, derives from the defensive reflex to shield against the creature helplessness of one's limitations by taking on an excessive burden of blame for causing one's own sufferings. For many individuals, their shames reflect the weakness of their limitations turned into fatal flaws and signify a uselessness or wrongness in their existence. If a person does not have the wherewithal to struggle uphill against these self-condemnations sufficiently in order to live, they may become mired perpetually in a despairing fatalism.

If we check in now with the older brother who was scolded harshly and sent off to his room by his mother, he is far from feeling guilty. Although in the immediacy of his mother's scolding the older brother may defend himself, as time goes by, he may feel the sting of her words more deeply and feel himself to be a pathetic failure for "not being good enough" for her. The implications of punitively shaming himself are quite significant; he is now not only victimizing himself, but also the victim of his own punitiveness. He may now feel he deserves pity for being a hapless victim of his parental fate. Indeed, in his self-pity, he may wait indefinitely for his mother to invite him back into her good graces and make him feel loved again. Whereas guilt often leads to a pro-social reparative sense of *owing* good works to make up for one's misdeeds, shame instead leads to an entitled sense of feeling *owed* consoling reassurances that one is not as "pathetic" or "bad" as one thinks.

Not surprisingly, then, when shame becomes too intertwined with guilt, the need to defend oneself by projecting an image of strength through pride crowds out any conscious acknowledgment that one has committed wrong. The mask of pride is constructed as a self-preservative defense to cover up the vulnerability of one's injured dignity. Our pride often will not allow us to lower our defensive guard sufficiently to prostrate ourselves, and open ourselves to the humility of guilt needed to apologize for a wrong that we may have committed. Instead of apologizing, our pride leads us sometimes to entrench ourselves even more deeply into justifying our original actions by replicating the same wrong again, as if to justify why we had a right to do what we did in the first place. In this sense, the best defense is to go on offense.

Piers and Singer's (1953) concept of a shame–guilt cycle well describes the self-perpetuating quality of this flight from conscience. An individual may first commit an act of aggression, which leads to self-divisive feelings of guilt. Since the person's shame is interwoven with guilt, and he cannot bear the "weakness" of being in the wrong, he commits an act of aggression again to prove he had a right to do so in the first place. Perhaps then, what often looks like a "superego deficit" would be more accurately seen as an obscured conscience, in which one uses the continued perpetuation of wrongdoing to silene the disturbing echoes of one's conscience.

For the guilty person who has accepted the limitations of being human, it is not as difficult to admit wrongdoing, since he has already acknowledged the fundamental imperfections inherent in being human. In contrast, the shamed person cannot disentangle the admission of a mistake from the revelation of a defective inadequacy that shadows him throughout his life.

Certain individuals may, at times, give lip service to the *mea culpas* of self-blame as a defensive strategy to preempt further attack from the outside world. This ritualized litany of apology takes on the appearance of taking responsibility for their actions, only to be followed by the same actions that call for the same *post hoc* apologies again. Rather than come face-to-face with the meaning and consequences of their actions, such persons may feel unconsciously justified in indulging their "irresponsible" actions to fend off the merciless ogres of self-blame with which their consciousness is burdened. Here, we see how the strange bedfellows of harsh self-shaming and unconsciously entitled actions mediated by self-pity obscure the deeper ethical roots of genuine responsibility. Indeed, whereas self-shaming and self-pity are intertwined in an enclosed relationship with oneself, genuine guilt and remorse are concerned with making reparations and reconciling with the individual one has wronged.

## Cycles of Shame and Self-pity

In previous chapters, I have emphasized that in the wake of a significantly disrupted relationship to an Other, we use our minds to dissociate from the embodiment of trauma and filter the "why" of our suffering through the lens of omnipotence, in which we automatically blame ourselves for "creating" rather than "finding" our own traumatic experience. From an evolutionary perspective, this automatic defensive reflex to bring threat into our "area of omnipotence" (Winnicott,1960b) is an adaptive means of transforming the passive impotence of a helpless creature into the activated potency of a creator who is in control of his environment. In attempting to fend off this sense of weakness, however, the individual takes on too great a burden for controlling interactions with an outside world that are unpredictable and uncontrollable, thereby leading to the problematic shame of "taking the fall" for his own suffering. Children, for example, who are sexually abused or suffer the loss of a parent at a very young age or who have a physical disability may feel that there is something *intrinsically wrong* with them that brought on their unfortunate fate.

Yet at the same time that a child dissociates and shames himself for "creating" his own traumatic experience, he also has an embodied sense of "finding" his experience, of being victimized, through no fault of his own. Whereas the shame response is an introjection of self-blame for the weakness in *not* preventing one's suffering, self-pity is an identification with a wished-for response of consolation and comfort that never occurred. In this sense, the self-pity is an attempt to compensate for the absence of a wished-for consoling Other by "licking one's own wounds."

It is not an exaggeration to say that everyone has some lingering pockets of self-pity that correspond to the times that they were hurt or disappointed to a significant degree. When experiencing psychic injury, we cannot help but yield, at least for a passing moment, to the reflexive urge to feel sorry for ourselves. At such times, when we feel too conscious of our hurt and helplessness, we are tempted to curl inward and "take our ball and go home."

In an American culture of stoic individualism in which feeling has traditionally been bypassed for action, there is not much tolerance for the thumb-sucking passivity that is evoked by the phrase, "You are feeling sorry for yourself." Our culture's pejorative view of self-pity reinforces a shame that one may already have in exposing the weakness of one's sensitivities to consciousness.

Yet our unconscious intentionality to feel sorry for ourselves will have its way "with or without our permission," as Loewald (1980) pointed out. We do, however, have a choice in the relational stance we take toward our own self-pity, and *that* makes all the difference. Whether or not we grant ourselves the tacit assent of consciousness to "feel sorry for ourselves" has tremendous implications for the behavioral alchemy of how that self-pity is ultimately expressed. If we are able to accept that we are feeling sorry for ourselves and acknowledge a sense of hurt and victimization without accompanying shame, our brief moment of consoling ourselves is more likely to pass into other emotions and experiences.

When we disown any shame-filled awareness of feeling sorry for ourselves, however, we are more likely to fetishize the unacceptable and "dwell" in our sorrows. The momentary experience of self-pity increasingly becomes too monstrous a shame to be spoken about and degenerates into a series of repeated moments of self-pity without answerability to a consciousness that wanted no part of it anyway. This cycle of excluding the fact that we are feeling sorry for ourselves from consciousness, and then various actions designed to dramatize our victimization, may go on indefinitely until feeling sorry for oneself finds an articulated, inclusive voice within the governance of the psyche.

The sense of being a wronged victim implicit in one's self-pity derives then not only from the original helplessness of trauma that one had experienced, but also in reaction to one's own self-shaming. The shame of blaming the victim in oneself for one's own injuries results also in the self-pitying sense of being wrongly victimized by forces beyond one's control. References to oneself as "pathetic" lead quickly to feelings of self-pathos. When the individual identifies himself as a helpless victim, he may feel persecuted by something outside of himself, when he is actually reacting to his own self-tyrannizing voice of shame. Punter (2014) articulates this paradox of shame and self-pity: "How will we assess whether we are 'pitiful' or not—whatever 'pitiful' might mean—does it imply that we are ourselves 'contemptible,' or does it mean we deserve pity?" (p. 86).

These cycles of shame and self-pity become perpetuated, because as Mitchell (2000) points out, they are "private arrangements with ourselves." The self-enclosed quality of these private arrangements with ourselves, in which we believe we are "not good enough" or "lower than," are entrapping precisely because they are static, closed systems that preempt us from new experiences. Instead, all new experience becomes swallowed up and incorporated by these shame-self-pity cycles.

Kierkegaard (1849) thus suggests that the despairing person is despairing, in part, because he cannot let go of the image he has of himself. His freedom to change is continually swallowed up by repeatedly adhering to the image or consciousness he has of himself. Hinting at the transfixing aspects of narcissism in self-pity, Kierkegaard's (1843c) character Aesthete A in *Either/Or I* writes: "I have only one friend, and that is echo. Why is it my friend? Because I love my sorrow, and echo does not take it away from me" (p. 33).

Rich is a 44-year-old, recently divorced man who is the youngest of five boys. Despite the fact that both of his parents have died within the past four years, he remains quite distant from his four brothers. When I asked him how he felt about his estrangement from his brothers, his response of "whatever" seemed to reflect a stance of angry indifference. He is much more invested in clinging to and pursuing various women in his life, even after they give him clear signals that they are no longer interested.

Rich often feels sorry for himself when he finds himself alone on week-ends and attempts to escape his loneliness by pursuing whatever woman had last rejected him. The cycle of rejection, self-pity, loneliness, and continued clinging is then repeated. Recently, Rich became painfully aware of this pattern and tagged himself with the additional label of "loser" for good measure. When I asked him about self-attack, he responded by saying his inability to tolerate being alone and his self-pity were pathetic. I responded that he seems to be in the no-win situation of feeling sorry for himself ("I'm a loser") for feeling sorry for himself, and that his self-contempt contributed greatly toward making his solitude intolerable. He could not use his self-contempt to spur a change in his behavior because his sense of victimization, as expressed through his self-pity, was still unacceptable to him.

When we examined his cruelty toward himself more closely, I noted how his indifference towards being ignored by his brothers contrasted so sharply with his strong feelings about the women who rejected him. He then began to cry spontaneously as he described his old feelings of being a tag-along for his brothers, and that more often than not, they went out together while leaving him, their baby brother, alone with his mother. He has introjected the experiences of feeling rejected and of desperately hanging on like "a self-pitying loser," and he has brought those introjections into his periods of aloneness whenever rejected by the women in his life. His masochistic actions of clinging to rejecting women are then designed both to dramatize the objective actuality of previous experiences of suffering and to flee a self-contempt for feeling sorry for himself.

### Proving What Happened Really Happened: Thinking in and Symptoms as Action Proof

Typically, trauma is differentiated from ordinary suffering on the basis of the belatedly constructed trail of post-traumatic symptomatology leading back to the experience of trauma, thereby creating a point of developmental arrest. In this sense, the only way we really know of the existence of fixation points or developmental arrests at all is after the created fact. Traumatic experiences and their subsequent residue of psychological symptomatology do not just stand alone as blanked-out islands of experience that inevitably determine our present state of being. It is we, in the immediate aftermath of trauma, who also reconstruct our own developmental arrest by defensively curling in upon ourselves and dissociating from the experience of trauma. This defensive cover-up of vulnerability, in turn, often forecloses any possibility of securing the external recognition needed to validate our experience of trauma, necessitating that continue to reenact our own trauma, often in indirect ways, to prove what happened really happened.

Elsewhere (Shabad, 2001), I have suggested that the child's defensive dissociation from embodied experience and disavowal of his traumatic injury of victimization may lead to obsessional "thinking in." Through the insulated lens of his mind's eye, he is subject to the process of thinking in, whereby he doubts and de-realizes his own experience as to whether he *really* was victimized or whether he imagined it. Maybe, he thinks, my parents really do love me, and I am just imagining that they did not.

Since the self-witnessing testament to the reality of one's victimization through the filter of one's own memory is so endlessly uncertain, the self-doubts of thinking in fuel its transformation into the need to prove the embodied reality of one's injury through the action proof of self-defeating symptomatology. Left to our solitary self-enclosure, we alternate between obsessionally undoing and compulsively proving our own traumatic victimization. Fixation points then are subsequently formed by repetitive unconscious actions that have the paradoxical aim of memorializing the same traumatic injury we are attempting to obliterate. Freud (1914) hinted at this link between de-realization and repetition when he said that repetition is simultaneously an obliteration of memory and a form of remembering.

In this sense, our particular constellation of symptoms is animated by the unconscious intention to return to the "scene of the crime" and to prove the *objective actuality* of our prior suffering. By means of self-defeating behavior, we attempt to secure a credible witness who will validate the event of our victimization, so we no longer have to carry the sole burden of memorializing our own traumatic experience. When patients attempt to rid themselves of their symptoms before understanding their reason for being, they risk losing the trail they have constructed leading back to their experience of suffering, thereby de-realizing the actuality of their injuries. Perhaps then, a primary reason for resistance to 'getting better" in treatment derives from a determination to give dignity to one's experiences of prior suffering through the persistent holding in to one's symptoms.

The more shameful and impermissible it is to integrate the sense of helplessness and vulnerability intrinsic to traumatic experience, and the more sealed off we are from consciously acknowledging that experience, the more intense will be the need to prove its actual occurrence. Like the parent who says to a child, "If you don't stop crying, I'll give you something to cry about," only to have the child intensify his wailing, the more we shame ourselves for our symptomatology, the more we will engage in those actions. The sequence that perpetuates symptomatic actions goes something like this: self-blame; shame for being victimized; dissociation from the experience of shame; thinking-in and the de-realization of one's own experience (was I really mistreated, or was I just too sensitive?); and finally memorializing actions designed to counter these doubts about the embodied actuality of one's victimization.

The seemingly self-defeating aspects of symptoms serve a memorializing and communicative function that is designed to combat the de-realizing effects of thinking in and proving that what happened actually happened. Without a validating witness to our traumatic experience at the time it occurred, we are left to show in our actions what we are unable to say in words.

This action proof is meant to solicit the consolation and comfort of an empathic witness who would testify and validate the experience of victimization because the sufferer cannot do that for himself. With a deep unconscious sense of indignity and victimization that has neither been acknowledged or found comfort in the arms of others, some persons may be tempted to act out masochistically to elicit from others a pity to which they feel entitled but cannot muster for themselves. The self-defeating tendency to "cut off one's nose to spite one's face" may be used unconsciously in this way as a perverse vehicle to bring attention to one's downtrodden condition.

The problem is that because the individual expresses her symptomatology from within the safe, insulated confines of her self-enclosure, the intimate creation of her symptoms has a very private language. The aim of creatively transforming her private sufferings into a shared, enduring language through the eyes of another person often continues to remain out of reach. In effect, the individual's attempts to memorialize and convey the actuality of her traumatic victimization through her symptoms fails because her self-enclosed attempts to communicate are so indirect and non-verbal that they never find their sought-for audience. Eventually, the more ashamed one becomes of one's own symptomatic message, and the more doubt-laden the memory of one's suffering, the more one must raise the decibel level of one's choked-off communications.

Robert's lonely trips to study at the library on Friday nights may thus be viewed as a self-defeating symptom designed to convey to the world at large how he always had to "work" compliantly on behalf of his mother's possessive needs while other children were free to play. His self-pity for being victimized unjustly is not articulated verbally but expressed through the dramatization of masochistic actions designed to elicit pity from others. Even though Robert also calls himself "pitiful" and "pathetic" because he views himself as a lowly "loser" for going to the library alone on Friday nights, his self-contempt fuels his pity for himself and the need to compulsively elicit a pity from others that he feels he deserves but cannot muster for himself.

Robert's sense of himself as "pathetic" is a means of accentuating a consciousness, even a pride, in his own weakness. Looked at in this way, Robert is unconsciously intending to present an image of himself as "pathetic" in order to solicit a witness to his mother's suffocation of his autonomous life. If Robert could gain conscious access to his underlying sense of injustice for his mother always pulling him away from his peers, he could replace his shame with an empathic understanding for the *raison d'etre* of his actions.

## Fatalism and the Repetition of the Enclosed Future

Our desires are indispensable personal compasses that guide our purpose and direction in life. If we assume with Freud that our wishes constitute the basic fuel that make us go, then we can never forsake our desires for a more neutral, dispassionate way of seeing the world. We cannot disentangle *any* view of reality from the personal filter through which that view is processed. Generally speaking, the fluctuation of our moods from joyful to despairing reflects to what extent our desires are fulfilled or disillusioned in the outside world. Ultimately, we tend to see the world through the projective lenses of our desires or defenses against those desires, through the positive illusions of hoping for the best or the negative illusions of fearing the worst.

In the immediate aftermath of traumatic experiences, we turn inward and shame ourselves for the weakness in the exposed vulnerability of our wounds. The avoidant qualities of shame often cause us to retreat from the vulnerability of our wishes and the hopes attached to them. We instead brace indefinitely for a repeat encounter with the monstrous embellishment of a suffering that already happened and which we project onto unknown persons who we have not yet encountered. These transferences of fear and mistrust, rooted in very personal experiences of trauma and disillusionment, are then projected on to the blank canvas of an essentially unknowable future as negative illusions. In his well-known paper Fear of Breakdown, Winnicott (1974) describes a person's persistent anticipation of impending catastrophe in the future because of unprocessed, traumatic ruptures in the past that never have been genuinely experienced or lived through.

The seeming childlike naivete of our positive illusions is not so much an attempt to deny an awareness of the difficult truths inherent in the external world as it is an attempt to ward off the despair of our negative illusions. Indeed, whenever I see an email or text signed off with a "happy face" emoji, I suspect the shadow of a lurking melancholia. Our illusory omnipotent control over the future and other persons is not a defense against an enduring *real* helplessness as much as it is a defense against the negative illusion that the sense of helplessness that was experienced in the wake of trauma will last forever. The post-traumatic chains of anticipatory anxiety that bind us into the slavery of self-enclosed prisons are not actual, but defensive reactions to the transference afterimages of trauma; we constantly anticipate and brace for in the future the experience of trauma that we have already endured.

Through the lens of one's self-enclosure, one does not live forwards as Kierkegaard recommends, but attempts to live backward into a future that seems to be nothing but a fated recurrence of the past. Since the self-enclosed individual cannot get beyond the circularities of his own mind, he becomes a prisoner of his own transference perceptions. Each stranger that is encountered becomes a revisiting of the introjected disillusionments of the past. He projects his shame and mistrust onto the blank canvas of an unknowable future and then retreats in trepidation and dread from encounters with an Other who has been inscribed with the monstrosity of his own phantoms.

Life becomes an anxious sidestepping of anticipated threat, such that the inertia of rest becomes a desired escape from the stresses and pressures of living. In a sense, for such individuals, life alternates between threat and the respite from threat. For persons terrified of falling into the abyss of their own shame, life alternates between a fear of failing and the relief of not failing. The possibilities of one's hopes being realized are not formulated or conceived; they are alien and outside the enclosed expectations of fearing for the worst. In Kierkegaard's (1843c) words, such individuals are "bound in chains, which are formed of dark imaginings, of anxiety producing dreams, of restless thoughts, of fearful presentiments, of unexplained anxieties" (p. 33).

In anticipation of encountering the projection of our own monstrous phantoms in the future, we continue to retreat from or wage war against this enemy Other. In the meantime, life continues to go unlived. We might then take heed from Franklin Roosevelt's wonderful words of wisdom when he declared, "The only thing we have to fear is fear itself."

The self-enclosed cycle of shame and self-pity perpetuates a despairing helplessness that one's fate has been pre-determined and that there is nothing to be done about it. In this sense, we may view the term "helpless" literally as meaning "without help." The self-enclosed individual remains helpless because she is not able to genuinely receive and let the help of love penetrate a deep sense of not being unlovable enough. This chronically per-petuated helplessness leads to a despairing fatalism concerning the useless-ness of effort. Dostoevsky's (1864) Underground Man, mired as he is in an inner cauldron of shame, self-pity, and resentment, expresses the perverse pleasure of this fatalism:

> The pleasure resulted precisely from the overly acute consciousness of one's own humiliation; from the feeling that one had reached the limit; that it was disgusting, but couldn't be otherwise; you had no other choice—you could never become a different person; and that even if there were still time and faith enough for you to change into something else, most likely you wouldn't even want to change, and if you did, you wouldn't have done anything, perhaps because there was nothing for you to change into.
>
> (pp. 6–7)

Perhaps the most problematic effect of self-pity, then, is how it engenders a sense of helpless passivity. Cartwright (1988) thus says: "Unchecked self-pity robs its agent of natural incentives to solve one's own problems. Self-pity is thus debilitating. We feel sorry for ourselves instead of facing that which generates our problems" (p. 556).

There may be unconscious rhyme and reason to what Nietzsche (1887) referred to as the "willed impotence" of self-pity. It has been my clinical impression that the passivity of self-pity reflects the sufferer's unconscious fantasy of passively waiting to be rescued from his downtrodden state by an idealized consoling mother. It is precisely because this wished-for mother does not materialize, that a person remains despondent and fatalistic. If this person were truly convinced that no such idealized mother can help in rectifying his suffering, I often have thought that the individual would move to help himself.

In this regard, there is something profoundly disrespectful and unhelpful when we respond to a person's suffering with pity rather than compassion, even if the sufferer seemed to have gone to great masochistic lengths to elicit that pity. Indeed, Nietzsche (1887) emphasized that pity expresses a contemptuous attitude toward the sufferer: "To offer pity is as good as offering contempt" (p. 135). Such offerings of pity do not recognize the self-pitier's potential sense of agency to do something to mitigate his or her own suffering. Since the self-pitier already suffers too much from the shame of his self-degradation, more pity only serves to collude with the sufferer's lack of self-respect.

For example, if a person were to announce that she had just been diagnosed with cancer and already feels sorry for herself because of the diagnosis, then maybe the worst thing another person could say, "Oh my God! That's terrible. I feel so bad for you." Even though these words may be offered in the name of love and empathy, the shared commiseration leaves no room for the possibility and hope to better one's condition. It is in this sense of pity masquerading as love that we can understand Graham Greene's (2006) words in the epigraph to this chapter.

In my clinical work, I am very conscious of *never* losing that sense of respect for the patient's freedom of attitude toward the givens of his or her life. It is of course important to balance that respect for the patient's underlying dignity inherent in his or her agency with a genuinely compassionate witnessing of what he or she has suffered. Yet since a person's sense of agency is centered primarily in her answerability toward herself, in that spirit I occasionally point out to patients, "I think that you are feeling sorry for yourself." Instead of avoid making that comment because of the patient's shame, I believe it is important to model a matter-of-fact acceptance of self-pity as a way the patient is conveying her sense of victimization.

Many clinical practitioners may believe that in making such a statement, I am causing my patients to be even more self-conscious about a self-pity that they already may be too ashamed to admit. Since patients often feel helplessly stuck in their cycles of shame and self-pity, I am trying to raise awareness of their active relationship with and implication in their own psychodynamics. To illuminate the active role that patients play in their own psychic life, for better or for worse, enhances their sense of personal agency and, ultimately, a sense of potentiality to improve their lot in life.

It has been my impression that factors such as tone of voice, timing, tact, and a trust in the therapist's goodwill make a huge difference as to how the phrase is heard by the patient. Since I am aware of the more pejorative meanings associated with "feeling sorry for oneself," I have occasionally attempted to qualify what I say by reassuring the patient that I don't mean the statement moralistically but more as a means of describing a self-consoling stance they are taking toward themselves. To my surprise, my qualifications often seem unnecessary. Perhaps this is because the matter-of-fact quality of my voice conveys my feeling that there is nothing unusual about feeling sorry for oneself, and most especially that one is not a lesser human being for it.

By confronting the mystique of the unspeakable under which shame hides, it becomes possible to integrate the fact of "feeling sorry for oneself" with compassionate understanding. If, for example, after suggesting to a patient "I think you are feeling sorry for yourself," I were to add "There was no one else to lick your wounds when your father abandoned the family, so you had to lick your own wounds," the shame of feeling sorry for oneself is placed consciously in a larger context of being victimized and consequent attempts to console oneself. In so doing, we can retain the proactive language of unconscious intentionality implicit in "*you* are feeling sorry for yourself," while softening its hard edges with an empathic understanding of the reasons that contributed to the patient's intentions.

## Claude: Overcoming "Doom and Gloom"

Three years ago, Claude returned to psychotherapy with me for the second time because he did not want to continue to be a casualty of his "doom and gloom" despair. Unlike his first attempt to move himself, he was determined this time to emerge from his comatose numbness to pursue his passions and make the changes he so much desired.

When Claude was originally referred to me 15 years ago for severe depression, he said that "doom and gloom" was all he had ever known. The same dark cloud that always had cast a pall over the living space of Claude's family in his childhood now seemed to have pursued him mercilessly and trapped him in its grip of foreboding heaviness.

Claude's father was a Holocaust survivor who did not speak much and had little to do with his family. His mother was a depressed woman who was quite overprotective of her son. She would not let him play with neighborhood boys, and when she did allow him to do so, she imposed a strict curfew on his returning home. Her own fears of what she perceived to be a dangerously threatening world infected Claude's views of his own future, and not coincidentally, bound him ever more closely to her symbiotic orbit. Here, in this insulated symbiotic circle of two, it was two orphans huddling together against the storms raging outside.

Significantly, it was his father, without his mother's participation, who escorted him to college. Perhaps she could not bring herself to give her tacit consent to her son's separation from his family and move toward autonomy. In not doing so, however, she made it abundantly clear to him that she would not recognize his fundamental independence as his own person.

Soon after college, Claude "drifted" into medical school and the profession of being a doctor. Far from feeling that medicine was his chosen profession, Claude felt that he somehow "fell" into a profession that had chosen him. During that time, his experiences with young women were quite limited; on the one occasion that he became physically intimate with a woman on whom he had a crush, he became humiliated when he prematurely ejaculated over himself.

In the meantime, his mother had fallen into a clinical depression after Claude went away to college. She endured years of severe back pain, until she finally committed suicide when Claude was 22. For Claude, however, his mother's suicide was just the culmination of a life of "doom and gloom." In a sense, he had become anesthetized to love and loss long before she killed herself. Without access to his passionate life force, Claude had no sense of purpose or direction.

Soon after his mother's death, Claude was matched up with a woman on a tour group. He was not particularly attracted to her and did not find her especially interesting as a conversationalist. Nevertheless, like Tolstoy's passive character Ivan Ilych, who when asking himself about whether to marry the woman he was courting or not, answered "Why not?" Claude, too, describes himself as "falling into" into a marriage to his wife rather than choosing her. They eventually had two children, but Claude says he never had romantic feelings for her, and yet has felt trapped in this unsatisfying and empty relationship for 30 years.

When Claude was referred to me for psychotherapy then at age 48, he was depressed, fatalistic, and pessimistic. Even though he was conscious of a different, better kind of life that other people lead, his numbness to feeling seemed to match up fittingly with the empty life in which he existed.

For five years, we struggled together to help him emerge from his bloodless existence of repetitively unhappy inertia. It became apparent how important it was for Claude to solicit a witness (my role) to the downtrodden life he had long endured. We spoke about his unconscious guilt for the "sin" of growing up, his attempt to separate from his mother, her inability to cope with his departure, and his feeling of responsibility for having caused her death. We understood how his self-deadened life was thus a sacrificial memorial candle he kept lit to her deadness in life and to her death. He came to the conclusion that his role of doctor to "sick" people, a role he did not find rewarding, was also a means of paying his reparative dues, and perhaps even a retroactive attempt to magically heal his mother.

When I pointed out to Claude how his cycles of shame and self-pity were perpetuating his continuing inaction and thus engendering further regret in the future about what he was not doing now, he often has pointed a finger of blame toward his parents. He especially resented his father for not teaching and guiding him sufficiently of how to cope with life adequately as a man.

As Claude continued to blame his parents for his lot in life, I said to Claude that I thought he was continuing to blame his parents as a means of sidestepping the pressure and challenge of overcoming his life anxiety in the here-and-now in the present. If he viewed himself with such major deficits and inadequacies, then he is off the hook from expecting anything too much of himself and is able to justify why he cannot leave his wife. He can absolve himself of answerability to himself and existential guilt for not living his life by displacing that responsibility onto his parents.

Despite Claude's enhanced awareness of his situation and his different opportunities for an exodus from his misery, he continued to complain about his work and marital situation, as if he felt helpless to change those situations. For those five years of treatment, he did not make any radical action changes to his life. In retrospect, Claude just wanted me to listen, to believe, and to bear caring witness to the story of his life experience until that point.

After a ten-year hiatus, Claude sought me out again for therapy. He was still a doctor and unhappily married, but now he was determined to finally attain a life of passion for himself. He had been awakened from his doldrums by his crush on a divorcee outside of his marriage. Even though his feelings were unreciprocated, his discovery of a passion in himself energized him sufficiently to want to love and be loved finally before he died.

Unlike the first time Claude was in treatment, we have not been focused so much on Claude understanding himself and his history, as on his anticipatory anxiety and use of obsessional thinking and pessimism about the future as a defense against his fear of actually experiencing major changes in his life.

In this regard, Claude himself, has been interested in how to navigate through his fear of transitions separating the present moment from the future. On numerous occasions, he has referred to his need to just push himself into action to bolster his confidence instead of indulging his "doom and gloom." Despite Claude's struggles with a fundamental fear of experiencing life, he has made slow, steady progress toward the life he would like to lead. Instead of "taking care of older, sick people," Claude decided to become a teacher in order to become involved with people at the "other end of the life cycle."

As has been his custom of excessive self-protectiveness and caution, however, Claude has attempted to forestall the implementation of his own decision-making with his endless predictions, preparations, and rehearsals for his transition into the future before its actual arrival. For example, before becoming a teacher, he wanted to follow a teacher in his son's school around to see if he would like it. At these times, I have attempted to provide Claude with an alternative perspective that was far more fearless about leaping into action, but one that seemed to resonate with Claude's own fragile hopefulness. In general, I have seen my therapeutic role to be a holder of auxiliary hope for Claude's future; somebody outside of the obsessional circles of Claude's thinking who is able to offer reminders, sometimes gentle, sometimes challenging, that he is mistaking the pessimistic predictions he is making about the future as a defensive substitute for actual experience.

Claude has now entered a graduate program for training high school teachers. He has also spoken to his wife about his wish to get a divorce. Perhaps not surprisingly, they have planned the death of their marriage as dispassionately as they have lived the life they have shared together. Claude continues to struggle against himself, his fears of the future, and loyalty to his past. But Claude has emerged from his waking nightmare of quiet desperation and at this writing, he and his wife have agreed to sell the house and part ways in three months.

# Chapter 7

# Resentment and Entitlement

## The Reversal of Giving into Taking

No more fiendish punishment could be desired were such a thing possible then that one should be turned loose in society and remain absolutely unnoticed by all the members thereof. If no one turned around when we entered, answered when we spoke, or minded what we did, but if every person we met cut us "dead" and acted as if we were nonexisting beings, a kind of rage and impotent despair would soon well up in us.

(James, *Principles in Psychology*, 1890, p. 293)

Oh, of all sufferings, none, perhaps is so torturing as being chosen to be the object of pity; there is nothing which so tempts one to rebel against God.

(Kierkegaard, *Papers*, 1972, p. 304)

## Robert: From Self-Pity to Resentment

As Robert's treatment proceeded into its second year, there were increasing indications that cycles of shame and self-pity were beginning to give way to subtle expressions of envy and resentment. On one occasion, these sentiments emerged in no uncertain terms. Robert had just completed a prolonged rant about how much he envied everyone around him for their ability to participate in a life of friendships, flirtations, and sexuality. I was relieved because in transforming his hidden resentments into rage, Robert was able, at least momentarily, to break out of his enclosed prison of shame and self-pity. He acknowledged how much he hated his fellow students, while he watched them walking around campus as if without a care in the world. *They* all had lives, while he did not. *They* all were laughing and flirting with their boyfriends and girlfriends, while he remained pathetically alone.

After Robert blurted out these bitter sentiments in a torrent of words, I said that I was relieved to hear him openly express feelings that were not easy to admit. Given his shame and self-pity of feeling unfairly targeted by

DOI: 10.4324/9781003559559-8

the arbitrary whims of fate, it was inevitable that he would envy so many others who seemingly escaped scot-free from incurring misfortune.

Soon after that important breakthrough session, in which Robert gave himself an expressive freedom to protest prior indignities, Robert was able to give voice more easily to his sense of exclusion and isolation. In one session, Robert described a party that he had attended, in which he found himself in a circle of young people who were talking about their first-time sexual experiences. Each person took a turn telling his or her story of initiation into the grown-up world of sexuality, but Robert remained silent because he had no story to tell. He recounted how he felt like a "loser" because he was still a virgin and envied everyone else for being "normal."

Robert had never been able to articulate his resentments toward his mother holding him back on those overnights in middle school. He had never expressed how envious he had felt of all his peers who did not have to endure the imprisoned isolation of his mother's overbearing possessiveness. Early on in high school, he had become interested in a girl who his mother would not allow him to date. Most importantly, though, Robert eventually became his own worst enemy; his introjection of his mother's prohibitions, as well as the religious prohibitions of his Catholicism, greatly inhibited his free access to his sexuality, which he perceived as "sinful' and "dirty."

Even before the onset of puberty, Robert viewed his mother as an overbearing presence who sadistically begrudged him the pleasure of his most hedonistic desires. Since she largely prevented Robert from playing with friends, his only pleasure within the entrapment of his home was to play video games, which he attempted to do at every opportunity. His mother, jealous of this rival for Robert's attention, severely limited the time Robert could spend playing video games. In response, Robert would wait until his mother went to sleep at night to sneak off—always on tiptoes—to enjoy the forbidden fruit of his passion. His enjoyment, however, was always compromised by a hyper-vigilant dread in listening for the creaking of the floorboards above him, which signified that his mother was about to catch him in the midst of his "illicit" activities.

Robert's growing conviction that reaching for pleasure would be inevitably overpowered by the punishment of sadistic withholding was captured in a dream he had when he was eight years old, which still remained vivid in his mind 16 years later. The dream consisted simply of his father giving Robert a candy bar, which made him very happy. When his mother became aware that her husband had given Robert the treat, she became enraged at his father for giving the treat and took the candy bar away. As she did so, her face turned beet-red with rage and transformed into a "dragon."

Robert had learned all too well that pleasure was a crime, which would incur the most frightening of punishments. The intimidating monstrosity with which Robert's mother enforced her separation envy of begrudging Robert his own individuated life as a man led to Robert's introjection of a self-punitive war against the sin of his own sexuality. Now as a young adult, after he engages in masturbatory activity, he compulsively cleans up all evidence that he ever pleasured himself. Crime and its punishment thus had become manifest in the obsessive-compulsive cycle of doing and undoing.

In putting a lid on the evolving power of his sexual desires, Robert also was attempting to delay burgeoning manhood and remain a little boy in order to re-find a loving mommy of his infancy—but it was precisely that unconscious "regressive" need which filled him with shame, self-pity, and envy when comparing himself with his peers.

It is not surprising, then, that given Robert's own self-envying inhibitions, he, in turn, would begrudge his peers the free play of their sexuality as well. Scheler (1912) describes the silent voice of existential envy that is directed against the envied person's very nature: "It is as if it whispers continually: 'I can forgive everything but not that you *are* you, that you are what you *are*—indeed that *I am not you*'" (p. 35).

When one pities oneself because of feeling like an immobilized victim of fate, it is difficult to acknowledge and take responsibility for one's own role in not "seizing the moment" that now is gone forever. There is a self-perpetuating circularity in focusing one's melancholy longing on opportunities that have already passed by, since while one is so preoccupied with what has been missed, one is continually manufacturing more regret as empty, unattended moments speed by mercilessly from the future into the past.

In a certain sense, the envy of others could be viewed as an externalization of regret for the missed opportunities of one's own life that have not been lived out. Such individuals then may fantasize that instead of their lost opportunities being dead and buried, they are now gone forever because they have been stolen and are being lived out by the more fortunate individuals around them that they resent and envy so much. The envious person thus keeps the despair of regret at bay by harboring fantasies that there is endless time to undo her mistakes by grabbing back from the envied person the idealized life of which she feels deprived.

## Reflexive Guilt, Inhibition, and the Emergence of Resentment

How do Robert's shame and immobilizing self-doubts about his fundamental right to freely actualize his individuated life, as manifested in his self-pity, regret, and envy, culminate in the sudden emergence of his rageful outbursts? To answer that question, I would like to differentiate between interrelated terms such as aggression, activity level, assertiveness, resentment, hostility, and rage. Many of these terms have overlapping meanings, but their interrelationships refer to distinctly different psychodynamics.

We all come into the world with a passionate life force, and that engine of passion draws from a reservoir of life energy for its impetus. Although human aggression and its sublimation into self-assertive expressiveness draws from this life energy, I am speaking about aggression in a very broad sense, and not as interchangeable with hostility. Indeed, I would like to explore the paradox of how when one feels cornered by shame, self-doubt, and the right to one's assertiveness, it is resentment, as a consequence of inhibited verbal expressions of aggression and anger, that culminates in explosive paroxysms of hostility and violence. An individual's free access to his passionate life energy, including the self-defensive instrument of aggression, is indispensable to the initiation of dynamic movement, as well as self-assertive and self-expressive activity. Winnicott (1950) thus states: "At origin, aggressiveness is almost synonymous with activity" (p. 204). He further notes that in the beginning aggression resembles a "life-force" (p. 216).

A child's aggression enables him to differentiate himself as a separate individual from his parents. The first "No" enables the child to set boundaries as to where the parents' sphere of influence ends and the child's individualized freedom of self-determination begins. The parental acceptance of the child's autonomy diminishes the his separation guilt and facilitates the courage to differentiate himself from parental authority. His secure sense of belonging lays the foundation for the sense of right to sustain his self-willed and self-determining activity.

When one's wishes to be accepted and to belong are thus fulfilled, the child develops a positive sense of omnipotent wish magic ("what I wish for will come true"), which often will become modified as the basis of self-confidence and optimism about the future. Self-confidence largely derives its power from an underlying conviction of one's moral rightness, which then gives one license to assert oneself spontaneously.

Yet since many parents view their children's growing up as a form of abandonment, they may hesitate to recognize their children's evolving autonomy as their own individual persons. There are numerous parents who accept and recognize their children as long as they stay within the parent's sphere of influence, but then don't recognize the child who has a mind and will of his own. Like Robert, since such children may come to believe that the disloyalty of individuated freedom sows destruction in its wake, their unrecognized desire to individuate may boomerang back as a self-punitive reflexive guilt for the sin of separation.

Whereas positive omnipotence of wish magic thus refers to the conviction that one's desires have the magical power to create the world around us, negative omnipotence of wish magic refers to our conviction that our desires will destroy the world of those closest to us. The basis of such magical thinking lies in one's conviction that there is an instantaneously boundless movement leading inexorably from a wish to thought to words, which then lead inevitably to material changes in the external world. Once one gives verbal expression to a wish, that wish is carried along and born into the world through the midwife of "word magic." Cassirer (1946) describes the mythical creative force in word magic: "The Word, in fact, becomes a primary force in which all being and doing originate" (p. 45).

Beth is a polite, pleasant woman in her late 30s who was referred to me for depression and anxiety. Her mother had been diagnosed with breast cancer when Beth was two years old and then died of her illness two years later. To all appearances, Beth has had a close, healthy relationship with her father. When in the privacy of her own company, however, Beth suffered mightily from harsh self-recriminations and self-hatred for what she believed was something deeply flawed in her. Isn't that why, she reasoned, that she had been punished by her mother's death?

As Beth and I delved deeper into her belief that she had done something wrong to have made her mother die, she remembered how disorienting and difficult it was to see a strange, sickly woman replace her "real" mother of vitality. This increasingly frail mother no longer played with her like she had in the past and eventually became too weak to respond to Beth as well.

Beth wanted to be rid of this imposter, so that her real mother would return. When Beth's mother then actually did die, it reinforced Beth's magical belief that she had committed the unforgivable sin of wishing her mother to her death for which now she must be punished for the rest of her life.

Beth's consequent ability to mourn her mother's death was greatly complicated by a self-perpetuating dread that her destructive word magic would harm close family members like her father and grandmother if she opened up about her reflexive guilt and grief regarding her mother's death. On the contrary, her outward demeanor of sunny generosity was meant to be a reparative antidote to her destructiveness. Although Beth's mother had died 35 years earlier, Beth's melancholic burden of wrongness had continued to percolate and intensify in the silent cauldron of her self-enclosed mind ever since then. It is only in open dialogue that she unfolded the confessional story of her guilt and grief in a mourning process to which I bore witness.

A child's reflexive guilt and anxiety concerning the destructiveness of her desires often leads to attacks on the life force that fuels her creative initiation of activity. Like a psychic autoimmune system out of control, the child clamps down excessively on assertive and expressive activity for fear of where it may lead, which then culminates in the self-inhibition of passivity.

In not trusting the creative spontaneity and "rightness" of her desires as a guidepost by which to act and live, she is left with no other option but to submit to the moral authority of her parents. In order to be safe and secure, she may put endless pressure on herself to comply with conditions of acceptability as defined by her parents. In so doing, she serves herself up as a *reactive* object to the parents' will and authority.

This shift from feeling and thinking of oneself as an active subject to viewing oneself from the outside as a passive object is revealed sometimes when a patient says to the therapist: "I think you are disappointed in me." Even though the statement itself is often prompted by the *patient's* disappointment in the therapist for deviating in some way from an expectant hope for how the therapist would behave, she immediately transforms the subjectivity of her own disappointment in the therapist into the reflexively automatic guilt of an object who must have done something wrong to disappoint the therapist.

Many forces within Robert's family conspired to keep him immobilized and stuck. His mother's persistent non-recognition of his evolving development, even after the onset of puberty, as well as his father's caution to Robert to "get along and go along" with his mother, made it difficult for Robert to see his sexuality as anything but a sinful temptation to rupture the idealized innocence of the mother-child connection in his early life. Filled with such tormenting conflict about the fundamental goodness of his life force to become an autonomous individual, Robert's freedom to determine his own future became foreclosed and narrowed by dutifully obeying the "shoulds" of his mother's authority. This self-enclosed prison then resulted in his sense of despair, fatalism, and self-pity.

The child, who doubts that he can be morally good *and* affirm the passion of the spontaneous, creative gesture at the same time, must compromise his integrity as an individual in order to be "good" through a self-abnegating compliance with the moral authority of his parents. This sacrifice of one's dignity as an individual in living as a reactive creature who automatically complies with the authority of others, however, leads to mounting resentment. One cannot forfeit one's freedom of self-determination without paying a heavy price of resentment for the indignities suffered in one's self-shaming prostration. Since one has handed one's moral authority over to the other, it is the other who is responsible for one's downtrodden position.

Otto Rank (1936), who was greatly influenced by Nietzsche, believed that neurotics cannot create for themselves because they are guilt-bound to their parents as procreators. As a result, they neurotically project their inhibited life force onto authority figures, and then resist those authority figures through a "counter-will."

For the child who has not disentangled himself from the parent's moral authority sufficiently to affirm his own passions and create his own values according to his own conscience, there is nothing left to do but negate the will of the parents. When the problematic tensions of domination and submission enter into the human equation, the subjugated fight back by destroying the corrupted relationship of exploiter and exploited.

Indeed, far from feeling guilty in reaction to punishment doled out by external authority or the sadism of one's own self-shaming authority, one has no choice but to resist in order to protect one's sense of dignity. It is for that reason that Nietzsche (1887) suggests that punishment may *impede* the development of the very feelings of guilt it is supposed to awaken:

> If we consider the millennia *before* the history of man, we may unhesitatingly assert that it was precisely through punishment that the

development of the feeling of guilt was most powerfully *hindered*—at least in the victims upon whom the punitive force was vented.

(pp. 81–82)

Nietzsche elaborates: "Punishment makes men hard and cold; it concentrates; it sharpens the feeling of alienation; it *strengthens the power of resistance*" (p. 81).

The passive reactivity of complying with and simultaneously resenting external authority often leads to masochistic self-defeating actions as a means of avenging oneself against the tyranny of the should. The perverse spite of "cutting off one's nose to spite one's face" has the purpose of hurting the creators on whom one feels dependently bound like a slave-like creature. Compliance and ressentiment thus are strange but inevitable bedfellows of passivity.

This intertwining relationship between compliance, resentment, and victimization is a self-perpetuating cycle: One must make up for the destructiveness of one's resentments through the reaction formation of repeated selfless sacrifices to the other's desires, which only leads to further resentment, victimization, and entitlement. As long as compliance and resentment are the only passive bedfellows of choice, one continues to search for an ever-elusive sense of goodness.

The contrasting predicament between passively inhibiting self-expressive actions and then resenting it afterwards on the one hand, or engendering the authentic guilt of remorse that emerges in the aftermath of asserting one's desires on the other, introduces interesting moral ironies into people's lives. Frequently, we have a choice between adhering to the rules we *should* obey and what we would *wish* to do—or so we frame it to ourselves. Since the reflexive guilt concerning the destructiveness of asserting our desires prevents us from initiating actions, we obey rules appropriated from a social framework, which then further inhibits the assertion of our desires. Paradoxically, these compliant attempts to be obedient and "good" often backfire, for now our selflessness leads to resentment, indignation, and an entitled sense that we are *owed* compensation for our sacrifices.

In contrast, the initial "selfish" affirmation of our passions often leads to the authentic guilt of remorse, in which because we have fulfilled our desires, we may feel that we *owe* others. This sense of indebtedness then fuels the reparative pro-social urge toward doing good for others.

Robert *first* needs the self-pitying sense of being a "pathetic failure" who has been unfairly victimized by the powers of fate in order to mobilize the self-righteousness of resentment to push back against the external authority that has constrained his existence. The feeling of being unjustly wronged thus provides a justification for entitlement to some form of compensation that otherwise would be difficult for Robert to feel he deserves in his shamed pathetic state. In fact, this sense of entitled self-righteousness that emerges from self-sacrificial compliance may become such an appealing alternative to the conflicts of struggling with the up-front self-assertiveness of one's own desires that one may be tempted as if ritualistically to first sacrifice oneself in relationships in order to put oneself in the morally self-righteous position of deserving payback. In this sense, we might understand the expression of resentment as the delayed reactivity to the indignities of a suffocated freedom to be and to become.

It is not the animal who roams free who exhibits defensive rage, but the cornered animal desperately fighting for his survival who is savage. It is the inhibiting constraints on the aggressive energy of one's self-expressive life force that gives rise to resentment and rage. Road rage, for example, is not the straightforward expression of aggression, but is instead the violent eruption of displaced "road resentment" for having inhibited oneself one too many times.

## "Holding On": Memory, Melancholic Interiority, and the Emergence of Resentment

One important way of highlighting the paralyzing effects of shame and the emergence of resentment is by differentiating between the implications of feeling like an active free agent who lives according to the authority of one's own conscience on the one hand, and feeling like a reactive object who is unreflectively obedient to external authority on the other. In an earlier chapter, I described how expectant hopes link feeling, thinking, and imagination in the service of activity that has the purpose of realizing those hopes. As Fromm (1997) states:

> To be active means to give expression to one's faculties, talents, to the wealth of human gifts with which—though in varying degrees—every human being is endowed. It means to renew oneself, to grow, to flow out, to live....
>
> (p. 76)

Foss (1949) emphasizes that this active flowing out is the essence of what we call a "self": "What we call a 'self' is such a dynamic unity, an outreaching in which character is the objective for which the self reaches" (p. 8). Kierkegaard (1849) also emphasizes that, strictly speaking, the notion of a static self does not exist because it is always in the process of becoming: "A self, every moment it exists, is in a process of becoming, for the self (*kata dynamin*—potentially) is not present actually, it is merely what is to come into existence" (p. 31). In the same vein, Nietzsche (1887) goes so far as to say: "There is no 'being' behind doing, effecting, becoming; the 'doer' is merely a fiction added to the deed—the deed is everything" (p. 45).

Nietzsche (1887) suggests that self-affirmation, which is implicit in one's ability to act and express oneself openly, is characteristic of what he calls the "noble person." Scheler (1912) describes the noble morality this way: "The noble person has a completely naïve and non-reflective awareness of his own value and his fullness of being, an obscure conviction which enriches every conscious moment of his existence, as if he were autonomously rooted in the universe" (p. 37).

It is only after we encounter rebuffs and frustrations to purposeful action that we are stopped in our tracks, as if mortified by the obstacle and turn inward, thus cultivating a sense of interiority. Nietzsche (1887) declares: "All instincts that do not discharge themselves outwardly *turn inward* that is what I call the internalization of man ... that is the origin of the 'bad conscience'" (pp. 84–85). He then elaborates:

> This *instinct for freedom* forcibly made latent—we have seen it already—this instinct for freedom pushed back and repressed, incarcerated within and finally able to discharge and vent itself only on itself: that, and that alone, is what the *bad conscience* is in its beginnings.
>
> (p. 87)

In Nietzsche's view, in our natural state as human animals, we resemble "verbs" that are actively moving through time and space, and it is only in reaction to the frustrating barriers to self-expressive action that we become mortified as "nouns," immobilized by a self-conscious interiority.

This immobilization of active self-assertive expressiveness, and then becoming stuck on one's own interiority through self-attack, is characteristic of what Nietzsche (1887) calls "slave morality." Scheler (1912) contrasts the inherent self-confidence of the noble person with the "pride" that characterizes "slave morality." He suggests that it is because the person with "slave morality" has lost his self-confidence that he needs a show of pride in its stead: "Pride results from an experienced diminution of this naïve self-confidence. It is a way of 'holding on' to one's value, of 'seizing' and 'preserving it' deliberately" (p. 37). Such "holding on" is characteristic of what Nietzsche (1887) calls *ressentiment.*

The word *ressentiment* derives from the French *re-sentiment*, to feel again and again. Scheler (1912) states: "Ressentiment is the repeated experiencing and reliving of a particular emotional responsive reaction against someone else" (p. 25). In order to feel the sting of an insult repeatedly, one must hold on to and nourish the remembered experience of a prior indignity such that the continually renewed memory evolves eventually into a grudge.

Many such individuals, unable to sustain a sense of right necessary to self-confidently assert themselves, may become paralyzed in the immediacy of the moment when they are insulted or attacked. They may instead stay silent and let themselves be dominated by the other person, until many days or many years thereafter, when they might ambush the offending individual and say: "You really hurt me back then."

Nietzsche (1887) views this contrast between the ability to express oneself openly and directly in the moment and holding on to one's self-enclosed interiority to be an important distinction between the noble morality and the slave morality of the resentful person:

> Whereas the noble man lives in trust and openness with himself, the man of *ressentiment* is neither upright nor naïve or honest and straightforward with himself, the soul *squints*; his spirit lives in hiding places, secret paths and back doors, everything covert entices him as *his* world, *his* security, *his* refreshment; he understands how to keep silent, how not to forget, how to wait, how to be provisionally self-deprecating and humble.

> (p. 38)

The covert "holding on" of resentments against others described by Nietzsche in this passage occurs because of the immobilizing effects of shame and the fear of consequences that would ensue if one were to express one's protests or recriminations more openly at the time that they were experienced. Scheler (1912) writes:

> *Ressentiment* can only arise if these emotions are particularly powerful and yet must be suppressed because they are coupled with the feeling that one is unable to act them out either because of weakness, physical or mental, or because of fear. Through its very origin, ressentiment is therefore chiefly confined to those who *serve* and are *dominated* at the moment, who fruitlessly resent the sting of authority.
>
> (p. 31)

The sense of rejection and indignity resulting from experiences of being insulted, injured, and ignored have a transforming effect on one's life force because one feels compelled to go back in time and change the mind of the rejecting party in order to restore the dignity of one's own existence. Whereas the forgetfulness of the noble person enables him to continually let go of the past and move into the future, the resentful person with slave morality cannot relinquish memories of injury and insult that forever haunt him wherever he goes. Nietzsche (1908) elaborates: "One cannot get rid of anything, one cannot get over anything, one cannot repel anything—everything hurts. Men and things obtrude too closely, experiences strike too deeply, memory becomes a festering wound" (p. 230).

It is interesting to note here that Winnicott (1949a) postulates how the newborn's intellect becomes segregated from the psyche in reaction to the intolerable impingements of birth trauma. The function of this segregated intellectual activity is to "hold on":

> It is as if the intellect collects together the impingements to which there had to be reaction, and holds them in exact detail and sequence, in the way protecting the psyche until there is a return to the continuing-to-exist state.
>
> (p. 191)

He continues: "The value of this defense is shown when the individual comes for analysis for in the analytic setting, we find that carefully collected primary persecutions can be remembered" (p. 192).

Since resentful individuals are not able to affirm their own life force, to say "Yes" to themselves, they are relegated only to the reactivity of negating the external authority with which they comply, but also which they envy and resent. The humiliation of one's continuing dependence, perpetuated by one's unrealized desire to change the insulting other person into an accepting one, accentuates one's resentment and the need for some form of revenge to restore one's injured sense of dignity. Within an internal dungeon of a pacified, stunted life force stymied from without and within, the residue of resentments over various indignities that have been endured settles into a cultivation of bitterness and plotting of vengeance. Nietzsche (1887) states:

> While every noble morality develops from a triumphant affirmation of itself, slave morality from the outset says "No" to what is outside, what is "different," what is not itself and *this* No is its creative deed. The inversion of the value-positing eye—the need to direct one's view outward rather than back to oneself is the essence of *ressentiment*; in order to exist, slave morality always first needs a hostile external world; it needs, physiologically speaking, external stimuli in order to act at all—its action is fundamentally reaction.
>
> (pp. 36–37)

An individual's ability to use her aggression actively and creatively with a freedom of imaginative ruthlessness is extremely useful in helping her obliterate the significance of a rejecting person, and thereby in letting go of her resentment toward that individual. I use the word *obliterate* purposefully, because if the resentment of holding on is fueled by fantasies of avenging and thereby undoing an insult, then the only credible way that the resentful individual can free himself from the past is by constructing a creative illusion of taking vengeance by diminishing the elevated importance of the source of the insult.

When one person rejects or breaks off a relationship with another person, the question often arises as to whether the rejected person will nurse her narcissistic wound indefinitely, or whether she is able to actively and mobilize her ruthlessness sufficiently in order to "kill off the importance" of the insulting person in her own mind. Holding on to the memory of an insult reflects the extent to which a person is still reactively dependent on the insulting person for validation and approval of one's existence. In contrast, to ruthlessly relegate the insulting person to the oblivion of forgetfulness requires the mobilization of aggression that is crucial to the ability to separate oneself from that external authority and stand alone.

Sometimes, the inability to free oneself from a rejecting person, especially when that person was a parent, will lead to one's entire life being dictated by repetitive fantasies of reversing the past injury in romantic love relationships. Many such individuals pursue others who do not reciprocate their affections and avoid those who do. In this sense, we can say such persons are more interested in the power of changing and conquering the other and less interested in a ready-made reciprocated love.

## Shame, Indignity, and the Passivity of Waiting: The Entitlement to Compensation

In an earlier chapter, I described how when one's attempts to give of oneself and be received by another are rebuffed, the sudden rupture of the hope for relationship triggers a dissociative shift of the self's center of gravity from living within an embodied self looking out toward the world to an identification with a disembodied outside vantage point, as if now turned around and looking at oneself. This self-enclosed stance can be viewed as the individual's reflexive attempt to fill the void left by an expected connection with an Other by closing the circle of relationship upon himself narcissistically. The evolving process of offering oneself and one's creations up to others for acceptance is thus inverted into a transfixing hypnotic spell of narcissistic self-preoccupation.

Inasmuch as this person's offerings have been rejected, however, he carries that experience of rejection within his self-shaming stance toward himself and in the negation of his own desires. This person now becomes the chief culprit targeting his own desires—not unlike a collaborator with an invading enemy that has chased the authentic representatives of the host nation into exile. Since access to one's desires is so central to the constitution of a dynamic self, the negation of desire within one's self-enclosing consciousness continually undoes one's subjective sense of having a real self.

Through the foreclosure of otherness, change, separateness, loss, and ultimately death, life is increasingly emptied of a transformative, spiritual meaning. Hyde (1979) says of the narcissist: "The narcissist feels his gifts come from himself. He works to display himself, not to suffer change" (p. 53). The narcissist's dilemma is to find a way to solicit the validity of his existence from the recognition of the outside world without making himself vulnerable to rejection again. Filled with self-doubt about the acceptability of his own desires, this individual labors mightily to comply with the desires of significant others who he makes into the ultimate authorities of his worth. In an attempt to exhibit himself as an object for sale, he creates an idealized image of himself.

The consciousness of one's desperate dependence on others for the validity of one's existence is humiliating, and this indignity always lurks underneath in the form of resentment. At the very same time that this individual alienates himself from the subjectivity of his own desires—the very essence of his being—he also may unconsciously sentimentalize them, as if in a protective embrace from imagined global enemies who have waged war against them, most especially himself.

Here then, again, is the paradox in Robert's self-shaming stance toward himself: The self-victimization of calling himself pathetic leads immediately to a self-pitying sympathy for being a pathetic victim arbitrarily targeted by an unjust fate, which then justifies an entitlement to some form of recompense. With a sense of righteous indignation and resentment, this person may then retrieve his shamed desires from exile and give them a rebirth as entitled demands.

How then are these entitled demands manifested? Since the resentment of not being accepted unconditionally as a unique individual is fueled by the humiliating desperation of working so hard to satisfy the needs of others, entitlement is manifested often in a passive resistance of inertia against the labor of extending oneself too much and too far to meet any and all external pressures. On the contrary, resentment and entitlement are expressed by passively *waiting* for others to do the giving, for others to labor strenuously to make the entitled person feel unconditionally welcome.

Imagine the older brother (described in Chapter 6), who after being harshly berated by his mother for bullying his younger brother, feels so injured by his mother's favoritism that he declares loudly "I'm running away" and races out of the house. Every few steps, he turns around to see if his mother will come after him. He makes it to the end of the block, stops, and there he waits to see if his mother will chase him down, ask for forgiveness, and welcome him home again.

At the same time that he awaits her apology, however, he holds onto himself tightly with arms folded in a self-protective ball as if to shoo away would-be comforters. "This sort of waiting at the end of the block" could be a passive moment of self-pity, resentment, and entitlement if the mother attends to her older son's hurt. If left unheeded, however, his indefinite waiting may evolve into a chronic pout. In this sense, a pout, reflected in a defiantly protruding lower lip, embodies the conflict between one's desperation to have one's wounds attended to and a stubborn defensiveness about letting anyone in again.

Sometimes, the self-righteousness of an initial suffering that justifies later entitlements may be more appealing than the self-doubts that one imagines would follow the assertion of one's desires. There is a rich mythological and psychological tradition to the themes of long suffering entitling one to a later "promised land" and of hard work earning oneself the pleasures of play. Here we see the martyrdom of victims accorded a moral virtue that then justifies a sense of a right to have good things come one's way.

One particular way, especially in intimate relationships, the self-enclosed individual conveys the passivity of entitlement is in the expectation that others will be able to "read" one's mind without one having to verbally convey one's meanings. Rather than suffer through the vulnerability of openly speaking one's desires, it is the other person who should know what one is thinking. If the other person should fail in that designated task, the scolding wrath of the silent demand emerges in statements such as, "How long have you known me?"

In clinical work, too, therapists may sometimes become frustrated by the passivity of their patients, because they find themselves working too hard to advance the treatment for the patient. In a sense, such patients have made themselves into inert stationary objects, who place responsibility on their therapist to find a way to get them moving again. Indeed, since some patients may feel that even expressing themselves openly through verbal communication may feel like too much work, they feel entitled that the therapist "read" the contents of their mind and desires.

When in social life there is a fluid interchange in giving of oneself, and being received by an Other it is difficult to sort out who is the giver and who is the receiver. In such situations, giving and receiving seamlessly meld into each other. When the interchange of giving and receiving breaks down, and an individual's resentment of constantly giving without being received gives way to entitlement, this person is likely to keep close track of the imaginary scoreboard of who is giving and who is receiving.

Many "parentified" patients, who have put much pressure on themselves in this way to "care" for a parent by meeting her demands, eventually may feel exploited because no matter what they did it never seemed to be enough to be received appreciatively by the parent. For such individuals, the interpersonal field of give and take may be constrained by the circular compulsivity of obligatory giving to those who are designated as less fortunate and weaker and entitled receiving from those who are designated as stronger and more fortunate. In this social arrangement, the obligated caregiver, often feeling resentful for endless giving of herself without ever being appreciated, proceeds with a sense of entitlement to another relationship with an implicit demand of getting her needs fulfilled. Here, we see the unwritten social contract governing the free mutual interchange of giving and receiving constrained by the coercively alternating means of ensuring that "what goes around, comes around."

## Kathy: Want and Feeling Unwanted

Kathy had rarely experienced the privilege of giving and feeling that her contributions significantly enhanced the lives of the people around her. She knew of that kind of self-fulfillment and very much wanted to taste of its sweet depth, but fundamentally Kathy did not believe that if she entrusted herself to others, then they would recognize her value or safekeep her well-being for her. Ultimately, she had little faith in the truthfulness of the saying, "what goes around, comes around." Since no one else looked out for her, in her mind she had to look out for herself, which then lead to a moral disquiet and despair about her own sense of selfishness.

When Kathy's baby was five months old, her resentment of being woken up from a dead sleep overwhelmed her. She resented her son's need to be nursed and comforted because it interfered with her fervent urge to stay in bed. That inclination toward her own immediate desires was not an unusual sentiment for Kathy. As she put it at various times in various ways: "I want my own way." "I want to do what I want to do." "I am selfish."

Her husband often was dutiful in his efforts to please her, but if he or her son strayed away from her fantasies of who they should be, she began to feel a perseverating "hatred" toward them. As Kathy put it, she was always "fighting" everybody in her own head. Getting her husband or her son or other people to do or be who she wanted them to be ultimately did not work for her. She remained chronically unfulfilled, empty, and desperately waited restlessly for something or someone to shake up her life and change it.

What then was Kathy searching for? How do we understand her restless "emptiness"? Did the experiences of "getting her way" *really* register inside of her; that is, did they satisfy her emptiness in any sustained fashion?

Kathy, a 39-year-old woman, sought psychotherapy with me a few years ago. Her parents had emigrated from South America when Kathy was 19 years old. She was a slight woman whose timid manner made her seem somewhat smaller than she actually was. She conveyed the impression of a young girl with alert and watchful eyes.

When she was eight years old, her mother sent her to stay with her grandmother on weekdays, including overnights. She returned to her parents only on weekends. Recently, Kathy's mother acknowledged that her primary reason for sending Kathy away at the time was because the grandmother had just become widowed and was "lonely."

Kathy described her grandmother as a harsh, controlling, and paranoid woman. One enduring memory Kathy had of this period—which she was not sure if she had made up or actually happened—was of her grandmother holding a sharp knife and "looking like she wanted to cut someone."

Kathy, like the children from Bowlby's (1975) classic study on separation, desperately longed for her mother to come get her and take her home, or to put it in Bowlby's words, she "pined for the lost object." Each week, however, the routine repeated itself: She was picked up from her grandmother's house on Friday nights and brought back on Sunday evenings. When she did return home on weekends, her mother was busily preoccupied with all things except for Kathy—cooking, cleaning, and vacuuming. This caretaking arrangement lasted about six years until Kathy was 14 years old.

Kathy's parents were suspicious of outsiders and overprotective of their daughter. Their wariness justified the huddling together of family enmeshment and overprotectiveness of their daughter. In their implicit warning to Kathy to "beware of strangers," they did not, however, extend their warning to the emotional incest lurking within the family. Kathy had few friends her own age and instead accompanied her parents to plays, symphonies, and operas. Although she eventually became somewhat more independent, the echoes of her mother's admonitions to be careful followed her around wherever she went.

Indeed, Kathy's family lived in a very small apartment. While Kathy stayed with her mother, she shared a bedroom with her mother; her father slept with her older brother. This sleeping arrangement dramatized a schism in the parents' relationship as well, which was reinforced by her mother's declarations to Kathy not to expect much from marriage. Perhaps most damaging in this regard, when Kathy got older, her mother confided in her about not enjoying sex with her father.

Kathy's mixture of pity, shame, and disgust about her mother had led to survivor guilt for wanting something better and has made it very difficult for her to embark on her own separate life path. A child cannot easily leave a depressed mother in good conscience. Since Kathy did not feel her contributions were sufficient to uplift her mother's life, she had to sacrifice more and give *all of herself* away in loyal commiseration of identification with her mother's downtrodden condition as a token of her love and to silence any echoes of survivor guilt.

Kathy was not able to receive anything of value for herself because whatever good she received was "ruined" if her mother could not be happy. Kathy recalled that once when she was a child, her mother spoke wistfully of her regrets in not dating a couple of young men in her earlier life. Kathy responded: "But Mom, then you wouldn't have had me." In recounting this incident, she added, "It was so depressing when she said that."

Kathy viewed herself as "deserving to suffer" for being a disappointment to her parents, for letting them down. Her proof was simply their unhappiness. Indeed, often when Kathy's mother gave Kathy a gift, she would say: "I don't have many years to live, my life is over. So, I am giving this to you." Kathy was quite frustrated when she told me this story, and said: "If my mother was not happy, then the gift was totally ruined for me." Her mother's unhappiness became a source of Kathy's feeling unreceived, unappreciated, and ultimately unwanted.

That sense of unfulfillment and shameful vulnerability for feeling "unwanted" was then covered up and reversed into a state of "want," in which Kathy felt selfish for being left continually "wanting" to take and fill up her "empty spaces." She never was able to give of herself and to be received appreciatively as a cherished object who had a uniquely constructive effect on her mother's life.

## The Despair of Emptiness: The Inability to Receive, Insatiability, and Taking

In shifting the self's center of gravity from the inside looking out to the outside looking in, an individual reverses her devotional stance of giving to and being received by the Other into an enclosed narcissistic self-preoccupation. In making this shift of identifications, the directional focus of one's purposes also shifts. The intangible *quality* of emotional unfulfillment in not being received as a treasured gift by an Other is turned inside out and reified into an interior, physical space, an "empty self" seeking to fill itself by taking in a compensatory *quantity* of tangible material. I would term this reversal of emotional unfulfillment in not being received into an "empty" interior space, *the despair of emptiness*. One would think that if we were genuinely speaking about an empty space inside, then one could just fill up that emptiness with love and recognition, and the problem would be solved. But within the cover-up of her self-enclosure, this person has already introjected her rejected gift offerings as self-shaming and consequently feels undeserving of receiving anything good for herself.

A primary problem inherent in the despair of emptiness is that the entitled individual covers up the vulnerability of her injury in not being received and feeling "unwanted" by reversing it into a state of "want," in which she wants now to take for herself. As a result, the wish to give and be received is reversed and transformed into a need to take and grab to fill up one's sense of emptiness. Brown (1959) thus states: "The modern psychology of taking is constructed, by a process of denial, out of its archaic opposite, giving" (p. 279).

However, the French philosopher Henri Bergson (1889) has pointed out that the emotional quality of intensity cannot be translated into a measurable quantity of what he called extensity. Measurability or quantification may often refer to visible, physical phenomena that cannot readily be applied to the difficult-to-grasp quality of emotional life.

To the extent that such individuals feel "empty" because they have been deprived, they may now feel justified and entitled to covet and grab back what originally should have belonged to them. Although to all appearances, kleptomaniacs are stealing, it may well be that they feel that they are just grabbing back what they feel belongs to them. Winnicott (1956b) thus views the antisocial tendency as a sign of hope that a person can overcome his sense of deprivation and emptiness. Similarly, when Robert voiced an envy of his friends who talked of their experience having sex, I viewed that envy as an acknowledgment of an activated resentment that was more hopeful than the passive fatalism of his self-pity.

Yet I would caution that the transformation of a passive sense of deprivation and regret for what was missed into envy and activated covetous entitlement also has its dangers. Now the wrath and resentful explosions of hostility for one's sense of unjust victimization are directed toward other human beings instead of only oneself. Blinded by one's grievance, this hostility may result in an abdication of one's conscience and the dehumanization of others.

Since no quantity of material can satisfy a missing emotional quality, the desperate short-term filling up of one's emptiness is insatiable and therefore repeated. Fromm (1997) says: "Mental greed—and all greed is mental—even if it is satisfied via the body—there is no satiation point, since its consummation never fills the inner emptiness, boredom, loneliness, and depression it is meant to overcome" (p. 97).

Symington (1997) notes: "Greed, I believe is hidden under shame" (p. 154). The problem here is that because in one's fundamental self-enclosure one is covering up one's vulnerability, one cannot truly receive what is offered because giving and being received must precede the capacity to genuinely receive and sustain one's own life. Instead, takes and grabs by conquering the voluntarism of desire in others through the entitlement of coercive force. But this quantity of material cannot fully satisfy the despair of one's emptiness that is based on one's fundamental sense of unacceptability and unworthiness. Symington puts it this way: "What is taken from the other is not digested, so what is done with it? It is, in fact, not truly taken in; it is taken but not digested" (p. 155).

The shame of feeling undeserving of anything good becomes an internal sieve, making it difficult even to internalize what is most desired: a feeling of being valuable to another person. It is one thing for a wife to hear her husband's declarations of love and know that he means them, and another for her to actually believe him, to feel his love inside of herself. For that to happen, she would have to feel lovable. It is thus not unusual that a person may be accepted by 19 people and rejected by 1, but it is that one who sticks in the craw, since it is that one rebuff which resonates with one's own sense of unworthiness. Taking in perpetual quantities of drugs, food, and even human beings who are transformed from free subjects in their own right into objects is a desperate compensation for the inability to genuinely receive or internalize the good, which itself derives from not being received.

Since one's resentments infuse one's entitled demands with a choosiness of how exactly those demands will be satisfied, the despair of emptiness is perpetuated indefinitely. When a person is desperately thirsty, it does not matter to him whether he is drinking water or lemonade or from which cup he drinks to quench his thirst. It has been my experience, however, in working with what are often referred to as emotionally empty patients, that such patients are tremendously selective in how and by whom their demands are gratified. This particularity concerning how, who, and what will fill up their emptiness reflects more a sense of entitled directedness than just the generalized desperation of emotional hunger.

I work with one patient who has many good friends who treat her with kindness and respect, while she perceives her mother to be harsh and rejecting. Rather than focus on what she can receive from her friends to fill her sense of emptiness, however, this patient struggles with severe depression because of feeling unloved and unacceptable to her mother. In a sense, this patient's sense of indignation and resentment fuels a determination not to let her mother "off the hook" of being the mother the patient thinks she should be. While she is waiting for her mother in particular to change, she misses the love that she deems essential from the friends she has. That love comes too easily and does not sufficiently reverse the indignities that she suffered at the hands of her mother. She therefore feels she has to conquer by coercing the love from her mother that felt she never received in order to restore her sense of injured dignity.

The entitled individual is often thus not interested in the easy accessibility to and internalization of love that is given voluntarily by others, since in one's self-enclosure one cannot use that love anyway to satisfy one's state of want. Instead, this entitled person is stimulated by a constant state of want, longing, and demand as manifested in the pursuit of grabbing at, and conquering a love from others that has not been offered voluntarily.

Perhaps this entitled pursuit of the unreachable ideal is one way of understanding why the alternating relational game of seesaw—chasing and winning over individuals who are rejecting and disinterested, and moving away from those persons who are accepting—pervades the singles dating scene. By seeking to attain the unattainable, these individuals hope to undo and reverse narcissistic wounds suffered many years previously. In resisting the mutuality of liking and being liked at the same time, individuals feel they must *prove* their worth first by coercing love from those who have rejected them and who are unattainable before they can feel worthy of a loving mutual interchange of giving and receiving. Instead of entrusting themselves to the win-win scenario involving the simultaneity of mutual love, such persons attempt to ensure the impact of their life through the mastery of others as controlled objects. If one is not welcomed in the front door of a house through the give-and-take of love, one has to resort to power and violence and break in a back window in order to make an impact on the surrounding world.

Chapter 8

# From Shame to Group Pride

Normality and the Construction of
Human Hierarchies

> Seest though these stones in this parched and barren wilderness? Turn them
> into bread, and mankind will run after Thee like a flock of sheep, grateful and
> obedient, though for ever trembling, lest Thou with draw Thy hand and deny
> them Thy bread.
>
> (Fyodor Dostoevsky, *The Grand Inquisitor*, 1880, p. 7)

> I tell Thee that man is tormented by no greater anxiety than to find someone
> quickly to whom he can hand over that gift of freedom with which the ill-fated
> creature is born.
>
> (Fyodor Dostoevsky, *The Grand Inquisitor*, 1880, p. 9)

## Active and Reactive: Rank's Character Typology

In the previous chapter, I described how shame transforms the active initiative of self-assertiveness into a reactive passivity toward one's life. This passivity is characterized by the fatalistic helplessness of self-pity, resentment and envy toward others, and an unconscious entitlement of feeling owed recompense for the suffering of one's prior indignities. Instead of actively expressing and living a passionate freedom of self-determination, such individuals reactively attempt to shape themselves according to the designs of external moral authority.

The distinction between active and reactive is a central aspect of Rank's (1936) character typology, in which he distinguishes between normal, neurotic, and creative character types. Without wishing to reduce the complexity of human character to an abstract typology, I think organizing human beings according to these character types is useful because they clearly delineate different implications between living life actively and reactively.

Rank (1936) suggests that normal character types erase their uniqueness as individuals by surrendering themselves to larger groups. Such individuals conform to their peers and adhere closely to the conventional norms of

DOI: 10.4324/9781003559559-9

their society. Although the consensual agreements that many individuals construct concerning what is virtuous and what is not, and what is of value and what is not, are arbitrary inasmuch as they have been created by human beings, "normal" persons nevertheless elevate these collective illusions into sacred truths. Becker (1975) referred to this process of "man taking himself and blowing himself up to cosmic importance" as "macrocosmization" (p. 18). By bringing heaven down to earth in this way, Dostoevsky's (1864) Underground Man thus states that "all plain men ... mistake the nearest and secondary causes for primary causes and in this way persuade themselves much more easily and quickly than other people that they found a firm basis for whatever business they have in hand" (p. 276).

For example, many "normal" character types are likely to believe that patriotism is an absolute virtue handed down by God rather than an idea that has been elevated to a virtue through the consensual agreement of many persons. Experimenting on animals to save human life could also be seen as a consensually agreed-upon "truth" that is elevated to the status of an absolute truth. Yet we well know that the values of different societies and different epochs are often fundamentally different; in Nazi Germany, whereas Hitler's speeches and pronouncements were viewed as morally justified because they were going to lead Germany to a needed renaissance, we would now view his words with horror.

In Rank's view, neurotic character types see through to what Becker (1973) calls the "vital lie" of these collective illusions. They are not able to surrender their individuality easily to groups and often find themselves feeling like a "square peg" attempting to fit into the "round hole" of the outside world. Such persons frequently use the non-compliance of inertia to rebel passively against expectations and pressures that have been imposed on them from the outside world. The neurotic thus depends on the imposed structure of external authority to sustain the reactive oppositionality of his resentful passive-aggressiveness. In this sense, the neurotic character type, who is inhibited by excessive shame and self-consciousness, is caught in a dislocating limbo between not being able to affirm himself as a unique individual, and yet also not able to fit in and feel sufficiently acceptable to the outside world.

On the other hand, Rank's creative character type does not live reactively, but like Nietzsche's noble morality, he is able to accept and affirm his unique difference as an individual in self-creative action. The creative type is able to integrate and shape his passion into the self-assertiveness of an active subject. Indeed, one could say that a primary difference between the reactivity of the normal and neurotic types on one hand and the activity of the creative type on the other, consists in their relative ability to mobilize, transform, and sublimate the aggression of their passionate life force into self-expressive action. In this view, it is not only the neurotic who is inhibited by shame and then must look reactively to external authority for guidance of how to live, but also the normal type as well.

Interestingly, Rank (1936) criticized Freud for the conservative therapeutic ideology of attempting to help neurotics adjust to the normal miseries of everyday life. Rank instead advocated that the therapist help neurotic individuals replace their shame and self-consciousness of their unique individuality by facilitating self-acceptance. From Rank's perspective, normal persons are less attuned to their own individualized desires and predilections, because they attempt to shape themselves too quickly in accordance with the conventions of society. In seeking refuge under the secure umbrella of the many, such persons give up the life force of their own creative will. As Becker (1975) puts it: "Man wanted a visible god always present to receive his offerings, and for this he was willing to pay the price of his own subjection" (p. 52).

While the neurotic's will is inhibited by self-consciousness, the normal character bypasses excessive self-consciousness by conforming unselfconsciously to the consensual norms agreed upon by the majority. The standards emerging from that consensus then becomes the moral guidepost by which the normal character type lives his individual life. It is noteworthy that Fromm (1941) adds:

> The person who is normal in terms of being well-adapted is often less healthy than the neurotic person in terms of human values. Often, he is adapted only at the expense of having given up his self in order to become more like the person he thinks he is expected to be.
>
> (p. 160)

On the other hand, Fromm (1941) describes the neurotic person as somebody who was "not ready to surrender completely in the battle for his self" (p. 160). Inasmuch as the normal person is not able to live according to the conscience of his own moral authority, he, too, in the need to take on the standards of external authority as his own. is shadowed by inhibiting shame and self-doubt.

For some persons, the reactivity of adapting to the external world becomes of such urgent concern that it may preempt one's access to one's own subjective world of feeling and desire. Winnicott (1971) speaks of individuals who are "so firmly anchored in objectively perceived reality that they are ill ... of being out of touch with the subjective world and with the creative approach to fact" (p. 78). Here, the individual's desperation to fit in at all costs risks that he will sell his creative soul for an appreciative recognition he never received and a sense of belonging he never was able to attain.

In fact, the normal person's obliteration of shame consciousness and reactive "slave morality" are embedded in the construction of the very norms and values to which most of us conform. It is precisely because the "normal" individual covers up the self-consciousness of being a unique individual so adeptly by blending in seamlessly with others that their shames and resentments influence cultural norms in more insidiously pervasive ways than the inhibitions of neurotic persons.

## Jerry: The Urge to Find His Own Path

Jerry is an intelligent, articulate 20-year-old man who came for psychotherapy because he had just been suspended during his sophomore year from the highly prestigious university where he had been matriculating. Since Jerry had not been going to class regularly and had also not completed assignments and term papers on time, he had received failing grades or incompletes on all his classes.

Jerry's parents accompanied him into the first session, and while Jerry remained silent and fidgeted uncomfortably, his mother grilled me about my religious beliefs. She made it clear that my level of religiosity (as opposed to secularism) mattered to her far more than the particular religion to which I belonged. While Jerry's father remained silent, Jerry spoke only intermittently in response to my questions. I was determined to give Jerry the respect and dignity of talking to him. Jerry's mother went on at length about her concerns that Jerry was suspended from his university and provided a roadmap of what they were hoping Jerry would get out of therapy. I then suggested that for the last half of our session, Jerry and I speak alone while they go to the waiting room.

When I asked Jerry how he understood his predicament, he said that he lacked confidence in expressing himself. As the youngest of their children, he said that he was much more in the habit of listening to his older siblings rather than speaking, and that he preferred it that way. In a similar way, when he attempted to write a term paper, his thinking would freeze when faced with a blank sheet of paper.

From the first sessions onward, Jerry insisted that he had been excited about the prospect of taking his courses at the beginning of the semester, and that he looked forward to doing the required reading. When, for example, he saw on the syllabus that Plato's *The Republic* had been assigned, he was excited because he had wanted to read the book for a while. When the time came to actually do the readings and write papers, he would instead find himself surfing the Internet and binge-watching Netflix. He insisted that he had no conscious intention to engage in those activities, but that they were just "impulsive" actions.

Jerry experienced tremendous shame about his inability to keep up with the norms set by his older siblings. He brooded about his own inadequacies. Given that he is a very bright young man, it is not surprising that he emphasized the virtues of rationality and could not understand how he could be sidetracked from his own plans by impulsive actions that led to his suspension. Indeed, in reacting with great distaste to the arbitrary moods and whims that governed his mother's domineering authority, Jerry had come to place a great premium on the guiding principles of rationalism to make decisions. As Jerry discovered to his consternation, however, the emotional life that he had dismissed for being so irrational kept ambushing him at the most inopportune times and thwarting his life plans.

Over the course of therapy, Jerry provided numerous examples of his mother's rules with which he either complied (he was forced to break up with a girlfriend during his junior year in high school) or bypassed without her knowledge. Often when he talked about her, he would punctuate his narrative with sardonic chuckles and a cynically mirthless laughter. The presence of Jerry's mother as a predominant figure in his mind was vividly dramatized in our third session together. With ten minutes left in the session, his cell phone rang; he glanced at the phone and said, "I have to get this." He listened for two minutes and then, after he hung up, he suddenly broke into tears. We both understood at that moment how suffocating his mother's presence had become in Jerry's mind and life.

The first months of therapy were characterized by some tension and conflict about how Jerry understood the original problem and needed solution for which he sought out therapy. He viewed his deviation from the expected norm of doing his schoolwork and graduating from college as an impulsive, irrational departure from how he had planned to live his life. I responded to Jerry that perhaps he also had resentments and rebellious desires that were embedded in his non-compliant "impulsivity." That impulsivity had always been prohibited by the authoritarianism of Jerry's mother and now was dismissed by Jerry himself. His actions seemed impulsive to him precisely because Jerry could not let himself know what he was doing, otherwise the sentry of "rationality" in Jerry's would not have allowed him to indulge his pleasures. Jerry remained unconvinced.

Jerry often would become silent during our early sessions, claiming that he did not have a lot to say. I wondered to myself whether Jerry felt comfortable and trusting enough to express himself during sessions. I began to realize that the adamant persistence with which I was pushing Jerry to acknowledge the motivated aspects of his "deviant" impulsivity for which he was suspended may have been viewed by Jerry as yet another moralistic judgment by an authority figure in the image of his mother. Through the boycott of his silence in sessions, he was, in part, transferring his cynicism about his mother's rigid authority to me, not without reason. In one session, I wondered out loud whether I had contributed to some of the tension between us because, like his mother, I had been too stubbornly opinionated about what I was saying. Ironically, by acknowledging my role in contributing to our tensions, I also somewhat differentiated myself from Jerry's mother in his eyes.

There were other important ways in which I was able to earn Jerry's trust as someone who was on his side, especially when I did not automatically ally myself with the therapeutic aim of returning Jerry to the "normality" of academic success. When Jerry asked whether I thought he should apply for reinstatement to his university for the following year, I asked him how he felt about returning to school, he acknowledged his own ambivalence. He then immediately said that he had an urge to go on a months-long hike on a well-known trail in the western part of the United States. My ears perked up at the mention of his spontaneous "urge," because already in our first session he had said that he felt most himself when he was engaged in the simple activity of walking.

So, here then was a clear choice between returning to a pre-set plan of culturally sanctioned academic and career success, or for he and I to take his spontaneous "urge" of embarking on the trail more seriously. I recognized that for most of his life, Jerry had gone through the robotic motions of following orders and complying with authority, and he had then attempted to adhere to the most rational way of implementing his plans for an abstractly successful future. Yet those plans were all head and no heart; Jerry existed, but he was not yet an embodied self who participated in his own life.

After listening to Jerry describe how going on the months-long hike would help him overcome his stranger anxiety as he learned to rely on himself while meeting new people whom he encountered, I realized that he viewed the marathon trip as an opportunity to give rebirth to himself, to conceive and discover himself perhaps for the first time. He also saw the trip as a way of giving himself a powerful boost of self-confidence that he sorely needed. Such self-confidence seemed to be precisely what "Jerry the doctor" ordered for himself the patient, because he was paralyzed by shame and self-conscious dread of making mistakes no matter what choices and decisions he made.

Whereas early in life Jerry complied with his mother's authority and judgments, now through the introjection of those judgments, he had become his own worst critic. As we explored Jerry's experience of self-consciousness and problems with decision-making more deeply, he spoke contemptuously of people who blabbered on pointlessly and wondered sometimes whether he too had any real purpose in expressing himself out loud. I noted that perhaps in hating and attempting to distance himself from his mother's narcissism of taking up too much social space without purpose, he had gone too far to the opposite extreme and had paralyzed his own self-expressiveness in the process.

When Jerry first came for treatment, he felt terrible about himself because in his self-conscious paralysis, he was attempting to fit the "round peg" of his own uniqueness into the "square hole" of conventional academic norms. I have largely supported his spontaneously creative urge to embark on his own "path," both literally and metaphorically. Indeed, eventually, Jerry's parents decided not to continue paying for any more of his sessions, because they did not see the "progress" that they had envisioned. I told Jerry I would be willing to see him for a greatly reduced fee if he felt that he was benefitting from the therapy and wished to continue. He thanked me and decided to accept my offer. Following Rank's (1936) therapeutic recommendation, I attempted to help facilitate Jerry replacing the shame and self-conscious lens through which he viewed his unique difference as an individual with one that was more self-accepting.

After completing his long hike of 1,100 miles in 4½ months, Jerry called me to schedule a session when he returned. I immediately saw a difference in the way he held eye contact with me. He seemed to speak with less hesitation and more confidence. He also said that as soon as he returned from the hike, he wanted to call high school friends with whom he long had been out of touch because he now felt that he had accomplished something that he could talk about.

When we spoke about the hike itself, he said that for the first month he ruminated much about his failures of the past and worries about the future, but that changed when the trail took him through the mountains. One morning as he watched the sun rise, he had a transformative experience. As he persevered through his hike, he realized that he could rely on himself to push through other kinds of adversity as well. In general, Jerry's long trek on the trail has helped him transform shame into pride in accomplishment. In the last session that I saw him, he matter-of-factly declared that felt ready to apply himself to his studies.

## Hiding in the Crowd: Shame and Conforming to Group Norms

Whereas neurotic individuals may not be able to separate from parents and construct a self-affirming individual life, "normal" individuals often seem to differentiate themselves sufficiently from parental authority in order to surrender their individuality to peer groups. Yet this apparent differentiation is compromised by the security of surrendering one's individuality to peer groups and eventually to the abstraction of societal authority. Kierkegaard (1847a) thus says that such normal individuals construct a social identity with only the "the outer garments of differentiation" (p. 95). For most such individuals, the loyal adherence to parental indoctrinations and tradition evolves eventually into the masks of conforming to group norms of peer relationships.

Through the mutual jeopardy of exposure of one's vulnerabilities and shame, the masks of conformity bind each group member's self-esteem to every other group member's self-esteem on the paradoxical basis of covering up and inhibiting one's individual differences. If a hypnotic trance is an unconscious collusion between the hypnotist and the willing suggestibility of the hypnotized person, then the loyal adherence to the moral authority of social norms may be viewed as a "slow-motion hypnosis" (Macalpine, 1950), in which each individual is able to surrender to the group the wearying hypervigilance of watching over his or her particular shames. Powerful loyalty pressures, with the coercive aim of enforcing uniformity, are brought to bear on each person to uphold a group pride in which all participants invest their hopes to transcend the inadequacy of their own limitations as separate individuals. As Becker (1975) emphasizes: "Each person cannot stand his own emergence and the many ways in which his organism is dumbly baffled from within and transcended from without" (p. 3). Freud (1921) speaks to these pressures not to stick out as an individual:

> What appears in society in the shape of *Gemeingeist, esprit de corps,* 'group spirit,' does not belie its derivation from what was originally envy. No one must want to put himself forward, everyone must be the same and have the same.
>
> (p. 119)

If the state of being self-conscious is a self-enclosed face through which we condemn our vulnerabilities excessively, then the construction of an outward-looking face or persona often is designed to cover up those shamed vulnerabilities by projecting an idealized image of pride and strength. Wurmser (1981) says:

> In shame one wants to change into another being or hide, not to be seen anymore. The mask changes the shamefully exposed into the shameless exhibitor, one who fears to be seen as weak into one who is seen and feared as strong.
>
> (p. 306)

This constructed social face is crucial to the normal individual, without which he is exposed to his nakedness as but one unique individual.

Already very early in childhood, we learn to collude with each other's defenses by constructing group standards of "cool" that are often based on nothing more substantive an agreed-upon image and appearance. We all want to be accepted for who we are as unique individuals, but we often defeat our own purposes when we don masks of cool to fit in.

Take the sixth grader who combs his hair a certain way and wears baggy pants and uses "cool" jargon to gain entrée into his peer group. In buying the approval and respect of his peers with the imitative mask of acting and talking in a certain way, he hinders his own aims to be accepted for who he is. He is still left in some doubt as to whether he would be acceptable in and of himself, if he were to reveal himself in greater individuated depth. On the contrary, he may observe how his fellow group members project their disowned shames and doubts about their own individual acceptability on the nerdy, parent-oriented kids who have not mastered the images of cool and who are teased mercilessly for their "geekiness" and "babyness."

Teenagers learn quickly enough, if they have not done so already, that it is not "cool" to wear their hearts on their sleeve or get too hot and bothered about anything since such open demonstrations of emotion reflect weakness that deviate from group norms. "Chill" is the watchword for, "Relax, don't show you care too much about anything. Be cool." The humiliations and shames experienced because of the pecking orders of high school culture, based largely on the ability to master the values and language of cool particular to one's peer group, still haunt many individuals long after adolescence and inform the norms of adult conformity.

Kierkegaard (1846) strips the emperor of his clothes to reveal the illusory quality of selves that are reflected images constructed from group and cultural consensus: "In order that everything should be reduced to the same level, it is first of all necessary to procure a phantom, its spirit, a monstrous abstraction, an all-embracing something which is nothing, a mirage-and that phantom is *the public*" (p. 59) Ionesco's (1959) play *Rhinoceros*, in describing how every person mysteriously turns into a rhinoceros, depicts the absurd lengths to which human beings will go to duplicate each other in order to cover up their exposed isolation as separate individuals. Jaspers (1933) says of such individuals: "He will regard himself, not as one endowed with independent selfhood, but merely as an exponent of the multitude which backs him up. At bottom, he is as powerless as any other individual" (p. 56). Kierkegaard (1846), too, states: "The fact that several people united together have the courage to meet death does not nowadays mean that each, individually, has the courage, for even more than death, the individual fears the judgment and protest of reflection upon him to risk something on his own" (p. 53).

In order to attain a sense of transcendent significance, normal individuals thus adapt to and immerse themselves in what Becker (1973) calls the "borrowed meanings of others" at heavy cost to their own truths. Furthermore, such individuals must erase the uniqueness of their difference without fully knowing what they are doing and how much they need others to prop up their self-esteem. After all, any shame consciousness of their profound limitations as self-sustaining individuals would expose the anxieties and sense of weakness that underlie unconscious conformity. This unconscious use of borrowed meanings prompted Becker to describe the narcissism of human character as a "vital lie." Narcissism is vital because the self-forgetful deception and ignorance as to the energies we really draw on enable us to go on living securely and serenely; narcissism is a lie because we do not want to admit how much our sense of individual significance depends on the meanings of others.

The problem here is that just as Narcissus's enchantment with his own appearance constricts his ability to actually live, the preoccupation with one's social image is an extension of narcissistic defenses in which we attempt to avoid the mortification of exposed vulnerability by not getting too deep, by lowering the stakes of our expressive life. As in a large, enmeshed family, the mutual possessiveness of one for all and all for one becomes a cultural mandate that narrows each individual's vision of what is possible.

Fromm (1941) describes the problem with such self-idolatry: "An idol is a *thing* that we ourselves make and project our powers into thus impoverishing ourselves. We then submit to our creation and by our submission are in touch with ourselves in an alienated form" (p. 42). Kierkegaard (1849) refers to such individuals as "spiritless." He likens the spiritless person to a "mirror in which he captures the world, or rather, in which the world reflects itself" (1847b, p. 23).

This socially constructed image thus can be viewed as a kind of narcissistic reflecting pool by which we become enamored with a mirror of ourselves at the expense of our actual individualized being. Kierkegaard (1846) says trenchantly:

> By seeing the multitude of people around it, by being busied with all sorts of worldly affairs, by being wise to the ways of the world, such a person forgets himself, in a divine sense forgets his own name, dares not believe in himself, finds being himself too risky, finds it much easier and safer to be like the others, to become a copy, a number, along with the crowd.
>
> (p. 36)

Bollas (1987) uses the term "normotic" to refer to a problematic normality: "Normotic individuals are unusually rooted in being objective, both in their thinking and their desire. They achieve a state of abnormal normalcy by eradicating the self of subjective life" (p. 56). In a sense, the abstract popular images of group consensus take on the reflected life of what is objective reality for this individual in sharp contrast to who he would be if he defined himself through the passions of his own subjectivity as an individual. Becker (1973) aptly sums up the problem: "It is fateful and ironic how the life we need in order to live dooms us to a life that is never really ours" (p. 56).

This tendency of looking to the consensus of the crowd for guidance of how to conduct one's life may be illustrated by the common homo-emotional tendency of filtering one's heterosexual choice of romantic mate through the perceptions and opinions of one's own same-sex peers. For example, a man may declare that he is attracted to women who have certain characteristics (slim, large-breasted, "fit") that conform to the group norms constructed by other men. I refer to this tendency as homo-emotional because for such men the woman is but a trophy object to be conquered and shown off to other men in order to elicit their approval and envy. In such situations, the man's primary passions and emotional concerns are not directed toward the person of the woman (hetero-emotionality) but are involved with other men. Of course, the problem with choosing a potential mate in this way is that 20 years later, all those other men who one was hoping to impress will have long disappeared from the scene, while the individual who filtered his perceptions and choice of life mate through the lens of group consensus must live with the consequences of his choice. The high-status coupling of the star quarterback with the homecoming queen in high school, who get married but then are divorced 20 years later, is the prototypical example of a choice that has been constructed as much by the expectations and pressures of the "crowd" as by the individuals involved.

Tolstoy's (1887) novella *The Death of Ivan Ilych* traces the spiritual bankruptcy of the normal individual in his main character Ivan Ilych. Ivan Ilych enters adult life without the passion necessary to live his own unique truth. Tolstoy recounts: "All the enthusiasms of childhood and youth passed without leaving much trace on him" (p. 11). He painstakingly avoids ways in which he would differentiate himself from the crowd. Without a sense of his own individuality, he seeks guidance of how to live from the "propriety of external forms required by public opinion" (p. 16). Even when making momentous life choices, such as whether to ask the woman who he was dating to marry him, Ivan Ilych seemingly drifts into his decision dispassionately: "Really, why shouldn't I marry?" (p. 14). Tolstoy summarizes the problem of Ivan Ilych's life with intriguing eloquence: "Ivan Ilych's life had been most simple and most ordinary and therefore most terrible" (p. 10).

It is only after a fall, which results in a mysteriously fatal illness, that Ivan Ilych gradually begins to come face-to-face with the falsehood of how he had lived: "It is as if I was going downhill while I imagined I was going up. And that is really what it was. I was going up in public opinion, but to the same extent life was ebbing away from me" (p. 53). At the end, it is only after Ivan Ilych stops attempting to justify the lie of his life that he can die in peace.

## Comparative Self-Value: The Construction of Human Hierarchy

Since shame originates in the self-consciousness of defining oneself from the outside looking in rather than through the subjectivity of desire from the inside out, the only way one can find one's one place in the world is by comparing oneself with others. Kierkegaard (1967) puts it this way:

> Everyone, everyone is so prone to set his mind at ease with relativity. Anyone who is a little better than his family and relatives or the others in the provincial town where he lives among his peers, etc. promptly sets his mind at ease and feels superior. The law of existence for the numerical or for mass men is that they live by comparison.
>
> (Entry 2966)

When one defines one's worth through the uniqueness of one's individual contributions to others, it becomes quite difficult to compare and measure the value of the $x$ quality of one's contribution with the $y$ quality of another's person's unique contributions. If human relations in our culture were to be defined more on the basis of respect for the unique quality of each individual, then comparisons between different individuals would be rendered nonsensical.

Instead of deriving a special intrinsic value from his qualitative difference as a unique individual, the normal character type attempts to maintain the defense of covering up his individual deficiency by defining himself in terms of the idealized reflection of what is valued by his peer group. Perhaps what is most unfortunate about the reactivity to the authority of social norms is the wide impact that culturally defined images of what is good and bad define the value of each individual on the basis of invidious comparisons to each other. It is only by abstracting part-attributes from whole persons—such as good looks, achievement status, amount of money, fame, intelligence, or slimness—that quantifiable criteria may be constructed through which one person can be compared to another person on whether one possesses a greater or lesser amount of that part-attribute than someone else. Rousseau (1755) thus states: "The one who sang or danced the best, the handsomest, the strongest, the most adroit, or the most eloquent becomes the most highly considered, and that was the first step toward inequality" (p. 149). It is sad that the unique quality of our different subjective lives is thus hijacked by a morality of power in pursuit of these abstracted images of the limited good as defined by the external authority of the normal.

Even something as simple as romantic attraction dictates the hierarchy of who is valued and who is not valued as much between individuals. If, for example, Joan is attracted to Bob, but Bob is attracted to Lily, Bob looks "up" to Lily as his better, while thinking of Joan as below him. If Joan then should become attracted to someone else besides Bob, he, taken aback by this "affrontery" that offends his narcissism, might feel something like: "How could this be? How can you dare like someone else besides me? After all, you are not my equal."

The word *hierarchy* thus derives from the Greek *hierarkhes*, rule of a priest. Perhaps by means of what Lynch (1965) terms the "absolutizing instinct" (p. 105), we try to bring the hierarchical distinction between heaven and earth into this finite life through the construction of hierarchies.

The striving to inculcate much of what is most valued by the many thus animates and provides meaning to the striving of the normal person. Yet there is an absurdity to attributing absolute higher value to someone just because that person gets into a better college or garners greater wealth or is a famous celebrity. Indeed, if we were to take a more humble, spiritual view of our place on earth, we would realize we are all just children in the eyes of God. Alternatively, if we were to take an atheistic view more seriously, we would view human hierarchies with some skepticism since we are all eventually only going to become dust.

Fromm (1941) stated: "The less he (an individual) felt he was being somebody, the more he needed to have possessions" (p. 141). When one thus seeks to define one's worth from the outside in on the basis of the constructed image one presents to the world, comparative worth as reflected by narcissistic hierarchies becomes of utmost importance. Fromm (1997) states: "We live in the mode of having to the degree that we internalize the authoritarian structure of our society" (p. 121).

In this light, it is interesting to note that the word *materialism* derives from the Latin *mater* or mother. Perhaps one must compensate for the emotionally qualitative sense of feeling "unwanted" and unfulfilled by emphasizing the proud appearance of accumulating around oneself a large quantity of "mother" or material things. It is fascinating that one historical narrative traces the value of gold to a cowrie shell found in the Red Sea, which later came to be identified with the goddess Hathor, the divine cow, the Great Mother.

Taking in becomes a vehicle of filling up the emptiness of an enclosed private space and building up a sense of self-worth that one can no longer attain through an open give-and-take with others because of one's defenses against the vulnerability required to receive love. Such openness would require that one let down the walled-off defenses one has constructed to cover up one's shamed vulnerabilities. Becker (1975) thus states: "Man has changed true giving to the one who passes things to the wholly taking and keeping" (p. 89).

The normal person strives to sell himself as a valued commodity by taking in much of what the many deem important. Through the tangible incorporation of money and material, one is able to build up the interiority of a three-dimensional bodily space, which also provides physical evidence of "I am somebody." Brown (1959) states insightfully: "We may therefore say that it is inherent in the money complex to attribute to what is not food the virtue that belongs to food" (p. 257). Roheim (1934), in referring to narcissistic capitalism, suggests that there is an equation of wealth with magic power. This substantive proof of possessing a material interior space, a self-enclosed autonomous self, as a means of combatting shame and doubt, has been described by Erikson (1950) as a primary struggle of the second psychosocial age of development.

Fromm (1997) describes how nations with capitalist economies are governed by the consumerism of accumulating material goods in what he describes as a "having" mode of relating to others. In contemporary American society, for example, the "normal" individual covers up his shame as an individual and constructs a proud self-image or "persona" of success by accumulating a large quantity of money. In this way, the normal person in a capitalist society is not unlike the narcissist who builds himself up as a valued commodity to sell for the approval of others. Fromm expounds on this theme in capitalism: "Since success depends largely on how one sells one's personality, one experiences oneself as a commodity" (p. 127).

In this same regard, Deleuze (1983) adds: "Ressentiment can only be imposed on the world through the principle of gain, by making profit not only a desire and a way of thinking but an economic, social, and theological system" (p. 118). Perhaps more accurately, we could say that it is not ressentiment specifically that motivates gain, but its inevitable consequence of entitlement that seeks its vengeful comeuppance of being on top after the oppressive sense of being on the self-shaming bottom.

Since resentment emerges originally because of the shame and self-pity that one cannot have a desired effect though one's offerings of love, one seeks to have impact through power, force, and coercion. When the shame-based morality of power (success vs. failure, winning vs. losing, strength vs. weakness) is applied to the notion of comparative self-value, then we can see that winning instead of losing also signifies taking in and possessing the defeated loser, and thus acquiring new power. For centuries, human beings have thus transformed persons into objects or "slaves" to accumulate as one's possessions. Indeed, Fromm (1997) says the having mode of behavior "transforms everybody and everything into somebody dead and subject to the other's power" (p. 77). Human beings routinely incorporate or "totalize" (Levinas, 1969) other persons as object representations in their mind's sphere of influence.

Yet if we viewed each individual through the three-dimensional lens of his or her unique complexity, we would probably experience much anxiety about the unmanageably chaotic diversity of the world that surrounds us. We instead master our anxiety with regard to the complexity of individual differences by creating templates of group stereotypes (Gilman, 1985), and then attempt to collapse the uniqueness of individuality into those stereotypes.

In the meantime, the courage of exposing one's all-too-human vulnerabilities in the service of open communication and mutual expressions of love is not celebrated publicly as a major virtue. We desperately need the respect of recognition and an openly expressed generosity of spirit from each other, but it would not be "cool" to publicly acknowledge those needs. There are many persons who speak of the necessity of love, but preciously few who are able to actually show their vulnerability to expressly give and receive love in defiance of all cultural forms of hierarchy based on power and status.

## Us and Them: Scapegoating and Killing One's Shame in the Embodied Other

Perhaps it is because differences connote exclusion and separateness, and arouse hidden anxieties of isolation as insignificant individuals, that we often feel compelled to distinguish hierarchically between "us and them." Adam Phillips (2002) poses a basic question: "Why is hierarchy a reflex response to difference?" (p. 6).

In retreating from the anxieties and self-doubts of shame exposure by taking shelter under the cover of loyalty to our own kind, we attempt to obliterate the limitations of our individuality by resurrecting our individual resentments behind the guise of group pride. Far from being fair-weather friends, the relations between rivalrous siblings of a given group or culture become governed, at least in part, by the misery-loves-company motto of rainy-day friendships. Bound together by the dangers of exposing one's individual passions to the envious judgments of others, culture ties the interests of its disparate members together through the loyalty of shared self-denial. Kierkegaard (1846) thus notes that: "In an age which is very reflective and passionless *envy is the negative unifying principle*" (p. 47).

Freud (1930) states: "It is impossible to ignore the extent to which civilization is built up on renunciation of instinctual gratifications" (p. 97). He emphasizes how this "cultural frustration" dominates the whole field of social relations. Indeed, he suggests that the necessities of social cohesiveness lead to a vicious cycle, in which each individual must inhibit the expression of his sexual and aggressive drives, which then engenders more resentment, which, in turn, then must be inhibited again. In an important postwar book about the ability of Germans to mourn the shame of their Nazi past, Mitscherlich (1975), following Freud's thinking, states: "It is anger over the prohibitions of *our* own society, which motivates our resentment against our private and collective enemies rather than the objectionable characteristics of the latter" (p. 92). It is not surprising, then, that

Scheler (1912) declares: "A potent charge of *ressentiment* is accumulated by the very *structure of society*" (p. 33).

Adhering to the moral judgments of group norms diverts each individual from his own freedom of conscience and the genuine remorse he may feel for hurting others. In order to brace for potential accusations from his peers for any deviations from group norms, each group member summons his energies to preempt the risk of excommunication, thus leaving very little mental space for the self-reflectiveness of a free conscience.

Whether one is hiding oneself within the collectivity of the tribe to which one is loyal, or whether one is encased within the safe confines of one's motor vehicle, or whether one is insulated behind the faceless distances of one's computer, sooner or later the resentment of feeling cornered by the demands of others may explode vengefully in violent rages. It is because of the danger that an individual's hidden resentments may suddenly emerge in the conscienceless anonymity of one group's demonization of another group that it becomes especially important to examine the reactive "slave morality" of the normal character type.

In his classic study of mob psychology, LeBon (1895) says: "The individual forming part of a crowd acquires, solely through numerical considerations, a sentiment of individual power which allows him to yield to instincts which, had he been alone, he would perforce have kept under restraint" (p. 9). Becker (1968) notes as well: "The evil that man has in himself and his world stems not from a wickedness in his breast, but from an uncritical allegiance to the program for actions which his society has fumblingly and blindly mapped out" (p. 142).

In our attempts to master the experience of our own shame, we externalize the dynamic of self-contempt and worthlessness by constructing hierarchies between people according to that same dynamic of oppressor and oppressed from which we suffer so much within. Such hierarchical distinctions allow *us* to distinguish ourselves from *them*—other lesser mortals—and, at least on this earthly stage, to strut around proudly for a brief period of time. Morrison (1989) states: "The subject projects his shame into the object (the container), treats the object with contempt and haughty disdain and thus distances himself from his own shame, while continuing to interact with it through the interpersonal relationship with the object" (p. 106).

Goffman (1963) describes how shame is related to the stigma of social pollution and has historical roots in the notion of defilement. Girard (1979) also suggests that the threat of being infected with defiling impurities through their contagious spread has played an influential role in social relations. In her classic study *Purity and Danger*, the anthropologist Mary Douglas (1966) describes the crucial importance the fear of contagion and the need to sharply differentiate between purity and impurity plays in social relations:

> Ideas about separating, purifying, demarcating, and punishing trans-gressions have as their main function to impose system on an inherently untidy experience. It is only by exaggerating the difference between within and without, above and below, male and female, with and against, that a semblance of order is created.
>
> (p. 4)

This mortal fear of being flooded over with impurities emanating from a monstrous Other helps us to understand the desperate need to demarcate rigid boundaries between the pure and the impure, between us and them. Whereas in shame we inhibit our self-expressiveness and objectify our-selves within, by projecting shame onto externalized "us and them" hierar-chies endemic to group narcissism, we objectify others as alien and Other.

Perhaps of most danger, Ricoeur (1967) states: "Dread of the impure and rites of purification are in the background of all of our feelings and all our behavior relating to fault" (p. 25). Under the cover of group loyalty to one's own kind, individuals attempt to undo the traumatized sense of defilement and personal shame through purification rituals of sacrificing the Other. They project their own disowned vulnerabilities onto others and attempt magically to kill off the existential insult of death, which is now inscribed in those frailties. The omnipotent defense of denying one's mortal limitations may become coupled with its projection upon a monstrous Other, such that a life-or-death struggle of "kill or be killed" must ensue between "them" and "us." Koestler (1978), speaking of the blind loyalty to our own kind, makes an important point:

> Even a cursory glance at history should convince one that individual crimes committed for selfish motives play a quite insignificant part in the human tragedy, compared to the numbers massacred in unselfish loyalty to one's tribe, nation, dynasty, church, or political ideology, *ad majorem glorian dei.*
>
> (p. 14)

Becker (1975) asserted that in the zero-sum logic of scapegoating, one becomes stronger through the death of the scapegoated victim by incorporating his life force. The scapegoat, embodying our disowned death, is sent off into the never-to-be-heard-from wilderness, so that we can continue to live deathlessly. Rank (1936) said: "The death fear of the ego is lessened by the killing, the sacrifice of the other through the death of the other, one buys oneself free from the penalty of dying, of being killed" (pp. 40–41).

These shame anxieties and the need to make sharp distinctions between them and us also are implicated in the rigid boundaries constructed between masculine hardness and feminine softness. Theleweit (1987) examines the fantasies of right-wing German storm troopers immediately following World War I. He notes that the overflowing, soft, fluid liquid of the female body was viewed as a dangerously contagious Other that the storm troopers feared would overwhelm their male identities. Theleweit suggests that these men, to whom he insightfully refers as the *not fully born*, were hell-bent on armoring their bodies with a physical "hardness" in order to ward off the contagion of being flooded from the outside.

Similarly, we might view germ-phobia as a fear of being taken over by the impurities of our shames that we project into the outside world, which then boomerangs back persecutory anxiety concerning contagion. It is not surprising that Adolf Hitler was a germaphobe; Donald Trump, also a germaphobe, was determined to build a "wall" on the southern border of the United States in order to keep out the "invading hordes" from Mexico and Central America.

Elsewhere, I have suggested that this fascistic idealization of hardness is an attempt to defend against the shame of being born of a woman from whom one never separated and therefore is feared as a presence who forever lurks within (Shabad, 2008). In subsequent years, Hitler played on this fear of the underlying symbiotic mother and feminized man to spur a reinvented, self-created Aryan superman whose firm musculature and emotional hardness delineated rigid boundaries to armor him in a genocidal war against the impure threat of the parasitical, feminized Jew.

## Understanding Friends and Blaming Enemies

It is not only Nazis and other perpetrators of genocide who divide "us" from "them." Many of the self-styled virtuous among us attempt to cleanse themselves of their shame by conveniently projecting their sense of "sin" onto perpetrators who already have committed crimes or wrongdoing. Looked at in this way, since our larger culture carries a hidden shame in each of its members, it must go through purification rituals, in which each individual places his or her shames onto an embodied scapegoat who is then sacrificed. These sacrificial rituals cleanse the normal members of the body politic of the sinful impurities and weaknesses of shame. The us versus them dichotomy of being loyal to our own kind and then externalizing shame onto a monstrous Other parallels our tendency to understand the motives of our family and friends when they do something wrong, while not extending the same benefit of the doubt to the strangers in our midst. We seek to understand those we love, and we blame our enemies.

Many people view criminals or sexual abusers or Nazis or serial killers as nonhuman "monsters" who must be held accountable for their misdeeds, but who are not worth understanding in depth. The punitive tone, often accompanied by a wagging finger, with which the word *accountability* often is uttered belies the displaced resentments and moralistic judgments of "innocent" bystanders, who are simultaneously exempting loved ones from their harsh judgments. If a parent were to say something sadistically hurtful, for example, one might hear something like, "Mom didn't really know what she was saying. Besides, she can be difficult sometimes because she had a really bad relationship with her own mother." In our desperate need to split the "good" of the pure from the contaminating "bad" of the impure, our inconsistent attributions of a punitive accountability often become manifest in rationalizations with which we erase wrongdoing in people we need or idealize, while clearly blaming those we have "no use for"

I have occasionally conducted a thought experiment when teaching trainees. I ask the class to imagine a picture of Adolf Hitler as a young kindergartner raising his hand to ask if he can go pee-pee. The teacher then escorts him by the hand to the bathroom. A number of trainees have said that they are quite discomforted by the juxtaposition of incongruent images of good and evil. Mixing Hitler's evil with the image of goodness normally attributed to a child's innocence can be challenging to the normal tendency to split good and evil. Some people may find it more difficult to hold the adult evil Hitler responsible for his actions if they actually picture that he was an innocent child at one time. This difficulty may be compounded if they were to conjure up an image of innocent little Adolf being beaten by his father.

For many who forego understanding in favor of condemnation, knowing why someone does something may be tantamount to excusing or condoning that person's actions. After all, sometimes explanations sound all too much like rationalizations, even justifications, for wrongdoing. Perhaps there is a fear that to understand the reasons behind a person's wrongdoing is to risk dissipating a sense of righteous indignation. As clinicians, many of us are well aware of patients who, not wishing to have their resentments softened, do not want to know the reasons why parents did or did not do the things they did. Or when patients attempt to quickly bypass their resentments by attempting to understand their parent's motives, many therapists may suspect that they are protecting an idealized image of those parents.

When perpetrators are understood, they are often transformed from monstrous targets of scapegoating and blame into three-dimensional persons. The further we probe into the depths of the human soul, the more we discover that we are all more human than otherwise. We cannot isolate understanding from its ethical underpinnings of empathy and compassion. In ways that words cannot describe, human beings have a deeply rooted sense of kinship with each other's suffering.

For those of us who study the workings of the human psyche, it is incumbent upon us to be curious rather than merely judgmental about the nature of evil. Without excusing untold cruelties or violence visited on individuals or groups, it is our responsibility to understand rather than merely condemn individuals who commit horrific crimes. In this chapter, I have attempted to show how the "might makes right" morality of shame colludes with the group narcissism of loyalty to one's own kind to make it possible to commit evil while obscuring the compassionate echoes of one's conscience.

Chapter 9

# The Nobility of Resistance
## Transforming Resentment into Active Rebellion

The eye of him who sees me will behold me no more...
Therefore I will not restrain my mouth:
I will speak in the anguish of my spirit,
I will complain in the bitterness of my soul.

(*The Book of Job*, 7: 8–11)

The whole meaning of human life can be summed up in the one statement that man only exists for the purpose of proving to himself every minute that he is a man and not an organ stop.

(Dostoevsky, *Notes from the Underground*, 1864, pp. 288–289)

## Acting-Out and the Freedom to Act: The Values of Psychoanalysis

A number of years ago, I remember reading a painfully sad article in the *New York Times* Sunday Magazine. The story was an autobiographical account of a man who had made a pivotal life decision many years earlier and now deeply regretted the path he had chosen. At that fateful point of his life, this man had been in a four-times-a-week analysis for five years when his fiancée, with whom he was deeply in love, received an offer for a great career opportunity on the West Coast. When he brought up the strong possibility that he would be moving with her and leaving the analysis, his analyst told him in no uncertain terms that if he did so, he would be fleeing from the unfinished work of his analysis and strongly advised him against making the move. After much deliberating, the man decided against moving with his fiancée in order to remain in analysis. Soon after, the fiancée broke off the engagement. His poignantly written account was full of misgivings for losing the love of his life, for the road he had not taken.

I open with this story to emphasize how much our views of resistance depend on the underlying values we hold with regard to the purposes of

DOI: 10.4324/9781003559559-10

psychoanalysis, especially on those occasions when the analytic and therapeutic don't always overlap. My own values lead me to view psychoanalysis first and foremost as a therapeutic endeavor of helping individuals fulfill themselves in love, play, and work before they die. In this view, Socrates notwithstanding, the *unexamined life can be well worth living*. There are plenty of people who don't know much about themselves at all who are quite capable of loving and being loved, working, and playing. Viewed through this existential lens, from the moment an individual walks into my office, I have a clinical responsibility to help that person make the most of the time remaining until the imaginary horizon of his or her death.

It is when people's lives are constrained by seemingly mysterious forces they cannot identify that psychoanalysis becomes an invaluable vehicle toward freeing individuals from invisible chains that bind them. When the instrumental goal of enhancing self-insight becomes a valued end in itself and is detached from its primary therapeutic purpose of *actually* living a fulfilled life, however, the consciousness-raising process of delving into the recesses of one's psyche may sometimes become an unending, circular endeavor.

From its inception, psychoanalytic treatment has not been informed so much by the aim of helping patients directly in making action transitions in their lives, but by the more indirect purpose of lifting repressions. Indeed, Freud (1914) viewed instinctual strivings toward action as a constant source of resistance that worked against the analytic goal of enthroning secondary process thinking and reason.

Freud's views of resistance derive directly from his metapsychology, in which he theorized that human motivation is propelled by the primary aim of conserving the past. In fact, he viewed the "adhesiveness of the libido" (Freud, 1937) to be such a potent force toward maintaining the status quo that he declares: "The finding of an object is in fact a re-finding of it" (1905a, p. 222). Years later, Freud (1920) elaborates on this line of thinking in greater detail in his positing of a death drive: "The elementary living entity would from the very beginning have had no wish to change; if conditions remained the same, it would do no more than constantly repeat the same course of life" (p. 35). Indeed, rather than conceive of an inherent organismic movement of growth toward the new and unknown, Freud writes that life itself only comes into being because of "external disturbing forces" (p. 36).

In assuming an inherent drive to psychic inertia in human beings, it followed that analysis must necessarily become a form of combat to overcome the patient's natural tendency to conserve the past through repetitive action. At two very different points of his life, Freud reiterates what he views as a battle with the patient's psyche: "When the investigation comes upon the libido withdrawn into its hiding place, a struggle is bound to break out" (1912, p. 102); and "The analytic situation consists in our allying ourselves with the ego of the person in order to subdue the id" (1937, p. 235).

Given the suspiciousness with which analysts have viewed unconscious motives that have not been thoroughly vetted by analytic examination, it is not surprising that any action in life that diverts from analytic self-scrutiny would be labeled as resistance. Freud's (1914) difficulty in conceiving that actions could potentially be fueled by an inherently voluntary exploration of the new and self-healing motivations led him to declare:

> One best protects the patient from injuries brought about through carrying out one of his impulses by making him promise not to take any important decisions affecting his life during the time of the treatment, for instance, not to choose any profession or definitive love-object.
>
> (p. 153)

The analyst's tendency to claim possession for the continuation and progress of the treatment process is most evident with regard to when and how patients decide to leave their analyses. The story with which I opened this chapter—of the man who was filled with regret for losing his beloved because of an ill-fated decision to remain in analysis—is unfortunately not an atypical occurrence in the history of psychoanalytic treatment.

Many analysts throughout the history of psychoanalytic practice have taken Freud's paternalistic recommendation too seriously. There have been many occasions in which the analysand has wanted to terminate for good life reasons, like taking a job in another state, only to be told that she is fleeing the analysis, also known by the oxymoron "flight into health."

To my mind, over-using interpretations to prevent the patient's attempts to separate in this way, often a countertransference projection of the analyst's possessiveness is not unlike that of a parent having a difficult time letting go of a child. Since most patients are already too guilt-bound to authority figures, such interpretations have had an insidious, "mind-fucking" effect of sowing further doubt in patients who already wonder if they have a right to an individuated life of their own. Under the guise of being "ana-lytic, such countertransference acting-in reveals clearly how the analyst views the patient as a possessed object rather than a freely willing subject in her own right. Unfortunately, Freud's recommendation backfired tragi-cally for the life of the man who lost his fiancée.

As analysts, we ultimately must decide what our values are. Is the patient's outside life secondary to the analysis, or is the analysis meant to serve the entirety of a patient's life therapeutically?

Rank (1936) has critiqued the Freudian concept of resistance for its ina-bility of conceiving constructive aspects of a patient's repetitive actions:

> The Freudian concept of resistance ... derived from the narcissistic placing of the analyst in the center, leads necessarily to a therapeutic pessimism, for, in terms of a theory oriented from the analyst, every reaction of the patient must be interpreted as resistance... Only if one permits the ego of the patient to have value as an independent power can one overcome this sterile concept of resistance, recognize even in repetition the constructive elements and prize the new as a voluntary expression of personality, even if it should contradict the ideology of the analyst.
>
> (pp. 104–105)

A few years ago, when I was invited to write a paper on the "difficult-to-reach" patient, I thought about how the history of psychoanalysis has largely been defined through the perspective of its practitioners. How many patients have there been in the unknown annals of psychoanalysis who have been presented as "difficult-to-reach" cases, who would have loved to put pen to paper about their difficult-to-reach shrinks?

Even though it is the patient who comes for help to alleviate her distress and often is looking for an accessibly reachable analyst to help with that task, the phrase "difficult-to-reach patient" turns the motivational impetus of the patient's will to change inside out and makes the frustrated analyst the centered agent who must reach the patient in order to facilitate change for the patient. It is as if the analyst were saying: "Stop being so difficult to reach so I can help you change."

On occasion, I have supervised trainees who have become anxious when-ever their patients express doubts or question the direction of the treatment. In supervision, these young professionals then sometimes ask me: "What am I doing wrong?" I often respond by saying: "Why not just ask the patient where she would like the treatment to take her?" Yet the supervisee's question to me reflects how much solitary responsibility she is taking for the course of treatment. Indeed, when therapists feel excessive disappointment, impatience, and even anger toward patients for not getting better, we may conclude that therapy has high personal stakes for the therapist.

The co-opting of the patient's agency is a testament to how much the therapist's own sense of ethical well-being depends on being an effectively loving agent of therapeutic change, and therefore how important it is that the patient be cooperatively receptive to her contributions. In the process of viewing herself as the responsible engine of treatment progress, the therapist risks denuding the patient of her freedom of self-determination and rendering her into a mere object of manipulation for a change that is for her own good.

## The Ethical Privilege of Helping: Power Differences between Therapist and Patient

With the intersubjective turn away from the impersonal authority of the analyst as knowing interpreter of the patient's "unconscious material," what then becomes of resistance? Aron (1996) has described the intersubjective relationship between analyst and patient as mutual but also asymmetrical because of "the inherent differences in the patient's and analyst's roles, functions, and responsibilities in the analytic process, such as free associating, interpreting, confronting resistances, establishing ground rules, and setting and paying fees" (p. 98). In my view, the primary asymmetry in the analytic relationship with regard to help seeking—patients are help seekers, analysts are designated helpers—is most relevant to the problem of resistance.

Perhaps there is nothing that runs deeper in a human being than the need to contribute and belong to the human endeavor. Elsewhere (Shabad, 2001, 2010, 2017), I have described how this drive to contribute is manifest from the beginning of life in the child's primary need to give and to be received open-heartedly by his parents. The appreciative parental reception of the child's offerings provides a form of ethical feedback on the fruitful "goodness" of the child's contributions, which in turn reinforces the self-confidence necessary to further development through the difficult transitions of life. Searles (1975) specifically links this need to give to universal psychotherapeutic strivings: "Innate among man's powerful strivings with regard to his fellow men, beginning in the earliest years and even months of life, is an essentially psychotherapeutic striving" (p. 380).

Whenever we attempt to help another person in need, our ethical self-image as capably loving and worthwhile human beings is at stake. As "expert helpers," psychoanalysts have a countertransference investment in the progress their patients achieve as validating feedback of their loving capacities and adequacy as constructive, contributing human beings. The multiple opportunities that analysts have to be of value to their patients are not only a means of discharging their professional responsibilities, but also provide them with a position of ethical *privilege* that reverberates back on a moral sense of themselves as "good."

In sharp contrast, Searles (1975) says: "The patient *is ill because, and to the degree* that his own psychotherapeutic strivings have been subjected to such vicissitudes that they have been rendered inordinately intense, frustrated of fulfillment or even acknowledged" (p. 380). More generally, Becker (1964) says emphatically: "People break down when they are not 'doing'—when the world around them does not reflect the active involvement of their own active powers" (p. 104).

The self-respect and confidence that analysts derive from this ethical privilege in being an effectively creative helper in contrast to the help-seeking patient translates also into a *privileged* position of power and authority. Aron (1996) thus states: "Psychoanalysis is inevitably asymmetrical because there are differences in power between analyst and patient" (p. 98). In this context, it is interesting to note that Brown (1959) also points out that in the archaic economy of gift exchange, the ability to give confers prestige and power.

These asymmetrical differences in power within the therapeutic alliance, founded from the beginning in the indignity of one person in a position of relative ethical weakness seeking help from another person who is in a position of relative ethical strength giving help, lead the intersubjectivity between the analyst and patient to degenerate sometimes into a hierarchical subject-object relationship. Kierkegaard (1849) thus states:

> As soon as the question of being helped begins ... especially when the help comes from a superior ... then comes the humiliation of having to receive unconditional help, in whatever form, of becoming like a nothing in the hands of the 'helper' for whom everything is possible....
>
> (p. 87)

As the authority who has the creative prerogative of subjectivity in this asymmetry, the analyst sets the ground rules and uses the defining power of language to interpret the transference-countertransference dynamic and name resistance.

More specifically, Rank (1936) has said that psychotherapy could be viewed as a Promethean life and death contest between the creative wills of the therapist and patient in which both participants attempt to mold each other in their image of a desired ideal. He suggests that because therapists are "creative types," they have an advantage over patients in this struggle of two wills. Kramer (1996) expounds on Rank's views: "Patients come to analysis because they cannot create themselves and are guilt-bound, unconsciously to their progenitors" (p. 210). On the other hand, he continues:

> analysts are artists, who use the patient—an artiste manquee (missed artist) as a living object onto whom they project their own creative urge. But this living object has the same creative urge—the same 'Promethean complex' as the analyst.
>
> (p. 210)

If we take seriously the idea that human beings derive a fulfilling confidence in themselves most of all from having their offerings and contributions received by others, then the way we define helping in analysis becomes more complex. That is, what if patients "get better" when analysts themselves are receptive, accessible, and reachable enough that they convey to patients, both implicitly and explicitly, how their own lives are enhanced by their patients' creative presence?

Perhaps it is Groddeck's (1923) hesitancy in giving up the powerful position of creative helping that prompted his discomfort when the roles of therapist and patients were reversed:

> And now I was confronted by the strange fact that I was not healing the patient, but that the patient was treating me. Or to translate it into my own language, the It of this fellow-being tried so to transform my It, did in fact transform it, that it came to be resolved for its purpose. Even to get this much insight was difficult, for you will understand that it absolutely reversed my position in regard to the patient.
>
> (pp. 262–263)

Ahead of his time, Ferenczi (1932) acknowledges this constructive impact of therapeutic helping: "We gladly allow the patients to have the pleasure of being able to help us, to become for a brief period an analyst, as it were, something that justifiably raises their self-esteem" (p. 65).

## The Tyranny of Should: Resistance and the Mandate to Get Better

The hierarchical subject-object relationship between analyst and analysand can be problematic because many patients come to treatment in the first place because of a history of being objectified by parents and a consequent inability to assert themselves confidently. Often, these individuals were recognized only as created extensions of their parents' conceptions and "cast out" as persons who had a mind and will of their own. Since as children they felt the gift of who they are to be inadequate to satisfy their parents, they dreaded the obliterating experience of being cut off and therefore attempted repeatedly to shape themselves according to their parents' specifications.

Just as such patients inhibit their own passion to grow and change in favor of submitting to the moral authority of their parents, they now reenact their historical passivity by investing an "expectant faith" (Freud, 1905b) in the analyst as the "subject who is supposed to know" (Lacan, 1964, p. 232) what is best for the patient. After all, the narcissistic extension of authority by parents is frequently imposed in the benignly loving name of knowing what is best for the child, as viewed of course from the parent's secondary process thinking about the long-term future as opposed to the primary process thinking immediacy of the child. Parents encourage eating vegetables instead of Oreo cookies and prioritize the great importance of doing homework to get good grades for a future success that is only vaguely understood as a clear priority over watching a favorite TV program.

If love, even parental love, is not moderated by a respect for the will of the child, however, it ceases to exist as love and degenerates into the self-expansiveness of unchecked power. A primary risk of setting the healthy and sensible against the immediacy of the child's passions too early in life is that the prohibited pleasures not being lived out are relegated to an unconscious realm of idealized desires and fantasies. The power of those forbidden desires then inform the rebellious dignity of a deprived freedom against what Horney (1950) calls the "tyranny of the should."

When such individuals enter Whole Foods, for example, if they were only to tell themselves they *should* eat kale but think to themselves that they really *want* to eat cupcakes, they would not be honest with themselves. They also *want* to eat kale since they would like to stay healthy and live long lives. But given the historical relationship of many children with the overarching reach of parental authority, it is difficult for many individuals to take genuine ownership of those long-term desires for an abstract future; they often are externalized and transformed into a superego authority of "should." Resistance now derives its potency from the unconscious idealization of rebelliousness against complying with what is experienced as an externalized authority.

When the problematic tensions of dominance and submission become intertwined with a too-rational mandate to do "for one's own good," there is nothing left for the subjugated to do but fight back. Compliance with authority and the resentments underlying passive resistance are strange but inevitable bedfellows when the objectification of persons is front and center in human relationships. This resentment may become manifest as a silent resistance against the coercive power of parental authority, such as when a child becomes determined not to give a parent the satisfaction of crying while being spanked.

On more than one occasion, I have been frustrated, as have many others, by having to wait on long lines at grocery stores. It seems, perhaps only in my mind's eye, that it is precisely because the clerk at the checkout counter knows that I am in a hurry that she dawdles, withholding from me the time I deem precious. Maybe though it is *because* I am in a hurry that she has the feeling of being passed over in a cursory fashion, as if she were only a trivial way station to some more important destination I have in mind. Through her resistance, I am forced finally to take notice of her and reckon with the dignity of a real person who is impeding me in my aims.

The therapeutic alliance is typically based on the unspoken assumption that patient and analyst are on the same page of working toward a better future for the patient. Yet, as patients seek change to become someone different, more capable, and healthier so they will be more acceptable to themselves and others in the future than they are in the current moment, they also may feel as if they are selling their soul in order to be "fixed." When this implicit agreement to work toward the patient's better future does not take into account the patient's underlying wish to be respected and accepted as is, symptomatic warts and all, the patient *must resist* the analyst's idealized authority and the mandate to change in order to reclaim her freedom of dignity.

For patients who have felt objectified all their lives, it may be therapeutically crucial to experience their own differentiated sense of agency by rebelling against the virtues of "getting better." In Dostoevsky's (1864) *Notes from the Underground*, the Underground Man is an apt spokesman for the oppressed sense of agency and resistance in the insulted, injured, and ignored. He says:

> Man can deliberately and consciously desire something that is injurious, stupid, even outrageously stupid, *to have the right* to desire for himself even what is stupid and not to be bound by an obligation to desire only what is sensible.
>
> (p. 286)

Many patients may verbalize compliance with authority in a litany of "I should do this" and 'I should do that," while, at the very same time, they resent and purposefully rebel against specifically *not doing* what they *should* do in their actual behavior. Unheard voices strive at the most inconvenient times for the dignity of realized expression against self-negating prohibitions through guerilla-like forays of rebellion in repeated symptomatology.

Elsewhere (Shabad, 2001), I have described how the formation of symptoms reflects a "silent loyalty oath" patients took with themselves never to forget the lonely sufferings that they experienced earlier in life. In this view, the patient's constellation of psychological symptoms is constructed as a memorial that is intended to communicate action proof of sufferings that had never been heeded or witnessed *at the time of their occurrence*. A patient's lived experience of repetitious symptomatology is pregnant with untold stories harkening back to an unwitnessed grief that had been buried in forgotten obscurity. It is precisely because everyone (including the patient herself) would be rid of these subversive symptoms that patients hold on to their "black sheep children," as if in sentimentalized embrace against all those who would do them harm.

These are patients who may exhibit what Freud (1923) called a "negative therapeutic reaction." Freud says of such patients:

> When one speaks to them or expresses satisfaction with the progress of the treatment, they show signs of discontent and their condition

invariably becomes worse ... one becomes convinced, not only that such people cannot endure any praise or appreciation, but that they react inversely to the progress of the treatment.

(p. 39)

A perfectionistic, bulimic patient who habitually complied with the high achievement standards of her parents emerged from a beauty salon feeling very happy about her new hairstyle. She was relatively satisfied with her weight at the time and felt more attractive than usual. On her way home, she received many looks that confirmed her feelings. When she arrived home, her roommate complimented her on the new hairdo. A few minutes later, when she was alone in her room, the patient found herself feeling extremely annoyed and irritable. Another patient, Jim, said soon after entering Alcoholics Anonymous, "If my parents say one word of praise about this, I will be in the nearest bar the next day." When all goes well, sometimes it goes too well.

The passive aggressiveness of resentment is often manifested in the perversity of going against the grain of one's own good. Such patients may attempt to exact a belated revenge against their parents by devoting their lives to the spiting of parental ideals that were never truly made their own by working against their own treatment progress. If the therapist does not take the dignity of the unreachable patient's personhood and freedom of self-determination sufficiently into account, then it may become manifest in the transference as a resistant "counter-will" (Rank, 1936) toward treatment. In resisting the forward momentum of a treatment shaped by the anticipatory fantasies of the analyst (Cooper, 2010), patients may be attempting to teach the analyst who is the real proprietor of their life. If one feels impotent to break invisible chains that bind by any other means, then at least the self-destructiveness of "cutting off one's nose to spite one's face" offers an attempt to liberate by destroying the corrupted relationship of exploiter and exploited.

Eventually, however, these individuals often find to their despair that through their habit of complicity with external authority and reflexive passive resistance against it, they have trapped themselves in a prison of their own reactive making. They have turned themselves inside out and wage a silently passive war against their own life force, now projectively embodied in the very same outside world that they resist.

As Nietzsche (1887) has suggested, it is a far simpler matter for individuals to say NO to external authority that they may view as unjust rather than say YES to themselves—that is, affirm their own conscientious authority of responsibility over the choices of their life. How then can a psychoanalytically oriented psychotherapy facilitate the transformation of I WON'T into I WILL? Since this experience of felt coercive pressure itself is the result of projecting one's own will to grow on the outside world, much of the essential work of treatment is the recollection and taking of responsibility for those projections so that one may move from the pathology of inhibited passivity to an actively expressed life force.

## Jane: A Life of Performance and the Resistance of Inertia

Jane is a 35-year-old single woman who has come in for a thrice-weekly analysis with presenting problems of depression and suicidal ideation. In the few months leading up to her first appointment, she had become distressed because she was breaking appointments with different people in her professional life. This "unreliability" alarmed her especially because she always had taken great pride in fulfilling her responsibilities and obligations. Rather than show up for these appointments, Jane only wanted to stay in bed and put the covers over her head.

From an early age, Jane had been groomed for a life of high ambition and success. Her parents demanded that she get perfect grades throughout school so that she could gain entry into the very best law schools. She eventually followed in her father's footsteps to become a very successful attorney and a partner at a highly prestigious law firm.

Jane's life of performance, achievement, and success was not only relegated to her work but spilled into her personal relationships as well. Jane grew up on the East Coast as an only child entrapped within her parents' marital divide. Virtually every evening at dinner, she sat helplessly by as her parents screamed at each other, seemingly uncaring and oblivious to her presence. In fact, on one occasion, she attempted to tiptoe away from the dinner table, only to be stopped short in her tracks by her mother's loud warnings to return to the table.

Jane felt enormous pressure to fill the void for both parents individually that neither of them could provide for each other. She was elevated prematurely into an adult role as "partner" to her father and caretaker of her mother. In addition to being a well-known attorney, her father also was prominent in local politics. On a number of occasions, she accompanied him to political functions instead of his wife.

Jane described her mother as an "anxious, intrusive, and childish" woman who was both "pathetic" and "quite demanding." Jane felt she often had no choice but to cater to her mother's demands and filled the role of dutiful daughter diligently. Unfortunately, her constant accommodations to her mother's needs came at the high cost of Jane's health and humanity. Jane had one memory from when she was 11 years old: Over the course of a few days, she complained repeatedly to her mother that she felt tired and dizzy, but her mother continued to ignore her and sent her to school anyway. She collapsed in class and was brought to the school nurse. Her mother came to get her and brought her to the emergency room of a local hospital where she was diagnosed with pneumonia.

Since her parents demanded so much time and energy from her emotionally and academically, she had very little opportunity to form a social life with her peers. She did her work diligently, performed at a very high level, and then spent much time hanging around her home.

For Jane, the public sphere of human relationships, emptied of desire, hope, and trust, had become a meaningless world of performing mechanically as an object shaped by the designs of others, while her own unmet needs and despair became encapsulated in an ever-shrinking private time and space in which she was left only to lick her wounds. Now, in this state of full-borne retreat, she no longer recognized herself. Indeed, she often referred to herself as a "failure" or "fucked up" or "sick" for not being able to keep up with the challenging pace of her life.

Jane's resistant inertia could be viewed as a symptom of silent protest against the mechanizing pressures that had governed her life. If I had viewed Jane's wish to stay in bed primarily as depressive pathology, and then viewed my responsibility as Jane's analyst to make her functional and tuck her back into her life again, her protest of inertia most likely would have resisted the coercive pressure of my efforts as well.

In this sense, I engaged in what Orange (2011) describes as a "hermeneutics of trust," in which the therapist trusts that the patient is attempting to communicate something important of her experience in her behavior. A hermeneutics of trust also entails a view that there is even a self-healing component in the patient's nonverbal communication of symptoms. Perhaps also, I don't think of symptoms only as troublemaking pathology, because ultimately I agree with Rilke (1934) when he says:

If there is anything morbid in your processes, just remember that sickness is the means by which an organism frees itself of foreign matter;

so one must just help it to be sick, to have its whole sickness and break out with it, for that is its progress.

(p. 70)

Like many analysts, I have often worked with patients to help provide their lonely sufferings with an articulated breath of expressive life. I have played the "sympathetic advocate for the devil" and sided with Jane's resistance by providing affirmative reasons for the symptom coming into existence in the first place. When Jane declared that there was something "sick" about her because she could not keep up the challenging pace of her life, I responded:

> You have been sickened by many coercive pressures through your life. You had to take the radical step of staying in bed and boycotting a life that was not yours, so if and when you do decide to get out of bed, you will be sure that future day and life will belong to you and you alone.

Indeed, I viewed Jane's suicidal ideation not so much as a wishful fantasy to end her life permanently, but more to destroy a counterfeit life that was not of her choosing and embark on a "new beginning" (Balint, 1968).

By allying myself with the orphaned voice of her lonely sufferings, I have earned some credibility in Jane's eyes that has helped keep her hopes alive for a renewable future. Yet her lifelong resentments for always having to adjust to the schedules of others has inevitably surfaced in treatment. On a number of occasions, she has cancelled her appointments and then attempted to reschedule for new appointment times. In addition, when she has cancelled, she has called frequently between sessions, and I have made special efforts to respond to her, even when I have been at out-of-town conferences. Most of the time, I have accepted her sporadic absences without interpreting the underlying meaning of her "acting out." However, on one occasion, when I did take note of her cancellations and attempts to reschedule, I suggested that she probably was sick and tired of showing up on my territory at a time of my choosing and may have been attempting to re-create a new time and place of her own choosing. She immediately provided numerous examples throughout her life when she had to accommodate herself to the schedules of others.

It has been very difficult for Jane to start over again at this point in her life because she must reckon with her profound regret for the opportunities that were missed and many years of life given away to the preferences and judgments of others. When through the insights gained in therapy, patients begin to see the glimmerings of their own agency with accompanying regrets of how they could have lived differently, they may paradoxically continue to act out the very symptomatic behavior that precipitated the regret in the first place in order to justify to themselves that they never had any other choice than to live as they had lived. Repetition of the same thus becomes a defensive means by which patients may evade an existential guilt for the missed opportunities of an unlived life. Self-justification here is not verbal; we repeat our actions imploring an imaginary arbiter to see that we had no other choice than to do what we did. What had to be, had to be; the proof is in the repetitious inevitability of the same. But this cycle of repeating symptomatic patterns of living to fend off one's regretful self-accusations keeps patients mired in a fear of change and despairing fatalism.

Jane, too, has struggled with a despair that her past life of robotic performance will overtake and foreclose all future possibilities with a fatefulness that she cannot escape. In part, these anxieties concerning her future reflect her temptation to maintain the symptomatic structure of an introjected parental superego on one hand and a passively rebellious non-compliance to that enemy within. As Jane struggles to relinquish the secure familiarity of her rule-bound superego and form a conscience based on the self-accepting freedom of her own desires and their emergent values, her analysis has evolved into the fundamental question of who and what will constitute the moral authority of her life.

## The Activation of Resentment: Affirming Fantasies of Revenge and Rebellion

How then might we more constructively liberate our patients from thwarting their own will, so that they do not have to resort to the passive-aggressiveness of resentment in order to make the dignity of their presence known in the world? Most patients come to see us because they feel cornered by the inhibiting self-doubts of their shame. Those self-inhibitions gradually become so powerful that such individuals feel helplessly unable to move forward with their lives. Entrapped within this sense of helplessness and fatalism, we thus often see patients who become resigned to the despairing futility of I CAN'T.

The rigid dichotomies of a selflessly giving therapist/helper and a receptively needful patient, based implicitly on a metaphor of physical emptiness, may not map on to the emotional lives of human beings so neatly. When we view patients primarily as "wounded souls" who have not received sufficient material "supplies," we risk perpetuating a fatalistic sense of their own incapacities. Or as Jane, always hyperconscious of her childhood deficiencies, says frequently: "Well, I guess I'm screwed."

Too often, the capacity to protest has been stilled in many patients because of being explicitly prohibited by parents or because of being inhibited by their own self-shaming. Parents stifle their children's voice of protest, especially when they run contrary to the practical necessities of what one "must" necessarily do. Yet the freedom to express one's inner life is of great emotional value in and of itself, It is precisely since this voice of the "lost cause" going against the realities of the external world has no niche for it to be received and heard that it is important for the therapist to attend carefully to it. Otherwise, the silenced capacity to express protest of "I don't want" toward a more powerful authority often resurfaces in the passive-aggressiveness of resistant inertia, as well as in adult anxieties.

There is a high cost to adult freedom for those children who were prohibited from overly protesting the external authority on which they depended. This impermissibility to rebel leads to the alienation from a life force that fuels the strength of passion in self-assertive expressiveness. Without this freedom to express oneself, one is relegated to very indirect expressions of bile from the shadowy recesses of one's resentments. That disallowed expression of unwillingness thus may become fetishized and surface in a different form many years later. Indeed, I have often wondered whether much of the anticipatory anxiety adults endure in facing the transitions and changes of their lives occurs because their stifled discontent is transformed into the nonverbal symptomatology of anxiety. Rank (1936) thus says: "The physical symptom makes out of a *not-wanting-to* a *not-being-able-to*" (p. 156).

For example, I have sometimes taken note of the anxiety many adults feel on Sunday evening or while driving to work on Monday morning. This anxiety seems to be a repeat of the trepidation that many children experience at the end of the weekend prior to going back to school. Yet many children do not feel free to express not wanting to go to school. I have often thought that if only such children would have been able to provide an expressive voice to their discontent—"I don't want to go to school tomorrow" or "I can't stand doing my homework"—and have a parent respond empathically—"I understand honey, but unfortunately you have to go to school anyway"—then the inhibition of rebellious protest would not become transformed into the hesitancies and the anticipatory inhibitions of adult anxiety.

As a child, Jane was denied the freedom to protest against the mandates that permeated her life. Like many children, she was not permitted to say: "I don't want to do my homework" or "I don't want to go to school today. Jane's protest against the "have-to(s)" of her life only was able to find passive-aggressive expression in the embedded and indirect communication of her staying in bed. If she is "disabled" by depressive pathology, she can say "No" to the outside world resentfully and no one will stop her. But this form of passively negating what is outside reflects Jane's obedient compliance with external authority and the impermissibility of rebelling more openly.

Shame takes a toll on the reach of our wish-fueled imagination to go beyond our limitations. In our shame, we inhibit the invaluable tool of curiosity and deconstructive questioning of the powers that be, which is a necessary gateway toward inner freedom. We need our curiosity because it casts doubt on parental indoctrinations that have been taken in on the basis of blind faith; curiosity inquires into the underlying sources of parental authority.

From this point of view, the internal act of rebelling would take the form of deconstructing the source of tyrannical authority that has been introjected in the aftermath of shame. Too many patients live helplessly at the mercy of a faceless authority to constantly measure, evaluate, criticize, and ultimately inhibit their creative initiatives. Such patients have never learned to talk back to their parents, to question authority, and do not feel permitted to talk back to what Fairbairn (1952) calls their "internal saboteur" (p. 101).

Indeed, Camus (1951) has made a point of distinguishing between the passivity of resentment and active rebelliousness. He describes resentment as "the evil secretion, in a sealed vessel, of prolonged impotence" (p. 17). In contrast, he says: "Rebellion ... breaks the seal and allows the whole being to come into play. It liberates stagnant waters and turns them into a raging torrent" (p. 17). It is for that reason that I think it is of great therapeutic value that the therapist model the courage to confront the monstrous and bring it down to size by introducing the idea of talking back to the tyrant within. Since the slavishly blind obedience to an invisible absolute authority of rules and "shoulds" in one's life is protected and maintained by a hypnotic mystique of a magical spell that forbids all dissident voices, the therapist's introduction of deconstructive rebelliousness against that inner tyrant breaks the spell, thus cutting the monster down to size. Nietzsche (1882) thus states: "Your insight into how such things as moral judgments could ever come into existence would spoil these emotional words such as 'duty' … for you" (p. 187).

A few years ago, a 17-year-old boy, Kenny, was brought in to therapy by his parents because he was "laughing inappropriately" at school, and it was reported also that he had been overheard muttering violent threats to other kids under his breath. When I asked Kenny about the threats, he said that he was just joking.

When Kenny began his individual sessions, we explored what was going on for him at school in detail. He talked about how much he hated the "popular" kids because they were all "fake." We talked about how he often ate lunch alone, his feeling of being very much on the outside of everyone at school, and how he was often a target of teasing and mockery by the same popular kids. Early on, with more probing, Kenny revealed violent fantasies of wanting to "shoot people" and his wish to "run over all the kids at school with a truck."

With the tragedies of many school shootings echoing in my mind, I took these threats very seriously, especially because Kenny fits the profile of shooters who are loners who are bullied at school and generally feel that they are on the outside of the human community. Nevertheless, I was convinced that his violent fantasies were originating more in the impotence of his hidden resentments rather than the straightforward self-assertiveness of anger. As a full believer in the healing elements of the talking cure, I thought that if Kenny and I could join together in understanding and activating his fantasies of revenge by voicing them out loud, their intensity could be diluted.

In response to my query about his home life, Kenny reported how his father dominated the house with an iron fist. At times, his father could be personable and friendly, but more generally his pronouncements were immediately transformed into the rules of the house. I got the sense that his mother was loving but fairly weak and only attempted to come to Kenny's protection in the aftermath of the father's excesses. More specifically, the father's temper made mealtimes difficult to get through. If Kenny were either to pick up his knife and fork the wrong way or utter a dissident opinion from his father's, he would get an immediate slap across the face. This was not an infrequent occurrence.

I very much wanted Kenny to see that because he was not able to fight his father back in the moment, he took the inhibited anger/resentments with him to school and to displace his vengeful need to splatter violence on the kids who already were not innocent in his eyes. In conveying this to Kenny, I made sure to let him know I was aware that his violent fantasies toward other kids was not only about what was happening at home because he certainly also was fed up with being insulted and excluded by kids at school.

Yet I did not discourage Kenny's genuine contempt for the robotically conforming kids at school. I also was generally supportive of his rage and revenge fantasies toward his classmates. I encouraged him to speak and even imaginatively elaborate upon these wishes for revenge. He did so with relish and probably with no small amount of surprise that an adult man like me was letting him fantasize hateful revenge to his heart's content.

I supplemented this support for his fantasies by suggesting that perhaps even though "they" were the popular kids who had each other to keep them company, maybe he has a leg up on them because he was unable to be a fake like they were. Perhaps, then, having "contempt" for them was a better way to go then revenge. In saying this to Kenny, I hoped to puncture the mystique that the popular kids had something valuable with each other from which he was left out. In so doing, I also was attempting to dilute the destructive power of Kenny's envy of them.

At this point, I think my serving as a participatory witness to Kenny's sense of humiliation and vengeful rage gained me credibility in Kenny's eyes, so much so that he wanted to share the music of his favorite bands with me, most of whom were very dark. He first wanted me to hear Nirvana and had me read the lyrics of a Kurt Cobain song. The lyrics were very cynical and dark, and I knew Kurt Cobain had killed himself with a drug overdose. I asked Kenny about Cobain's suicide and asked him directly whether he wanted to follow in Cobain's footsteps. He replied: "Not really."

I then took my turn as well and asked him to listen to my favorite classic rock anthems of the early 70s, especially the Vietnam protest songs. After he listened, he said they were "pretty good." He then raised the level of dark morbidity with me by having me listen to Death Metal bands and one extreme Norwegian Black Metal band. After I exclaimed quite spontaneously "This is not music!" and "Where is the melody?" he laughed at my discomfort and seemed very pleased that he was able to shock me.

Eventually, Kenny left therapy and seemed to calm down sufficiently at school to finish his senior year. I then heard from him again in the middle of his freshman year at college. He wanted to let me know that he was doing well there.

The questioning of parental or cultural indoctrinations, as well as the dogma of tradition and pressures of social conformity, are a crucial way station toward safekeeping an individual's freedom of self-determination and consistent skepticism of the canons upon which power insists. Spitz (1959) has noted that the first "No" is a hugely important step in the emergence and development of the self. Schafer (1983) emphasizes that it is important that analysts focus on "what resisting is *for* rather than what it is *against*" (p. 162).

From this perspective, we might consider that Jane's active protest of resistant inertia is a first step toward self-healing in what Tolpin (2002) has described as the "forward-edge transference": "Transferences of still-remaining healthy childhood development in the unconscious depths, albeit in the form of fragile 'tendrils' that are thwarted, stunted or crushed" (pp. 167–168).

We all are well-acquainted with the long, noble history of the oppressed resisting their oppressors, and the voice of the individual standing up for the dignified freedom of her subjectivity against the objectifying indoctrinations of totalitarian uniformity. Oscar Wilde (1891) was moved to declare: "Disobedience, in the eyes of anyone who has read history, is man's original virtue. It is through disobedience that progress has been made, through disobedience and through rebellion" (p. 10).

Resistance is the lonely, isolated voice of the forgotten that goes against all expectations. By way of defiance against the status quo—whether obeying parental dictates transformed into one's own introjected commands of "I should," or conforming to social conventions, or adhering to the rationality of doing "for one's own good"—resistance cries out its displeasure at being overlooked, its voice of dignity unheeded.

If we consider the fact that the Hebrew word Satan means "The Adversary," then we might view resistance as the demonic cry of protest from the insulted, injured, and ignored for being cast out to exile for "one's higher good." When in Milton's *Paradise Lost* (1667), Lucifer is excommunicated from heaven, he remains ever the proud rebel and declares upon surveying his underworld exile, "Here at least We shall be free" and "better to reign in Hell than serve in Heaven" (Book I, pp. 257–259).

The two-year-old who throws food off the high chair is resisting the pressured indoctrinations of what is "good" as transmitted by parental authority. When my son Ben was five years old, he took a more direct, verbal approach to resisting authority. On one occasion, when I asked him to clean up the mess he had just made in the living room, he looked me in the eye and asked: "Who made you the boss?"

I was amused and pleased by Ben's question because I knew that his rebellious spirit of skeptical questioning today would help him carve out his own pathway tomorrow. Perhaps that is also why Rilke (1907), in a letter to a friend, declared upon leaving psychoanalysis: "If my devils are to leave me, I am afraid my angels will take flight as well" (p. 123).

To respect the "rightness" of the patient's resistant stance of I WON'T ultimately helps to transform the patient's fatalistic helplessness of I CAN'T into the rebelliousness of pushing back against authority and begins to lend the dignity of free agency to the patient. In accepting and not pathologizing the patient's freedom to resist, I hope to help the patient open up the self-creating free space of I WILL.

# Chapter 10

# The Dignity of Freedom

## Countertransference and the Importance of Respect

> The part of himself that he wanted to be respected he proceeds to place above everything else and proclaims it preferable to everything, even to life itself, it becomes the supreme good.
>
> (Camus, *The Rebel*, (1951), p. 304)

> There is no other equality possible than the equal right of each individual to become and to be himself, which actually means to accept his own difference and have it accepted by others.
>
> (Rank, *Beyond Psychology*, 1941, p. 267)

## Phillip: From I Can't to I Will

Phillip is very much a man-child. Although he is quite tall and bulky and possesses a deep voice, he also often has a vaguely frightened and frozen look on his face, not unlike a deer in headlights. On this particular occasion, as at the outset of many other sessions, Phillip lumbered dutifully into my office and immediately began to recount the ups and downs of the previous week. He had monitored his moods closely so that he would have all the necessary information then ready to share with me—the expert—in order that I care for him appropriately.

Phillip is a 66-year-old white man, just retired from his position as a high-powered attorney, who sought out therapy because he did not know what to do with the rest of his life. He lived alone and had been struggling with bouts of depression, anxiety, and much regret for key decisions he had made in the course of his life.

Almost immediately upon beginning therapy, Phillip spontaneously began unfolding a narrative of his early life. He said he had been very close to his mother early in childhood but rarely saw his father, a taxi driver who often worked long hours. When he was four years old, his mother told Phillip

DOI: 10.4324/9781003559559-11

that he would begin pre-school. Even though he very much did not want to go, she nevertheless.insisted. He remembered feeling much anxiety about the impending transition, but never really protested openly to his mother and instead complied with her wishes. This same difficulty with separating and then holding on tenaciously to the familiar also was evidenced in his memory of his first friendship at that same period of time. He had a best friend, James, but James was also friends with a couple of twin boys. Phillip felt very possessive of James and felt quite antagonistic toward the twins because of James's relationship with them. A theme began to emerge of Phillip's deeply enmeshed attachment to his dyadic relationship with James (and probably already his mother), and not wanting to share that relationship with a "third" party. Perhaps most importantly, the frequent absences of Phillip's father left him without a template of forming his own relationship with that third party in a triadic relationship. For Phillip, the emerging problem was that "third" was first transferred to the antagonist of school and then eventually to the outside world. Developmentally, from a separation-individuation perspective, this also meant clinging to past attachments and viewing the unpredictability of the unknown future as an antagonistic outsider or Other.

It turned out that Phillip's worst fears about going to school were realized. He was very pudgy and had a large birthmark on his neck for which he was teased mercilessly. Each day he dreaded waking up and going to school, but nevertheless he did not tell his mother about the bullying. Evidently, she had already lost all credibility for him as a caretaker to whom he could entrust his deepest feelings of vulnerability.

By the time Phillip left elementary school, life had gradually improved. His birthmark had been removed, and he had lost some weight. He made superficial friends at school, but they never really made a significant impact on his underlying loneliness. During that time, he also became fascinated with walkie-talkies and ham radio, and through these connections, he was able to alleviate some of his sense of desolation by making contact through short-wave radio with a whole community of individuals in far-off places.

As Phillip reached early adolescence, he grew taller, lost more weight, and discovered that girls were quite attracted to him. His confidence grew steadily, and his adolescent and young adult years went far more smoothly than his early life. He had a few girlfriends and formed some friendships, but nothing ever very deep.

By the time he was in his mid-20s, Phillip met his wife, Eve, who was six years his senior. She was very maternal, and he also found her to be very attractive. Soon after they got married though, she developed a rare and very painful disease that ravaged her body. She had to have her breasts and ovaries removed and developed severe chronic pain. For a little while thereafter, she would often cover up her body when coming to bed so that he would remain sexually interested in her, but increasingly he disengaged from sex and eventually divorced her. Phillip said that he divorced her at the time because of wanting to have sex with other women and because of a vague feeling of claustrophobia he felt during the marriage. Although she later remarried, Phillip and Eve have remained very close, devoted friends since the time of the divorce.

In the ensuing years, he would go to bars and pick up young women for one-night stands. Throughout those years of one-night stands, Eve's health continued to deteriorate, and her physical pain became worse. Even though she moved out of state and got remarried, Phillip has continued to visit her and her husband consistently every few months, sometimes for a couple of weeks at a time. During those visits, he would accompany Eve on her numerous appointments to doctors. Most recently, Phillip and Eve acknowledged to each other that they had been the love of each other's lives. Nevertheless, Phillip has repeatedly gone on internet dating in the hope of finding a romantic companion for himself.

Soon after Phillip came to therapy, his despair and regrets about his life worsened, and at times he would express suicidal ideation. When I asked him what he regretted the most, he responded that he had never really tried to form a serious relationship after the divorce and now finds himself all alone. He wondered aloud whether his deep emotional attachment to Eve had hindered his motivation of finding a new dating interest.

As treatment evolved, it became increasingly evident that Phillip's expectation of therapy was that he would bring his problems in to me, and I would fix them. He often began many sessions by informing me of the adjustments that his psychiatrist had made to his medication and by detailing the ups and downs of his moods over the course of the week.

Sometimes Phillip would tell me how he stopped himself from doing activities that he would probably enjoy because of his anxieties. Even though he enjoyed jogging, he said he did not like to jog while the temperature was in the 50s because he much preferred to run when the temperature was in the 70s. Although he loved movies and joined a film club, he said he did not follow through and go to film group meetings because of his anxiety. On a number of occasions, Phillip said he should volunteer for tutoring so that he would not be bored and "overthink" with all of his free time, but he nevertheless did not act on his stated intentions. Sometimes Phillip would punctuate his frustration about his inaction and various conflictual feelings by declaring: "I must be mentally ill" or "It must be my mental illness."

There are many patients like Phillip who present themselves in therapy in these self-inhibiting ways while at the same time implicitly asking the therapist to do something to fix their inaction problem. Given that many therapists enter the profession in the first place in order to help those in need because of their own personal and developmental reasons, the therapist often experiences a primary countertransference pressure to fill the complementary role of designated expert helper to the patient's need requests/demands. This pressure on the part of the therapist often leads him to take excessive responsibility for "fixing" the patient who is viewed as having too much pathology to help himself. Some therapists may respond to questions from patients about what they should do and what they should not do in a given situation, only to find that the patient often does not heed their advice anyway. Since in the therapist's mind, the patient's pathology derives from being fixated at one or other phase of development, it is understandable that the patient needs expertise and guidance for life decisions.

I would suggest, however, that a child's original dependence on a parent is fundamentally different from the dependence that is conveyed in adult passivity. Whereas childhood dependence is a phase in healthy development, the dependency of adult passivity is frequently complicated by feelings of self-inhibiting shame, resentment, and a sense of entitlement to some form of compensation for the guidance and caretaking missed in childhood. Many such adults do not view themselves as active agents of their own lives and refuse to act accordingly, because that would take the would-be caretakers who never cared for them adequately off the hook for what they should have done. In this sense, ironically, what distinguishes a child's dependence on caretakers from adult passivity is the adult's sense of resentment, indignation, and entitlement for NOT having been adequately cared for as a child.

When Phillip punctuates the end of a session with the parting doorknob question "Do you think I need to be hospitalized?" he is expressing annoyance and fear that once again he is being abandoned to his own self-sufficient devices. In a sense, he is letting me know that he is fed up living within the obsessive circularities of his own mind. Yet I believe that Phillip does not want me to say "Yes, you need hospitalization," *but* that he does want me to take his distress seriously and, like a good parent, provide him with hope that he can get better. Indeed, on one occasion, I asked him to consider how he would feel if I said "Yes, you do need to be hospitalized." He thought for a moment and acknowledged he probably would not cooperate with me anyway.

Eventually, I discerned that Phillip's view of himself as mentally ill was inextricably intertwined with a paralyzing anxiety of facing the future. Viewing himself as mentally ill relieved him of the pressure and anxiety of living his life by enabling him to retreat into a self-enclosed sanctuary. However, no matter how much many of us feel deserving of a future that will invite us into its embrace with the open arms of a welcoming mother and thus provide us compensation for past sufferings, life unfortunately takes no mercy, remaining indifferent to our developmental hardships. This confrontation between an individual's passivity that will not budge and a future that will not reach out to beckon him kindly leads often to a tragic stalemate, eventuating in a despairing fatalism that brings an individual in for psychotherapeutic treatment.

Even though Phillip did not see himself as an agent who had any control in determining the course of his life, I thought it very important that I nevertheless held hope for his capacity to heal himself with my facilitating help, even if he did not believe it at the time. I wanted to respect the dignity inherent in Phillip's potentiality as a free agent, even if he did not feel that himself. When he declared he was "screwed up" or had mental illness, I told him that I did not think he had mental illness but that he was trying very much to navigate through problems in living. I added that to view himself with mental illness took pressure off of him from having to live his life, and yet it was precisely that feeling of I CAN'T, which also entrapped Phillip in his life predicament in the first place.

Indeed, when individuals view themselves as emotionally incompetent, they invariably will lack hope or confidence that they will be able to navigate their way through the anxieties of encountering unfamiliar and uncomfortable situations. They may then retreat from their anxieties, only to realize that what they thought was the sanctuary of the safe and familiar becomes a source of imprisoning despair because of emptying their life of new opportunities and experiences.

Phillip's decision to jog only when the temperature was exactly to his liking bespoke a kind of self-pampering, as if he had become stuck on an introject of an infantilizing maternal imago, which then greatly influenced many of his life choices. In this sense, Phillip still lived as if he were still fixated on a wished-for, pre-school mother, an idealized mother who would not have pushed, prodded, and compelled him to go to school before he was ready. His sense of being prematurely evicted from the comforts of home and his sense of helplessness in navigating life covered over a deeper refusal of the future as antagonist to which he had been cast out. Phillip's view of himself as mentally ill and incompetent to move toward the future was a means of rationalizing and justifying a demand that before he would move forward, he first be cared for properly in a way that his mother had neglected long ago. This demand to receive his just due of caretaking came at a great cost for Phillip: his loss of self-respect and the missed opportunities of an all-to-brief mortal life. It is this struggle in Phillip—between that to which he feels entitled and the unhappy real-life consequences that ensue from waiting for his just due—that has become the grist for our therapy sessions.

Most recently, after returning from a three-week trip to visit his ex-wife, in which he devotedly escorted her to numerous doctors, Phillip felt isolated again. Again, he expressed deep regrets for divorcing her. When I then inquired whether he would want to be with Eve now for the rest of his life if he had his way, he paused and said one part of him very much wanted to be with her, but that there was another part that imagined it would be "scary" to be with her. When I probed deeper, he said he would be afraid of feeling trapped in a life of constant caretaking. I wondered out loud to Phillip why he used the word "scary" instead of "I don't want" to describe his ambivalence about taking on a life of constant caretaking. I added that the moral impermissibility of hearing himself say that he did not want to take care of someone he loved transformed his sense of free choice of unwillingness into a sense of intimidated incompetence.

Phillip has begun to bring his early central conflict regarding separation from mother and going to school without any sense of *rapprochement* (Mahler, Pine, & Bergman, 1975) into the present therapeutic situation. Indeed, he recently revealed that every time he attempts to conjure up an image of Eve in her absence, he keeps seeing an image of his mother instead.

Immediately before the past winter holidays, Phillip reported how his mood improves often in December. His birthday is in December, and he loves the holiday festivities. He can walk alone in a residential neighborhood but not feel alone because of the Christmas lights adorning many homes. I said how making contact with some form of life in the distance reminded me of the role short-wave and ham radio played in his childhood in allowing him not to feel so desolately alone in the world. As therapy continues, I am hoping that Phillip's deepening trust in our relationship can continue to facilitate his burgeoning confidence in himself.

## Naming and Objectification: Diagnosis and the Alchemical Power of Words

It is to Freud's great and lasting credit that he recognized how the haunting significance of prior wounds and developmental conflict have powerful unconscious influences on human behavior. His discovery was a necessary corrective to the narrow emphasis that pre-Freudians placed in the power of the conscious will as a propellant of human motivation. One of the unfortunate effects of Freud's discovery of psychic determinism has been, however, to throw out the baby of personal agency with the bathwater of conscious control over one's actions. In psychoanalysis, our diagnostic designations of adult character have been replete with the developmental determinism of oral, anal, and phallic fixations and, eventually, pre-Oedipal and Oedipal-level character disorders.

The diagnostic reductionism of human character to particular stages of developmental arrest is far too mechanistically deterministic to account for the complexities and choices governing therapeutic change. Furthermore, many patients, firmly in the grips of self-dehumanizing introjects formed in the shadow of parental exploitation, already tend to objectify themselves too much, and certainly can do without diagnostic labels that aggravate the problem. I have seen a number of patients over the years introduce themselves by declaring "I'm bipolar" or "I'm borderline." Given the normalizing of these sort of objectifications, it is not surprising that at clinical case conferences, the case presenter may often omit personal pronouns of a patient's family members, such that "her mother" is rendered into the shorthand of "mother."

It becomes tempting for such persons who have habitually thought of themselves as objects at the beck and call of others rather than as active human agents in their own right to appropriate a self-objectifying identity by way of professional jargon, so that at least finally they can attain a sense of belonging to the powerful designators of their diagnostic identity.

Names, then, are not just names. Cassirer (1946) says: "The name does not merely denote but actually *is* the essence of its object" (p. 3). Freud (1913b) points out that from a primary process thinking point of view: "If you know the name of a person or a spirit you have acquired a certain power over its bearer" (p. 81). In a sense, the representation of a person in the form of a name coopts that person's sacred essence. The very same process of naming, which is used to such profoundly constructive effect in psychoanalysis to dissolve symptoms that derive their demonic power from their exiled independence from consciousness, also has the potentiality to conquer and efface the souls of real people, transforming them into colonized objects of another person's imagination.

The fairy tale *Rumpelstiltskin* reveals the life-and-death importance of names. The princess in the story is about to have a baby, and Rumpelstiltskin is a little man/dwarf who will take possession of the new child unless the princess can guess Rumpelstiltskin's correct name. If we consider that Rumpelstiltskin is identified with the new child, then this guessing game is a deadly serious power struggle for ownership of his soul. If he wins, he can retain control over his name and essence and create a new beginning for himself. On the other hand, if she succeeds in guessing his name and capturing his essence, as she succeeded in doing, he evaporates in a tantrum of mortification.

To the extent that patients already have objectified themselves too much throughout their lives, developmental determinism and the catch-all labels of diagnostic nomenclature further strip away the dignity intrinsic to the patient's personhood as a free human agent. It is not uncommon for therapists to use words like "damaged" and "disturbed" to describe patients. I'm not sure how such terms are helpful, and they often collude with the patient's own view of himself as "screwed up" or, as Phillip referred to himself, "mentally ill."

These "metaphors of the baby" and "metaphors of defect," as Mitchell (1988) described them, permeate our visions of therapeutic action and the techniques we employ to effect change. When the therapist, governed by a countertransference eagerness to help effect change, views the person of the patient as a "damaged" or "defective" object, he may view the patient as hopelessly and helplessly unable to determine the course of his own life.

Moreover, in psychoanalytic theorizing, these diagnostic labels are greatly influenced by what Mitchell (1984) refers to as "the developmental tilt." The developmental arrests and fixations to various stages of early childhood thus lead directly to diagnostic categories neatly tied together by group labels.

The developmental tilt has also accentuated what I would refer to as "metaphors of fragility", which are in great evidence in case conference presentations of patients. This fragility can be heard in statements like "She won't be able to hear that" or "He cannot tolerate that." These declarations, and the metaphors of breakage that they imply, are an often assumed but unexamined aspect of what is conveyed in analytic training about patients. It is precisely because these metaphorical conceptualizations of patients as fragile are handed down one analytic generation to the next through the authority of one's training and supervisory analysts, that they are perpetuated and being enacted upon with patients without fully delving into what they actually mean. Patients may have many sensitivities and strong emotional reactions, such as getting angry or breaking into teary sobs, but they are not China dishes who will break. Ultimately, I suspect that a therapist's constructions of patients as fragile are intertwined with unresolved aspects of the therapist's own aggression, resulting in countertransference fantasies concerning his destructive word magic (words doing untold harm). These countertransference fantasies are then projected on to the patient's ability to survive the analyst's words.

Many patients, like Phillip, come in for psychotherapy because of their despair for feeling helplessly at the mercy of external forces and inner torments beyond their control. One primary aim of psychoanalytic treatment has been to illuminate these inner conflicts through greater clarification and understanding and thereby relieve some degree of distress. Nevertheless, psychoanalytically inclined clinicians well know that such insight is often not sufficient to facilitate real-life changes for patients, whose enslavement to the tyranny of deeply insulated negative introjects often remains impenetrable to analytic interpretations. In a certain sense, the self-shaming authority of these negative introjects seems most especially constituted by an impenetrable, enigmatic quality that allows them to cast a hypnotic spell over the person. Indeed, we could say that the chronic helplessness that a child often feels about changing a real parent who is rejecting into a wished-for parent becomes transferred onto the adult's sense of futility and passive fatalism about altering the course of his own life.

These patients then transfer their lifelong passivity to the relationship with the therapist by projecting responsibility for transforming their lives on to the therapist. Their view of their own helplessness thus reinforces the analyst's countertransference views that they are too damaged to participate in their own healing. In this way, therapist and patient collude on the view that the patient is a helplessly inert object to be moved from pathology to health by the therapist rather than a freely willing subject in her own right. Indeed, sometime when a treatment is stalemated, and the therapist becomes annoyed and frustrated or even angry that the patient is resisting all attempts of therapeutic help, it becomes evident that the therapist's countertransference need to be of use has blurred boundaries regarding motivation and responsibility for treatment outcome. The therapist would be well to ask himself then: "Whose treatment is this?"

Since the analytic endeavor in particular is a deconstructive process of "shrinking minds" through interpretively reducing the manifest integrity of a patient's subjective self-presentation to its latent unconscious motives, it is especially important that respect for the patient's freedom of dignity as a whole person be a fundamental aspect of the treatment.

In these moments, we would be well to remember Kant's (1785) view of a human being: "A human being … is not a thing and hence not something that can be used merely as a means, but must in all of his actions always be regarded as an end in itself" (p. 38). Drozek (2015) thus speaks of the importance in the therapy relationship of a *mutual recognition of dignity*; he refers to dignity as our "ascription of unconditional or intrinsic worth of value to ourselves and others as human beings" (p. 432).

In my view, the recognition of a patient's sense of dignity must also include a recognition of the patient's freedom of self-determination, that the patient's life belongs to the patient, not to the therapist. No matter how much a therapist strives to save a patient from himself, she has to recognize and respect the boundaries that separate the therapist's provision of help from the patient's ability to receive that help. If the therapist were to pity her patients, even those who have suffered greatly from their traumatic experiences, the therapist would risk colluding with the patient's helpless sense of I CAN'T.

In viewing the patient's suffering with pity, the therapist risks depriving the patient of a certain dignity inherent at least in the POTENTIALITY of hope, attitude, and choice—that is, of learning how to cope with one's legacy of suffering and take responsibility for one's intentionality toward the future. This potentiality of hope to give rebirth to oneself at any given moment is possible because everything—life, time, and the human mind—is a dynamic process rather than a static thing What looks like developmental fixation or character structure is actually a repeated process. In this sense, it is of central importance in any treatment to convey hope and respect the capabilities of patients to move toward the open horizon of the future that need not be but an endless repetition of a traumatic past.

Rather than group patients into a category tied together by a diagnostic label, for example, perhaps we can fully individualize what we consider to be diagnoses of emotional life. After a patient presents her distress, and I eventually gather more information about the patient's history, I construct an always-provisional understanding of how the patient came to be who she is today. Most importantly, like the life of each individual and the treatment relationship itself, these diagnostic formulations are always evolving from session to session. Moreover, although I may be aware of the patient's history, at the beginning of each session, I revisit, by means of curiosity, a process of inquiry, and a consistently applied ethic of understanding, the patient's complaints of anxiety, depression, or regret. At the beginning of each session, I address the patient's symptomatology anew, as if I have not heard her complaints prior to that session. What specifically are you anxious about today? What makes you feel despairing? Through these inquiries, the my aim is both to understand and to help the patient participate in her own treatment by listening and being answerable as best she can in the moment—without blame—to the echo of her own words. Diagnosis is thus an ever-evolving understanding and treatment of the patient' distress.

For example, a number of therapists treat patients who have chronic suicidal ideation. For such patients, their suicidality has become almost a routinized way of coping with life's setbacks and adversity. Too often, in the attempt to be empathic, many therapists unknowingly join their patients in accepting the chronic "normality" of their symptoms. Some therapists often want to make sure first that peripheral safeguards are in place, such as signing contracts, promising to contact the therapist before doing anything extreme, and ensuring that there are hospitalization options available. Although these interventions are understandable, too often they become a primary mode of treatment that does not treat the suicidality directly itself. In these situations, especially if the patient has a history of suicidal attempts and suicidal ideation, the therapist implicitly believes and accepts that the patient has been chronically suicidal and will remain that way for the foreseeable future to such an extent that he has unknowingly joined the patient's fatalism.

Yet if the therapist were to step back from her habituated cynicism about the patient's suicidality at the beginning of each session, she would turn the question of living and dying on its head. Through curiosity and deeply penetrating inquiry, she would ask the fundamental questions: "Why today do you wish to die and not live? Is there another way to alleviate your painful sufferings?" In a sense, these questions put even to a chronically suicidal patient imply that even the patient's ongoing wish to die is such a deviation from the expectable wish to live that the reasons why it is necessary have to be revisited again.

## Analytic Respect for the Actuality of the Other Person

In order to overcome the foreclosed circularities of fatalism then, it is important to balance the analytic love of compassionately witnessing and validating the patient's past experiences of suffering with an analytic respect for the patient as a human agent who has the will and capability to move his life forward. As Camus (1956) emphasizes in the epigraph to this chapter, the very essence of a person's life, his very dignity as a human being, depends on being respected by others.

Benjamin (1995) has written extensively about the developmental paradoxes inherent in recognizing the fundamentally different subjectivity of others. She suggests that whereas primal identification with an inner representation of an outside other (a fantasy object) contributes to the empathic bridging of difference, it is opposed to the recognition of the other as someone who is essentially unique in his or her own right.

Whereas the concepts of empathy and love are familiar to many psychoanalysts, the idea of respect often does not get its proper due. To paraphrase Benjamin in terms of love and respect, the empathic bridging of difference characteristic of love must be balanced by a respect for the boundaries separating one unique individual's subjectivity and freedom of self-determination from that of another individual. Within a relationship between two persons, Benjamin (1995) thus speaks of mutual respect as the capacity of each person to "treat the other person as an equal" (p. 80). Such respect necessarily entails respecting the differences between each individual.

The word *respect* derives from the Latin verb *respicere*, "to look back at, to look again." How then might we understand the conceptual meaning of this etymology? Perhaps there is a spontaneous "first look" tendency in human beings to incorporate other humans as transference objects of their visual minds. Levinas (1969) has referred to this spontaneous tendency to incorporate what we see as a process of "totalization" as opposed to the recognition of the infinite mystery and difference of a uniquely other individual.

For example, we may tend to deny the death of loved ones and thus take for granted that they will be around forever because we see them as closely attached extensions of our own deathlessness. When we thus view them as beloved object representations of our minds, we may deny their mortality as we deny ours. This sort of denial allows us a peace of mind that enables us to go on living without excessive or paralyzing anxiety, but it may cost us an ability to value the preciously fragile presence of those that we love. The dimension of respect, however, requires us to do a double-take and take a second look of respect at a separate person whose destiny may differ from our own. This different person has a mind of her own as a free subject in her own right rather than someone who is attached on a yo-yo string to our mind's eye.

The meaning of "look back at" or to look at something again refers to realizing the other is "not a given object of sight," as Merleau-Ponty (1945) says, but must be realized as a subject in her own right. This second look, now informed by an accepting respect for the boundaries circumventing the other person's unique individuality, enables us to genuinely empathize with the other person's life and death from that person's vantage point. In the most fundamental sense, respect is empathically according the same freedom of self-determination to another being that one gives to oneself. One does not always understand or agree with why another person does or does not do what he/she does, but according respect means that we accept that person's freedom to live life as he or she sees fit. Without the dimension of respect in human relations, love can degenerate into colonizing attempts to subject another person's difference to the omnipotent reach of one's loving control, often manifest in the condescension of "I know what is for your own good."

The ancient Greek term *aidos* refers to an awe-filled reverence for the divide that separates the sacred from the profane. In some religions, God is neither to be represented by visual images or icons, nor have his name be uttered or spelled out. The God of the Old Testament, Yahweh, literally means "no name." The boundaries separating appearance from essence are meant to protect the sacredness of unimaginable mystery from being corrupted by the false representations of human imagination.

Perhaps we can bring the concept of *aidos* down to earth and use it as a necessary adjunct to love in human relations in its respect for the semipermeable boundaries that separate and protect the essential mystery of each different person. By highlighting the boundaries between appearances and essences, *aidos* provides meaning for the construction of a public sphere that shields the essential vulnerability of the private. This public sphere of social interaction lends a protectively respectful distance to the spaces between people and prevents them from knowing each other's essence prematurely without each other's consent. *Aidos* challenges us not to colonize other individuals, to kidnap their personhood and transform them into hostage fantasy objects of our inner worlds, but instead to respect the sacred mystery and freedom of self-determination of each unique person.

I use the term "semipermeable boundaries" purposefully to highlight the paradox that the self's boundaries are simultaneously open and enclosed. Whereas the openness of the unbounded self reflects a relational fluidity with other selves that could be described as love, the enclosed aspect of the self's circumscribing boundaries protects the privacy of each person's subjectivity, lending the uniqueness of individuality a dignity of freedom to create and choose that is characteristic of mutual respect. If a world of loving, boundless passion without respect for Otherness would degenerate into an objectification of other different persons, then a world of *only* respect for difference without any common bonds of fellow feeling and language would degenerate into the absurdity of relational indifference.

When Levinas (1969) emphasizes that each human being has an inherent ethical responsibility of care for the face of the Other, he is especially emphasizing a respect for the "face" as the presentation of the Other's unique subjectivity. Most importantly, the Other's subjectivity is not reducible to ways in which we may conceive of and represent that person in our own minds. He says: "The way in which the other presents himself, exceeding the *idea of the other in me*, we here name 'face'" (p. 50).

Derrida (2008) challenges Levinas's tendency to attribute this respect for the face of the Other only to other human beings and not animals. I take Derrida's challenge to Levinas quite seriously. After all, why would we not extend Levinas's notion of respect for the "face" of the other to the vast unique diversity of animal species and each individual animal?

It is worth noting here, as Derrida (2008) points out, that human beings claim colonizing dominion over the animal kingdom by grouping all animals under the abstract name of Animal. He says: "They have given themselves the word in order to corral a large number of living beings within a single concept, 'The Animal,' they say" (p. 32). From that colonizing abstraction, it is but a small leap to claim dominion over a now-rendered inferiority of "dumb" animals who cannot speak in defense of their dignity and freedom of self-determination.

Derrida's (2008) title for his book, *The Animal That Therefore I Am*, is itself a playful critique of Descartes's axiom of dissociative thinking, "I think therefore I am." It is because we are ashamed of and disavow our own animal heritage as embodied beings, who pee and poop and reproduce just like other animals, that we project that shame onto animals who are viewed as "things" to be mastered through domination and exploited as a means toward our own ends. When we lose the respect for the sacred essence of each living being to have an equal right to pursue its own destined actualization, we are apt to do violence to that being. Derrida describes this reasoning that distinguishes between the rights of persons and the rights of things:

> The person is an entirely different being, in rank and dignity from these things, which are irrational animals. One has power and authority over these irrational animals because they are things. One can use them and lord over them as one pleases.
>
> (pp. 92–93)

Indeed, as Freud (1913b) theorizes, civilization initially was founded on a detachment from our animal origins, which then returns from the repressed in guilty indebtedness and repayment through the worship of ancestral totems. Eventually, however, civilization dissociates from this sense of indebtedness and guilt toward our common animal origins as living beings, only for this disavowal to be projected in the image of an Other who is mastered through hierarchy, power, and sometimes eradication of the animal Other.

I am making this somewhat prolonged detour into our attitudes toward animals and our animal bodies because I have wondered whether the psychoanalytic relationship derived in part from the analyst's attempt to project the disavowed irrationality of his bodily needs onto the otherness of the "hysterical" patient who acts out her emotionality excessively.

As I have noted previously (Shabad, 2001), the prototypical psychoanalytic dyad between obsessional male analyst and hysterical female analysand, as exemplified by the case of Anna O. (Freud & Breuer, 1895) is dichotomized into male and female and into thinking versus acting. These binaries have not occurred by happenstance.

Elsewhere (Shabad, 2008), I explored the momentous effect that being born of woman has had on the male psyche. throughout history. With regard to the association of men with thinking and women with embodied action specifically, it is interesting to consider an example from Greek mythology. Zeus creates a number of Olympian gods from his head, the seat of rationality rather than emotionality. It may not be coincidental that at least in the English language, the original meaning of the term *conceive*, to create from one's body, is given a new meaning of conceiving or creating from one's thoughts. Have men coped with the envy of the maternal body's creative capacity by infusing thinking with a creative importance in its own right?

Looked at in this way, in the early days of psychoanalysis, the male analyst's disavowal of his own body is projected on the emotional acting-out of the female patient from whom he attempts to distance himself, and over whom he attempts to achieve hierarchical mastery by raising the consciousness of an unconscious creature. In this sense, psychoanalysis originated largely in the male analyst attempting, not unlike Henry Higgins in *My Fair Lady*, of making a woman be more like a man.

## Honoring the Patient's Curiosity: The Person-Person Relationship

Whereas the principle of "free association" has been central to the analytic enterprise and certainly would seem to encourage a freedom of curiosity, too often that process has applied only insofar as the patient inquires into the workings of her own mind. Should the patient's attention wander off and become a relational curiosity that seeks to pry behind the analyst's professional persona, the analyst has often skillfully deflected and deftly parried the patient's inquiries by means of return inquiries or interpretations about the patient's motives.

Many patients enter treatment in the first place because they cannot break out of the isolating but comfortably familiar haven of their own self-enclosed minds. The therapist's shutting down or deflection of inquiries about himself as a person perpetuates the patient's "resistance" to her exploratory curiosity and growth. As I emphasized in Chapter 5, an individual's self-enclosure reflects the degree to which the omnipotent burdens of shame have shut down one's passionate movement of generously opening up to the unknown.

When, for example, a depressed parent cannot enjoy her child's offerings or rebuffs his numerous attempts to lift her mood, the child may fall back on fantasies of omnipotence to compensate for his actual helplessness. The torment of perfectionistic demands to always do more to alleviate the parent's distress weighs heavily as a gnawing burden of responsibility for a sense of indebtedness that never gets paid. The process of being curious—with its concomitant dangers of inquiring, discovering, and knowing—therefore becomes linked omnipotently with a shameful consciousness of one's inadequacy and a despairing sense of futility. It is better "to see no evil nor hear no evil," rather than to be burdened chronically with one's sense of failure.

Patients who show no curiosity about who the therapist is as a person may obediently comply with psychoanalytic technique and don't challenge the professional persona of the therapist—but is this really optimal? Perhaps there is a clue as to why such patients focus on the professional and show no curiosity about the person of the therapist in the following statement: "I don't want to know anything about my analyst, because then I would have to take care of him." For certain patients, to know the foibles and frailties of the person of the therapist is tangled up with the automatic mandate to take care of him.

In returning to the beginning of Chapter 4 and my lack of response to Linda's curiosity about whether or not I was married, I denied Linda the respect of a response that her inquiry deserved. When the patient's probing quests for a more intimate, less formal relationship with the analyst are viewed as resistance rather than as self-healing attempts to satisfy a relational hunger and take on the responsibilities of knowing, it is counterproductive to discourage those inquiries. Without dialogical responsiveness, the exposed vulnerability of the patient's curiosity to inquire, discover, and know what was not known is left to grope in a relational void. There is something disingenuous about a fundamental analytic principle that encourages the patient to "know thyself," while discouraging a curiosity to know about the person of the analyst, who is inextricably linked to one's view of oneself. One must wonder, then: "Who is *resisting* whom in that encounter?" It is incumbent on the therapist to respect the patient as a human agent by responding to her curiosity about the person with whom that patient is speaking so intimately. The patient's curiosity toward herself *and* toward the therapist indicates a readiness to take responsibility for what she comes to know.

Johnny originally came to therapy with his wife for marital problems. They met in college, and soon afterward, they got married and had two children. When I first met Johnny, he struck me as someone who was very young, but also as someone who felt very burdened, which perhaps he carried metaphorically in his extreme obesity.

A number of years later, Johnny came back for individual therapy because of problems he was having with his boss at work and also because of some vague feelings of depression. Significantly, his father had died suddenly when Johnny was eight years old, and thereafter Johnny felt responsible for his mother's emotional well-being because he was now the "man of the house."

On one occasion, during the 2008 presidential campaign, Johnny, who had been a double major in political science and history as an undergraduate, mentioned how much he enjoyed watching *The Charlie Rose Show* because he liked politics. He then told me he was a Newt Gingrich supporter and asked me whom I liked. I said Obama, and he then began to criticize Obama's policy positions. I entered the fray with him, and we engaged in a friendly political debate that never got too angry or heated. In fact, Johnny often would have a pleased smile while we argued, as if he were amused that he was able to bring his "doctor" down to earth sufficiently to engage in a verbal sparring match. For a number of sessions thereafter, he often would initiate a repeat of our jousting sessions.

Whereas, from one point of view, Johnny and I were engaged in an extra-analytic enactment, I viewed our mutual participation in debating as the relational body that grounded the mind of our analytic work together. In remaining open to the unbidden aspects of my relationship with Johnny, I was attempting to promote the elasticity of "relational freedom" in the interpersonal field described by Stern (2015). Through our verbal wrestling bouts, Johnny also was attempting to work through an admixture of love and hate through which he had never been able to gain closure in his relationship with his father. Within the good-natured lightheartedness of our debates, not unlike the play wrestling between a father and son, the love reflected by the play contained the competitive aggressiveness of the wrestling itself. Perhaps more importantly, instead of adhering to a hierarchical relationship of idealized analyst and passive patient, or father and son, my entry into a debate with Johnny in the first place implicitly conveyed to Johnny a respect toward him as an "equal," with whom it is worth debating our differences.

## Will and the Facilitation of Answerability without Blame

Too often, the intertwining notions of will, freedom of choice, and personal responsibility have been exiled from psychoanalytic discourse, because I suspect such terms can be easily distorted into degenerated meanings of punishment and blame. Yet the recriminations of self-shaming have quite different, even antithetical, consequences than does the owning or disowning of one's inner life that is intrinsic to personal responsibility. Can we not understand the developmental experiences that strongly influence the trajectory of adult character *and also* respect—*without blaming*—the unconsciously intentional actions of a patient within which are embedded the seedlings of individual dignity, freedom, and responsibility? Mitchell (1988) thus writes that it is a fallacy to believe: "Influence and choice are opposed and inversely proportional to each other" (p. 255). He further states: "The analysand is not just the fly caught in the web, but is the spider, the designer of the web, as well" (p. 257). In my view, it is important that we hold in paradoxical tension the dignity inherent in having freedom of choice, while at the same time compassionately witnessing, validating, and understanding the influences that have contributed to those choices.

In this view, the sources of freedom, choice, individual dignity, and responsibility are embedded within the unconsciously intentional actions of a patient. As May (1969) says: "The act is the intention and the intention is the act" (p. 240). In referring to clinical work then, May insists that we are mistaken when we assume that a patient develops a sense of identity and then acts. He says: "On the contrary, he experiences the identity *in* the action" (p. 242).

Farber (1966) referred to this sort of unconscious intentionality as the "will of the first realm" in contrast to the more consciously purposive will of the second realm. According to Farber, "the unconscious will of the first realm spontaneously moves in a general direction, not toward a specific thing. And its predominant experience is freedom" (p. 8). In this sense, the will of the first realm is similar to a personal life force or energy.

There is a fundamental truth in the simple saying: "Actions speak louder than words." In the broadest sense of the word "want," we do what we want to do. Rather than think of a self who rationally plans_his or her actions ahead of time, perhaps it is more accurate to infer who we are from what we do. In this sense, our freedom of intentionality and choice as human agents of our lives are embedded fundamentally in the action decisions we make from one moment to the next. As a corrective to a consciousness that is permeated with rule-bound moralisms and directives to be "good," there is something refreshingly non-ideological about recognizing the urge toward freedom inherent in actions.

One way of understanding why patients often enter treatment is that they habitually find themselves living without a sense of integrity. Many persons discover to their consternation that they are not always saying what they mean, and their actions often do not follow what they say. Their stated aspirations to love, play, and work successfully are consistently undermined by self-defeating actions. For Schafer (1978), this problem of integrity derives from "disclaimed actions."

Such patients are trapped in a polarizing internal dynamic between consciously planning to follow "shoulds" that seem rational and sensible and in one's own self-interest, but which then they persistently resist either through opposing impulsive actions or through a resistant inertia. In the aftermath of their own inaction or "acting-out," they often shame themselves mercilessly and dissociate from the alien quality of their actions, only to repeat the cyclical dynamic all over again. In their minds, their inaction or fault-laden actions are "nuisance" symptoms, which many patients want to eliminate because they will not comply with the plan to be "good" and "sensible." As Farber (1966) emphasizes: "The problem of will is the temptation to force conscious intentions down one's throat instead of heeding one's freedom ... will becomes distorted under such conditions" (p. 15).

In such situations, it is important that the therapist then be fully aware of his own countertransference biases toward what is considered "good," even his ideas of the good for the patient getting better in treatment. As I highlighted in Chapter 9, the greater the responsibility the therapist takes on for pulling the patient toward treatment progress, the more the patient is tempted to resist the treatment in order to prove her life belongs to her, not the therapist. I frequently take a sympathetic view of a patient's actions because they are often a powerful, but often disowned, expression of the will and dignity of the patient. In looking at the patient's actions, I often point out that there are good reasons that underlie why the patient is doing what the patients is doing.

When I speak of respect, then, I believe it is important for the therapist to put his own conventional morality aside and pay heed toward understanding the often silently rebellious actions of his patients. When our patients berate themselves because their actions don't coincide with their best-laid plans, it is most likely because they have not empathically understood and accepted the affirmative motivations for their actions. For example, affirming the underlying motivations for the self-injurious behavior of "cutting off one's nose to spite one's face" would recognize the good reasons for wanting to avenge oneself passive-aggressively against exploitative authority figures, but one might also point out how the understandable desire to hurt the other may be backfiring in the form of hurting oneself. In emphasizing an accepting view of the patient's actions rather than words, I am also attempting to ally myself with the silent inner resistance of the patient against the tyranny of her should.

The individual who is twisted into a moralistic pretzel between the obligatory "good" of his shoulds and the disavowed "badness" of what he is afraid are his selfish desires would benefit from the healthy clarity of a three-year-old who knows very well what he likes and what he does not like, and then pursues the actualization of his desires quite directly. That clarity would help many adults, at least in terms of enabling a straightforward acquaintance with their fundamental desires.

To return to my treatment with Phillip then at the beginning of the chapter, through my own active and straightforwardly respectful attitude toward Phillip as an active agent of his life, I was attempting to model what he could do in his own active participation in relation to his own mind. Yet I was aware I was up against Phillip's history of impotent protest against separating and going to school prematurely, where he faced constant humiliation from peers. In his subsequent retreat from a chronic anticipation of a threatening future, he became locked in a self-enclosed prison of shame and self-pity, as manifested in his not feeling capable of facing the future on his own. In his resentment, the only thing that was left for him was to demand from life the caretaking that he was denied in the first place, even at the cost of his self-respect and dignity as a human being.

I then see my clinical responsibility as attempting to open an inner life of possibilities to Phillip that he had thought had been forever buried. Where he feels his anxiety or depression is disabling him into stasis and there is nothing to be done about it, I am attempting to cultivate his active relationship with his depression and anxiety as an ongoing process. In the following chapter, I will elaborate further on the all-important emotional flavoring and potential self-healing quality of that relationship with oneself.

# Chapter 11

# Letting Go and Holding On

## Mourning and the Paradoxes of Emotional Life

As Lucretius says, "Thus each man ever flees himself." But to what end, if he does not escape himself? He pursues and dogs himself as his own most tedious companion.

(Seneca, *On The Shortness of Life*, 60 A.D, p. 76)

Real generosity toward the future lies in giving all to the present.
(Camus, *The Rebel*, 1951, p. 304)

## Sarah: "I Am Not Good Enough"

Soon after the Covid pandemic began, Sarah, a 46-year-old divorced white woman and mother of two small children, began twice-a-week teletherapy with me over Zoom. After going through a long slew of psychotherapists over many years, Sarah said that she still felt depressed. Sarah said that no matter what she did, she never felt good enough. For most of her life, she felt that she had to be perfect, and as soon as a conflict occurred in a relationship with others or even minor things went wrong in her own life, she felt immediately that she had done something wrong and then became depressed from her sense of inadequacy.

Sarah's memories as an only child growing up with her parents were quite bleak. Her father was an alcoholic who got into a motorcycle accident when Sarah was five years old despite her begging him at the time not to drink. After he ended up in a wheelchair from his injuries, in the accident, he did finally stop drinking. Nevertheless, already early in therapy, Sarah said she was still "very mad" and "hurt" that she was not important enough for him to listen to her. I sensed that Sarah's hurt and seeming lack of sympathy for her father's consequent plight covered up other deeper feelings of love and closeness. Indeed, when I asked her about her subsequent relationship with her

DOI: 10.4324/9781003559559-12

father, she said that he was really the only parent who loved and supported her. He died while Sarah was at university, and she spoke tearfully about how during one of their last phone calls, he told her he loved her.

Even though Sarah described very little if any expressions of love between her parents, she was often inseparable from her mother. Her mother took her everywhere. Yet she also described how critical her mother could be and that she constantly had to be "perfect" to avoid her mother's wrath. She did speak with much fondness though, of how her mother took her for horseback riding lessons.

The mood governing the bleak, loveless marriage between her parents permeated her early years. The marriage eventually ended when Sarah was ten years old. Soon after, Sarah felt completely dropped after her mother got remarried. Her stepfather was often critical, and her mother often took her stepfather's side. She spoke resentfully of how it was constantly the two of them against her.

When Sarah first came in, she also informed me that she had been intimately involved with a married man. Even though he was apparently miserable in his marriage and kept promising to leave, he did not act on his words, and the affair continued seemingly with no end in sight. The relationship was quite volatile, fluctuating often between angry arguments and passionate reconciliations. Even though Sarah was aware of this very mercurial quality of the relationship, she saw it as a corrective for the relatively bloodless relationship she had with her ex-husband.

Nevertheless, Sarah paid a high price for the intense volatility of this relationship, since every time she and her boyfriend fought and he blamed her for one thing or another, she doubted herself constantly and wondered whether she was at fault. In her self-doubt, she was very acutely aware of how fearful she was that if she stood up for herself, he would break off the relationship and she would be alone.

Soon after treatment began, it became clear that Sarah's conflicting feelings toward her father of resentment, hurt, pity, and love were difficult for her to sort out. As she talked through her confusion, it seemed that she had used her residual hurt and resentment about his accident to defend against her anticipatory dread that she would fall apart if she were to gain access to her softer, more loving feelings toward him. In fact, each time that we even began to broach the topic of his love for her, she reddened visibly, became speechless, and began to tear up.

These more positive feelings toward her father led Sarah into a deep well of sadness and pity for him and herself from which she had long attempted to keep a safe emotional distance. Yet without gaining conscious access to her loving relationship with her father, Sarah could not mourn his life and loss. To bathe in the disillusionment of a love relationship or relationship with parents does not constitute a process of mourning; it only serves as a defense against the painful sadness of how something that was good at one time was lost. It is ironic then that in order to mourn, one must elaborate upon one's most precious memories in order to work through the loss of the good. In so doing a person is able to replace the bitterness of being stuck in the disillusionment of mainly negative memories with the bittersweetness of recollecting and reintegrating the love that was left behind.

Sarah's relationship with her mother was a very different and more difficult story. Sara seemed genuinely bitter at how much her mother had turned against her after she got remarried to Sarah's stepfather. The memories of how primary she seemed to be to her mother in their inseparability and then her mother's betrayal after getting remarried, now filtered through her subsequent resentment, cast the earlier apparent closeness in a bitter retrospective light. She now felt that she had been exploited as an object by her mother's selfish needs at the earlier time.

Even though she no longer talked or saw her mother very often, especially because they lived in separate cities, her loyal accommodation to her mother's exacting authority had done its damage. It now resided as a potent "should have done this or that" inside Sarah's mind—which she constantly felt she had to follow through with perfectly. Any shortfall of perfection became a fatal flaw in Sarah for which she would berate herself mercilessly for "not being good enough."

Sarah's conflation of an ideal version of herself and her far less ideal lived experience as a real self was a deep-seated problem. Her construction of a "perfect" self, derived from Sarah's repeated experiences of conforming to her mother's desired conception of a wished-for daughter, and from her determination not to incur her mother's withering criticisms if she fell short of that mark. Sarah's vision of and identification with living up to a perfect idea of herself has shadowed her throughout life. It is that conflict between the unreachably "perfect" self who she desired to be and the constant actuality of not feeling good enough, which became the primary focus of treatment.

Psychotherapy did not go smoothly at the beginning. Sarah presented her sense of chronic inadequacy to me, her unhappiness with herself, and then she would wait silently for me to make her feel better. Although Sarah had been in many therapies previously, she did not seem to expect that she would or should probe the workings of her own mind. Instead, she would tell me how she attacked herself and waited for me to make her feel better. On those occasions, when she attacked herself for not being perfect, and I inquired more deeply about what she had done wrong, she seemed often taken aback by my questions. The rather stilted interactions we had at the beginning were compounded by the fact that we began treatment doing virtual psychotherapy because of the pandemic.

I began to discern that Sarah more generally was very much entrapped in a cycle of berating herself mercilessly and then searching out selected trusted figures in order to save her from herself and make her feel better. Instead, we attempted slowly and painstakingly to help Sarah take a step outside of her introjected dynamic of self-shaming and self-pity, and becoming more aware of how her relationship with her own mind works. Moreover, this relationship would not only be a self-observing consciousness, but also one that actively interceded in her own mind's functioning. I did this by consistently using an ethic of curiosity, inquiry, and understanding in my attitude toward whatever Sarah brought in, with the hope that she could use my curiosity and inquiry to internalize a relationship with herself that replaced self-shaming with self-understanding.

In a very recent session, Sarah had just returned from a trip to Florida. She had traveled there to spread her father's ashes at the Daytona 500 speedway because her father had been a huge auto-racing fan. Before making the trip, Sarah had a difficult time overcoming her painful regrets for not having previously accompanied him while he was still alive. She was frozen in the self-scolding of 20/20 hindsight. Since in this particular year, Daytona fell on the date of her father's birthday, she decided to make the trip as a reparative gift of her devotional love to him.

To her surprise, she found herself identifying with him by enjoying the race herself. After she noticed her pleasure, she berated herself for enjoying it too much. She and I noticed how she deliberately interfered with her enjoyment of the race for fear of momentarily lapsing into a forgetfulness of the depression she had experienced for the bulk of her life. These symptoms of chronic unhappiness were sympathy pangs to her father's enclosed misery in a wheelchair, and also to the lonely suffering of her own desolation in reaction to the bleak family atmosphere in the aftermath of her father's accident. If she were to relinquish her symptoms that were formed as a testament to her prior experiences, then why did she suffer in the first place? Sarah's depression at least lent some sort of meaning to that prior suffering.

Kierkegaard (1849) has said: "What feelings, understanding, and will a person has depends in the last resort upon what imagination he has—how he represents himself to himself, that is, upon imagination" (p. 32). Our self-image can become so spellbinding, not unlike Narcissus's stare at his own image in a pool of water, that it becomes difficult to yank ourselves away from who we have always been and imagine becoming a different person in the new horizon of a wide-open future. Instead, too often we expect who will be in in the future will be constantly swallowed up by who we have been.

Indeed, one's loyalty to the way one always has been becomes its own kind of entrapment. In the introduction to Ferenczi's *Clinical Diary*, Dupont (1988) describes well how the process of identifying with the aggressor (what I am referring to as self-shaming) can evolve eventually into its own prison:

> The trauma victim, the child, or the mentally ill person reflects back to the aggressor a caricatured image of himself, this expressing simultaneously his own suffering and protest those truths which the aggressor is striving to evade. Then, little by little, the traumatized person becomes so caught up in his own scenario he closes for himself all avenues of escape.
>
> (pp. xviii–xix)

One of the hallmarks of shame is how automatically it leads to doubts about one's essential goodness as a human being. These self-doubts wreak havoc insidiously on one's confidence to make decisions, resulting then in the need to search out and depend on absolute moral principles and/or the authority of others to guide one's life. Without an external authority to which to adhere, and without access to the guidepost of one's own desires and values, such individuals often feel disoriented as to how to live.

For example, individuals escape the freedom of their decision-making by constructing "objective" rules to obey. Most typically, we stop at red lights without thinking about it because there is a rule or law that must be obeyed. In our minds, there is no freedom and no choice but to stop. Yet we can go through a red light any time we choose, though of course there are a variety of consequences that could ensue. Nothing might happen, or we could get into an accident, or we could get stopped by the police. In a similar sense, there are no "absolute" rules in life; there are just choices and the consequences that follow from those choices. A sense of responsibility derives from the freedom to make choices often between trade-offs of two imperfect alternatives and accepting the consequences of those decisions.

Sometimes, however, it is easier for patients to take refuge in the moralisms of self-shaming authority and continue to blame themselves for their problems because then there is an endless potentiality of hope to "make themselves better" rather than to struggle with the freedom of making pivotal real-life choices between imperfect trade-offs. For example, an unhappily married individual who is having an extramarital love affair may struggle with the question of whether to remain in an unhappy marriage and "intact" family *but* thereby lose a once in a lifetime chance of romantic love, *or* to move toward that love *but* then lose one's children and intact family. Such a patient may be more than happy to grab on to any interpretation of her own pathology in order to defend against the disturbing implications of an actual either/or choice that would emerge out of acknowledging her life dilemma.

Much of what makes holding on to one's self-enclosure so hypnotically entrancing is the anticipatory fear of change and its consequent confrontation with the 20/20 hindsight of self-punishing regret for not having moved earlier. Kierkegaard (1849) puts the fear of letting go of who one has always been this way:

> A person of this kind infinitely fears any inconsistency, for he has an infinite conception of what the consequence can be: that he can be torn out of the totality in which he has his life. The slightest inconsistency is an enormous loss, for it means that he loses that consistency.

> (p. 133)

Elsewhere (Shabad, 1987, 2001), I have written that the maintenance of one's symptomatology becomes a way of warding off the anticipatory fear of change and consequent pain of intense regret for missed opportunities.

One's maintenance of self-sameness becomes a way of justifying to oneself why one never had any other choice but to be who one has always been. It is not hard to see how the loyalty to one's prior being and powerful need to justify the road that one has taken can eventually become its own prison of despairing fatalism. For someone like Sarah, holding on to the certainty of an image of a self she had been for a very long time had become its own guiding authority to obediently follow, but one that has also kept her locked in a prison of despair.

What, then, can we use as an authority to live by? Many individuals use compliance with "rules and shoulds" as derived from conventional moral norms to make decisions. Here though, I would like to return to the idea I proposed in the Introduction to this book of using the projected image of our selves on our death bed as a mirror to each moment of how to best live our one and only life. I have referred to this deathbed image and mirror as our conscience, as our internal authority to live by. This conscience has nothing to do with shoulds, but is only derived from our short-term and long-term desires. If we lived according to our wants, we would still want to love the people that we love and treat them well. We would also not have much to do with people we don't like. If one of those people happens to be in our extended family who we see on holidays, we would know that we don't like him but realize also that we have a long-term desire (not a should) to remain as an accepted member of the extended family so we would have to cope with our dislike.

Looked at in this way, for example, a genuine gift to another person is not done out of obligation, but because we are following the dictates of our conscience, within which our social desires are embedded. As Derrida (1995) points out, the true gift is not at all transactional and does not expect any reciprocity from the other.

## Breaking the Spell: Communication and Awakening the Relationship with One's Own Mind

In describing Sarah's loyalty to her prior suffering and holding on to her symptomatology, I am making an assumption that the chronicity of her dynamic of self-shaming and self-pity does not perpetuate itself in an isolated compartment of her mind. I am assuming instead that she has an intentional, if not conscious, relationship to her own psyche that has its own purposes and reasons. Yet because that intentionality with regard to her own mind has always lay dormant, she feels helpless and fatalistic in relation to her enclosed dynamic of victimizing herself and feeling like the victim of her self-victimization. This lack of a felt relationship with her self-enclosed introjection of self-shaming and self-pity has led to a chronic sense of help-lessness of being able to do anything to ameliorate her own suffering. An essential part of Sarah's treatment has thus been to awaken her sense of agency in relation to herself.

In emphasizing an individual's relationship to her own mind, I have been greatly influenced by Kierkegaard's (1849) seemingly contorted, but vitally complex, definition of a self: "The self is a relation which relates to itself, or that in the relation which is relating to itself..." (p. 9). He then contin-ues: "Such a derived established relation, is the human self, which relates to itself, a relation which relates to itself, and in relating to itself relates to something else" (p. 10). The last phrase in this quote, "in relating to itself relates to something else," shows the extent to which a person's relation-ship with the contents of her own mind is a conduit between her mind and the outside world. For Kierkegaard, the "something else" ideally was each human being's relationship to God. Yet perhaps we can also see the "some-thing else" in the world as an individual's relationship to a therapist.

When a person tells a therapist of her shame or despair or paralyzing anxiety, she is revealing that she is not only mired within the confines of her feeling state, but that she also has an awareness of her distressed feeling state, and through that awareness she also has a relationship with the feeling state about which she is reporting. For many patients, the potential sense of agency in this relationship with one's own mind not at all conscious, which is probably why so many patients feel hopelessly entrapped within the introjective cycle of self-shaming and feeling victimized by their own shame. Frequently, the experience of agentic intentionality has become folded into the tyranny of self-shaming.

There is a great therapeutic value in awakening a patient's awareness and relationship with her own mind as the agent of active intentionality. Given how influenced one's relationship with oneself is by its simultaneous relationship to "something else," as Kierkegaard puts it, the therapist's way of being with the patient is of enormous importance in how a patient will subsequently relate to herself. If we believe that it is not only of great ben-efit to raise the consciousness of the patient's "observing ego," but also for the patient to learn how to intervene in that mind when bullying is occur-ring, then we, too, as therapists have to become active participants in our relationship with what our patients bring in to us. The therapist's respectful attitude of recognizing that the patient is always in relationship to her own injuries, sufferings, and actions as a human agent is necessary to any eventual self-healing capacity of the patient learning to live with her own mind.

The analogy that comes to mind for the uses of this relationship in treatment occurs if we were to walk out on the street and see somebody beating up a homeless person. Virtually each one of us would be aghast at the spectacle in front of us and waste no time in intervening. Yet unlike this active intervention in stopping the bullying of the homeless person, many patients who come for treatment just watch as the chronic bullying of self-shaming goes on in their own minds. Constructing an observing ego that only watches what is going on in one's own mind then is not enough: there are too many examples throughout history in which the perpetration of violent acts was permitted because "mere" observers did not intervene. In this sense, the therapist has to model a way for the victim inside to talk back, to protest, to rebel, to challenge the faceless self-shaming voice to come out of hiding and show its face. In this sense, we are speaking about promoting a "self-participating ego" instead of an observing ego. The therapist's use of the therapeutic relationship to awaken the patient's awareness and active relationship with her own dynamic of self-shaming can be used to promote a sense of agency and facilitate self-healing.

If we further remember that everything having to do with one's mind is a continually evolving process, then that means this relationship with oneself is also always being renewed and is renewable into the indefinite future. This view of the patient's mind as malleably renewable rather than rigidly static can lend an optimism to both the therapist and patient that which was always true has the potentiality to change.

Many patients come to treatment because they either feel very depressed or anxious or make plans and don't follow through with them. They feel helpless and hopeless about things getting better, often because different parts of their mind remain compartmentalized and incommunicado. In order to help facilitate the patient's sense of agentic freedom and become more responsible for her own decisions, it is of crucial importance first and foremost to open all lines of communication. Open dialogical communication between therapist and patient provides a model that facilitates greater intrapsychic communication between parts of the patient that normally remain compartmentalized and incommunicado. What often keeps these compartmentalized parts of the mind split off from each other is the process of self-shaming. Direct, straightforward communication expressed with tact is especially important, because the inchoate, general quality of shame thrives in the dark shadows of what is covered up.

Instead of prioritizing self-observation, understanding, and insight, I have come to appreciate the importance of "seizing the vital moment," of valuing the ongoing therapeutic experience of each evolving moment, especially as grounded in my relationship with the patient. As a therapist, I become a participatory witness to the patient's life experience. I attempt to model through my own spontaneous active participation and implicit valuing of a self-accepting self-awareness in dialogue with the patient that one need not be afraid of making mistakes because of incurring shame. It is better to jump in and to make mistakes of commission in living life than incur the unforgiving misgivings of avoiding the living of one's life in order to not make mistakes. Self-awareness is grounded only when it is based on a body of actual experience. Symington (1983) thus emphasizes that the analyst's inner act of freedom causes a therapeutic shift in the patient.

It is important, for therapists not to assume so much fragility in their patients that they can barely talk to them for fear that they will shame them and be responsible for their fragmentation. Through the influence of my own upbringing and my own clinical experience, I have become a firm believer in Freud's talking cure. As therapists, we have the responsibility not to be in such awe of the prior sufferings and shames of patients that we don't even help them put those sufferings into words. I am much more concerned about leaving patients alone in the enclosed isolation of the shames that they dare not speak. The intimidating spell of shame thrives in the unspeakable darkness of mystification.

If the therapist is too fearful of speaking straightforwardly to patients because of an anticipated fragility, the therapist risks leaving the patient isolated in a self-enclosed prison of self-shaming and self-pity. If we as therapists don't speak truthfully to patients, who else in their lives will? In this view, I have a responsibility to respect patients sufficiently to speak honestly with them.

When a patient complains of feeling "overwhelmed," I immediately ask what she means by overwhelmed, to elaborate on her internal experience. If a patient speaks too much in global terms or generalizations, or I don't really grasp what the patient is referring to, I immediately will ask her to be more specific.

Instead of colluding with a patient's attempt to undo or erase actions of which she is ashamed, I often give those actions the benefit of the doubt by applying an affirming ethic of inquiry toward understanding the motives for why one did what one did. For example, if a person is determined to remain on a diet and then shames herself for eating a piece of cake, I will support the good reasons for eating the piece of cake so that they are included in the psyche. This repeated application of a curiosity, inquiry, and affirming ethic of understanding gradually can supplant the patient's repetitive self-shaming that reflects the enclosed isolation of her mind.

My primary therapeutic aim is to facilitate increased intrapsychic communication and replace self-shaming with self-answerability that is informed by an ethic of curiosity, inquiry, and understanding. In fearlessly conveying this ethic, the therapist's relationship with the patient models a pathway by which the patient also does not merely only observe her mind, but also can actively participate in its evolving alchemical makeup. The therapist's active participation in speaking with the patient *without blaming* provides a model for the patient's own active participation in altering the sado-masochistic structure of her internal life and replacing it with an answerability to herself for her actions.

In highlighting the importance of understanding rather than shaming oneself for one's undesirable thoughts, feelings, or actions, I am ultimately attempting to illuminate a responsibility of answerability we all have in relationship to the internal authority of our own conscience. As soon as we are conscious of our depression or anxiety or misgivings about our behavior, we have a relationship with the focus of our consciousness. Within that relationship, we are responsible for our own self-inquiry: "What am I depressed about?" "What am I anxious about more specifically?" Whereas shame closes down self-inquiry, curiosity opens up an internal space to self-understanding.

I have noticed that the opportunity to intervene in this way often occurs when patients come in after a wild weekend and berate themselves in hindsight for what they did over the weekend. For example, one young woman, Pam, repeatedly would go to bars over the weekend, get very drunk, and then have sex with a random man, after which she would feel very cheap and very embarrassed. Rather than in any way colluding with her self-blame that always occured in hindsight, I inquired whether she was getting drunk so she could get away with having sex that otherwise would be morally impermissible for her if she had known what she was doing. I also asked what specifically she was thinking and feeling on the way to the bar and before she began drinking. Who was she before picking up a guy and having sex?

Another example: On more than one Monday morning, John came to therapy and complained about how he was an idiot for drinking way too much on Saturday night. I responded that his "Monday morning quarterbacking" is similar to looking at the answer key after taking an exam and then getting angry at himself for not knowing the answers beforehand. I then asked John whether he knew what he was doing in the moment before he had his first drink on Saturday night and whether he recognized the danger of his binge drinking predilections. I said very directly to John that blaming himself after his hangover waa much easier than holding his feet to the fire of answerability in the moment of decision prior to having his first drink.

When we actually went back in time to what he was feeling before the first drink, he talked about the peer pressure of drinking and not wanting to feel like a "party pooper." At certain times, we might explore what underlies his fear of not drinking and keeping up with the fun his friends were having. There are other times, however, when I directly juxtaposed the choice of trade-offs between enduring the suffering of his hangover on Sunday and even on Monday morning or not drinking excessively Saturday night and not conforming to his friends.

When Sarah initially entered treatment with me, it was evident that she had not been in the habit of interacting with her own mind. She presented her distressing symptoms to me, then fell silent, as she waited for me to save her from herself. So, at first, I actively participated in helping Sarah return to the non-communicative and desolate bleakness of her childhood home that she experienced in the immediate aftermath of her father's motorcycle accident. That atmosphere had evolved into the melancholic backdrop of Sarah's experience as an adult.

Sarah and I also reconstructed how as a child, she had obediently followed her mother's guiding authority, always with the trust that she was of primary importance in her mother's eyes. That trust was ruptured after her mother divorced her father, remarried another man, and then sided with the new husband against Sarah, all of which left a bitter aftertaste in her.

However, in addition to our joint reconstruction of Sarah's childhood, we also spent time speaking very specifically about her constant critiques of herself for "not being perfect." Who, I asked, was this mysterious voice scolding her for not being perfect? How did this voice acquire so much power over the rule of her mind? Could she (as my five-year-old son once asked me) defiantly question this tyrannical voice: "Who made you the boss?"

Sarah seemed both taken aback and bemused by these questions, but they achieved their purpose of jump-starting Sarah's inquiry into her own mind's workings. Lest she become concerned that she had to be a "perfect" patient and learn to become aware of and interact with her own mind within an urgent timeframe for me, I reassured her that her awakening to a relationship with her own self-shaming was new to her, and I had no expectation of a time frame of her mastering autonomous self-healing. I would be here available to her for as long as she needed.

Sarah has gradually opened up to the possibility of interacting with her own mind, and she has begun to weaken the hold that shame and the urgency to be perfect has had on her mind. Most importantly, she no longer feels a despairing fatalism of helplessness in relation to what occurs within her own mind. Her felt sense of I CAN'T has evolved more often into a sense of agency and the choice of I WON'T or I WILL. Over the past couple of years, Sarah has become less vicious with herself. She still can be given to moods of melancholy, but she has been able to view herself much more through a prism of understanding rather than shame.

Not surprisingly, as this evolution has occurred, she has also been able, when needed, to gain access much more to her anger rather than reflexively turn that anger into shame. Sarah has become stronger in holding her own in the relationship with her boyfriend. She became more conscious of him taking so long to leave his wife and more overtly annoyed at him. She stopped immediately protecting him and immediately taking on the burden of responsibility for everything that went wrong in their relationship. Indeed, Sarah broke off the relationship four months prior to this writing.

## The Paradoxes of Emotional Life: Self-Acceptance and Self-Knowledge

When we examine the polarized dynamic between a person's conscious compliance with life plans he "should" follow and the rebellious inertia of non-compliantly following through with those plans, it becomes clear that this individual has disavowed a forbidden desire that then is indulged through his inaction. It may seem like a strange thing that human beings idealize and yearn to reintegrate (often through disavowed actions) those aspects of themselves from which they have dissociated and exclude from the governance of their lives. In my view, learning the basic tenets of human psychology entails becoming closely acquainted with such paradoxical principles of emotional life on their own nonlinear and non-rational terms.

In my experience, the metaphors that I consider most relevant to emotional life, growth, and living a good life have to do with inclusion and exclusion, both interpersonally and intrapsychically. The inclusion/exclusion metaphors are fundamental precisely because they are intertwined with the metaphors of letting go and holding on, which are so fundamental to psychic growth. More specifically, when we include and accept ourselves, we more readily let go of who we had been in the past and give ourselves over generously to new experiences and new people. On the other hand, when we exclude something significant about ourselves or our prior experiences, we hold on and become stuck on what was excluded.

When one has been excluded from human relationships, for example, one tends to fetishize the self that was excluded by means of a self-preoccupied narcissism. Within this narcissistically enclosed relationship with oneself, one appropriates the sense of relational exclusion through the process of introjection by now shaming oneself after being excluded by others. What has been excluded by others now becomes the target of a repetitive self-exclusion as well. Yet paradoxically, the excluded, dissociated aspect of oneself inevitably and repeatedly ambushes us when we least expect through symptoms and unwanted actions, as if in silent protest to make sure the dignity of its excluded voice be included in the governance of one's life as well. Until these shamed and excluded aspects of the self are included, one holds on indefinitely.

On the other hand, when one feels received and included by others, it is also easier to include one's own inner life of spontaneous desire. That self-acceptance provides a generosity to let go of oneself to the unpredictable otherness of transitions and growth into the future. The intertwining metaphors of inclusion and exclusion are thus centrally implicated in developmental growth, the generosity of letting go so intrinsic to the mourning process, and the movement of therapeutic action.

I emphasize these contrasting pairs of metaphors, inclusion/letting go and exclusion/holding on, because I wonder to what extent Freud genuinely included the passions as a primary vehicle within the ideology of psychoanalysis. When Freud (1923) declares "Where the id is, the I (Ich) will be,"how much of the id is left intact? A key question for psychoanalytic clinicians to pose to themselves in understanding their own therapeutic ideology and values is to what extent do we believe in helping patients gain an enlightened rationality and mastery over the passions? Or to what extent do we believe that the passions and desires of our patients should remain intact as a dynamic propellant and guide to their lives?

After all, Freud placed a great faith in the Enlightenment ideals of rational self-knowledge as a means of civilizing the inherent selfishness of the patient's animalistic drives. When Nietzsche (1882) pronounced God to be dead, it became relatively easy for the analyst, with the aid of the patient's idealizing transference love, to slip into the residual vacuum by becoming a secular deity not just as one "who is supposed to know" (Lacan, 1964, p. 232), but as one who actually does know. As dispassionate observer and neutral interpreter of the patient's unconscious, the analyst modeled for the patient how she, too, can acquire the power of self-knowledge so that she can master her runaway impulses.

Yet Freud (1933) himself hints that it is not possible to use rationality to rise above the subjectivity of one's inner passions when he declares of the id: "No alteration in its mental contents is produced by the passage of time" (p.73). What I believe Freud means here is that we cannot want something different than what we want through any self-moralizing propaganda. We are left only with the choice of accepting what we desire and facing our fundamental wants directly, and perhaps in doing so, we can modify the urgent intensity of those desires. Winnicott (1949b) too, suggest that a cerebral braininess that aspires to objectivity and rationality is not a neutral ideal but a defensive dissociation from an impinged upon body. This detachment from emotion is evident in the abstract jargon of psychoanalytic discourse, which is far removed from the flesh-and-blood experiences of people's lives. I don't think that many analysts ask their patients how their "affects" are today. Or for that matter, how did your "object relations" do this week? If we analysts don't talk to patients in this way, then why do we continue to use such jargon with each other, even though it is detached from the emotionality of human experiences?

As spiritual animals who are driven both by our animal passions and passion for transcendence, I would like also to emphasize that emotional logic does not adhere to any rational or conventional moral principles. In distilling what I consider to be the most valuable insights of Freud, it is wise for us to agree with Freud that emotional logic is inevitably conflictual, counterintuitive, and paradoxical. We fear the shadows of our wishes and then project those shadows into the world from which we retreat in anxiety and dread. Many of these fears of our wishes often manifest themselves in such counterintuitive ways that they may elude the interpretive grasp of many therapists.

For example, a patient who has great trepidation about failing the bar exam may be fearful of her own seemingly counterintuitive wish to fail for the first time in her life. It is only after failing she can give herself the opportunity to receive the unconditional love she never received. In similar ways, the fear of heights may be viewed as a fear of one's own counterintuitive temptation to jump, or the fear of losing a loved one to a third person may sometimes reflect what seems like a self-defeating temptation to give one's loved one away. Yet all of these seemingly counterintuitive wishes probably all have elusive, but good emotional reasons underlying the temptation.

It would be helpful if all of us, not just the clinicians among us, if we learned how to be more attuned to and accepting of the strange amalgam of desires and fears residing within us. Why do we teach our children to prepare for career and work, to learn math and science and grammar, but not how to become aware of themselves while navigating through the hazardous shoals of their emotions, relationships, and the fragility of love and loss so basic to all of our lives?

It is clear that psychoanalysis has used the ideals of rationalism, objectivity, and neutrality as a means of masking a hermeneutics of suspicion (Ricoeur, 1970) regarding the primitive emotionality and unconscious actions rooted in a body from which one is alienated. The very process of analyzing or destroying the manifest integrity of what a person presents to us up front in favor of discerning latent underlying motives reflects an aggression toward the object of one's analytic focus. When we don't like what other people do or don't agree with their opinions, rather than go to war with them, analysts use the more intellectualized combat of uncovering the various unknown determinants that led to the behaviors they deem unacceptable. Through the enlightening power of consciousness, we use language to name, and thus acquire mastery over, the faceless antagonist of the unconscious before the otherness of the unconscious "hurts" us. In this sense, psychoanalysis used the counterphobic magic of naming and conquering persecutory anxieties of being ambushed by the unpredictable and untrustworthy unconscious.

In fact, I, too, have noticed this sublimation of aggression at the root of my own passionate interest and curiosity in posing the core question of psychoanalysis: "Why do people do what they do?" When I was very young, my mother frequently would begin crying when she spoke about her father's death at the Nazi extermination camp Auschwitz. At the time I wondered to myself: "Who were these evil Nazis that hurt my mother?" I channeled my outrage and wrath into an active curiosity to understand the underpinnings of the Nazi-Jewish relationship. What was it about the Jews that the Nazis hated so much? How did the conscience of Nazis evaporate so quickly?

I believe my motivation to become a psychoanalyst has been influenced by this sublimation of aggression into the idealistic aim of subjecting the nature of evil to my ethic of curiosity, inquiry, and understanding. I took the lessons my mother taught me about talking through and facing down the witch I dreamt of very seriously. Perhaps at times, I have taken these lessons too far. Early in my career, I was asked in a job interview with which three people in history would I like to have dinner. One of the three I chose was Hitler; I did not get the job.

I have introduced the anecdotal flesh of my own childhood here because I know how much it informed my clinical values and theory, not to mention a general philosophy of life. When psychoanalytic teachers and supervisors impart their knowledge of analytic theory and clinical expertise to their analytic trainees, we must ask what values, both implicit and explicit, are being taught and modeled at the same time.

Buechler (2004) has critiqued psychoanalysis for its excessive intellectualism at the cost of leaving out one's life experience as a source from which to learn about oneself as an analyst. She instead describes the importance of fleshing out the clinical values that have emerged from what one has learned from one's experiences. Maroda (2021) also has emphasized how critical it is for psychoanalysts to be more honest about how their own early experiences have shaped their countertransference vulnerabilities in treatment.

As psychoanalysts, we often are quite fluent with the theories into which we were indoctrinated during our training, but we don't always understand the personal countertransference investment we have in holding to the clinical values and ideals on which those theories are based. Our countertransferences of ideology and value are, I would argue, fundamentally non-rational choices that are reflective of our personal journeys of suffering, despair, and the pursuit of personal redemption. Even if we would wish to escape from ourselves into the secure certainties of agreed-upon theory, our concrete interactions with patients are so fraught with subjectivity, emotion, and value that we must inevitably fall back on the wisdom gained from our own experiences of suffering and healing as our primary instrument.

To the extent that we therapists can affirm our passions and view our experiences of disillusionment and renewed hope as humbly learned sources of potential wisdom rather than as shames to be disowned, our ethical ideals and theories become embodied articulations of the experiences through which we have lived. At other times, however, when we have not been able to actualize redeeming hopes for ourselves, we may rely too much on the idealization of theory and jargon to defensively cover up painful experiences of disillusionment and the introjected shame residue of those disillusionments. Whenever we are unaware of the underlying bases of the emotions or values or particular political tint we bring to bear on the facts of life, we pretend that external reality itself can be split off and abstracted out from the flow of our subjective lives. In so doing, we run the risk of creating a split between the passionately embodied basis of our existence and the abstract disembodied theories that describe those experiences, which themselves are an intellectualized transformation of that emotionality; we just don't know why or how.

Our minds are not neutral, information-processing machines that are detached from what we feel when we discover something new about ourselves. The process by which analytic patients come to know themselves is not conducted in an emotional vacuum devoid of value and meaning. Each new insight is flavored with an emotional valence that is transformed immediately into a moral self-evaluation of its being good or bad, such that all self-understanding may be viewed, to a greater or lesser extent, on a continuum ranging from self-acceptance to self-condemnation.

In a certain sense, the only way one can indeed know oneself is by first accepting oneself. Given the fundamentally phobic, avoidant quality of shame, one may immediately disavow a new discovery about oneself if it is viewed through the prism of shame and self-contempt. In this sense, self-contempt leads to the dissociation of not knowing oneself (excluding what is condemned by consciousness). Of course, rather than any permanent eradication of the unwanted part of oneself, this attempt at self-exclusion only results in holding on tenaciously to what has been excluded. Again, we just don't know how or why.

## Participatory Witnessing: Mourning and Bringing De-Realized Phantoms Back to Life

A primary aspect of what makes a trauma traumatic is a person's inability in integrating or including the traumatic experience as one's embodied lived experience. In the process of dissociating from embodied traumatic experience, the individual attempts to spit our or exclude what she could not tolerate living though. In so doing, she becomes fixated on what cannot be metabolized emotionally.

The traumatized individual becomes stuck specifically on the disruption between what one's expectant hopes of a relationship or of life and the actual traumatic experience that occurred instead. Since this fissure in one's experience is not integrated, a split takes place between consciously acknowledging the traumatic experience and attempting to adapt to the disillusioning bitterness of its aftermath, while at the same time tenaciously holding out fantasied hope, often unconsciously, for the restoration of a new beginning and a parallel trauma-less life that never occurred. From a temporal viewpoint, this split entails a continual attempt through the self-erasure of shame to undo one's traumatic experience and restore the wished-for, idealized pre-traumatic state of being. Yet since this annulment of one's traumatic experience is impossible, the individual becomes stuck chronically attempting to restore a pre-traumatic innocence that cannot be restored. The psychoanalytic view of fixations and developmental arrests most often views a person's sense of stuckness from this developmental point of view.

Yet a person can also become fixated relationally. Elsewhere (Shabad, 1989, 2001), I have described the cumulative developmental trauma of a psychic loss of a physically present parent, in which a child's eternal hope for the materialization of a wished-for parent is continually frustrated by the all-too-real reappearances of a frustrating actual parent. Even though the child, and then the adult, consciously acknowledges/resigns herself to the actual parent, this individual has never relinquished the hope that the parent will transform into the wished-for figure. The stuckness of relational fixation derives from the unmourned, relentless wish to change the frustrating actuality of a parent (and eventually other individuals) into the parent one would have wished-for. Frequently, in adulthood, these relational fixations become transferred from parental figures to other significant figures like spouses.

Through the compulsion of repeatedly attempting to change the unbudging wall of another person's reality into who we want the other to be, we become stuck in the attempts to heal the traumatic fissure of the past, often to self-injurious, masochistic effect. I suspect that the relentless steadfastness of retaining one's hopes for a wished-for parent or spouse is a means of protecting the relationship from the rage that would emerge if one indeed were to acknowledge the actuality of the frustrating other individual.

Since in the dissociative and self-shaming aftermath of trauma, this person takes on the omnipotent burden of causing her own traumatic experience and closes down access to her disillusioned wishes, this person never engages the mourning work of modifying the omnipotence of magical thinking, of disentangling her desires from their automatic links to fantasied gratifications.

Such incomplete mourning, in which wishes are not disentangled from their fulfillment, may be glimpsed in the following exchange: Therapist: "Would you like your father to say he loves you?" Patient: "That will never happen." The patient's response is something of a non sequitur, in that the therapist does not ask *what will* happen in the future, but what the patient *wishes to happen*. This relatively commonplace clinical example reveals how the patient automatically connects the mention of the wish to the actual fulfillment of the wish, as if she could not imagine one without reference to the other.

Many individuals thus fear acting immediately on what they think or say because, in their minds, affirming or acknowledging a desire's right to exist or have its say means automatically doing something about it. Since such persons have not modified their omnipotence sufficiently to draw a boundary between the morality of feeling, thinking, and imagining and a more public life of action, they rule their inner life with an iron hand of shame and exclude the impermissible. Ironically, however, it is precisely this exclusion from the governance of our lives that enables the omnipotence of unmourned desires and the unbounded connection to their fantasied gratifications to wreak inhibiting havoc on our lives through the circularity of the compulsion to repeat.

The process of being responsible for ourselves necessarily means listening to and accepting the cacophony of diverse voices within—all the thoughts, feelings, and desires clamoring for attention and inclusion in the governance of our lives. Listening to and affirming the dignity of each voice does not at all mean we will act on what we feel. I can take heed and validate my wish to eat a piece of chocolate cake without indulging that wish in action. Indeed, I have less urgency to act on that desire if I let my affirmation of my wish breathe life within the governance of my inner life.

If we view mourning as a process whose aim is to be relatively free from the compulsion to repeat the past, then we see how the dissociative defenses that arise in the wake of trauma work against mourning. When hopes are disillusioned or positive experiences turn sour, we dissociate from the good. This dissociative exclusion of the good often occurs because it is the good especially that is too painful to face in its disillusioning, bitter aftermath. These dissociative defenses then have a derealizing effect on the memory of the good, such that we now continually doubt whether the good and meaningful aspects of a relationship that no longer exists actually occurred or whether we made the whole thing up like a dream. As a result, we are compelled to return again and again to the derealized actuality that we doubt in order to once again restore the breath of realized life to what was actually experienced.

What then does facilitate a patient's process of mourning and the integration of derealized experiences of lonely suffering? The credibility of the therapist as an empathic witness to a patient's suffering cannot be conveyed by words alone. In the patient's mind, it is too easy for the analyst to discharge her therapeutic task oh so correctly, to nod her head empathically, to make clarifying interpretations to show that she understands. She will go home that night and enjoy her family, her patient's tales of woe blending in with the other stories of the day that she left behind. To the patient who has huddled in self-enclosed isolation for too long while waiting for someone to retrieve her, words are insufficient to make up for the lonely times she has endured. It is too late for all talk and no action; the desolation of nonbeing has wormed its way too deeply into the blood.

Perhaps what inspires the generosity intrinsic to letting go more than anything else is the patient's trust that there is someone out there who cares enough to take heed, to catch receptive hold of her experiences of suffering if she lets go of them. When we speak of a therapeutic holding environment, we are speaking of a relationship that contains the patient's sense of meaningless isolation, one in which she feels she belongs to the therapist's heart, mind, and soul. The therapist's credibility as a witness who cares and invests her personhood in what she is hearing provides patients with the conviction that they are entrusting their experiences to an enduring posterity rather than to the oblivion of deaf ears.

Many years ago, I saw Charles, an acutely suicidal 40-year-old man, who was in despair because the beloved girlfriend with whom he had a 25-year-long extramarital love affair had become sick with cancer, at which point she decided to break off their relationship so she could retrench in her family. In his early sessions, Charles would walk in and before even sitting down, he would exclaim: "I don't care! I don't care! I just don't care anymore." He would then launch into repetitive tirades, in which he would disavow his girlfriend's significance to him, punctuated only rarely by nostalgic, dream-like reminiscences of better times they had shared together. However, there was some quality in these brief instances of remembered intimacy that prompted me to believe that in his bitterness, Charles had rewritten history and had deprived himself of a preciously meaningful memory from himself.

Sensing that he was killing off experiences of passionate love once shared with his girlfriend, I said that no matter what had happened since, no one could take away the genuine intimacies he had exchanged with her at one time. They were not just a dream he had, but a reality that had existed and would always exist, and one to which I could now bear witness because of his communicating it to me. His obsessional rage subsided immediately and gave way to bittersweet tears, as he declared rather proudly: "We did have something pretty good, didn't we?"

Mourning is not only a matter of working through trauma and all the nasty things our parents did to us, but to reidentify the abandoned hopes for a wished-for parent that we once had or to elaborate on the pre-traumatic life that we once genuinely enjoyed before being traumatized. It is those disillusioned and excluded, but relentless hopes for the restoration of the good that holds us hostage in our lives.

Mourning need not, indeed cannot, entail a person renouncing unrealistic desires. On the contrary, mourning is a paradoxical process in which a person must affirm precisely those orphaned, disowned desires that are most unrealistic and impossible to fulfill in order to relinquish the persistent demand that they be fulfilled. By validating those desires, we remove them from a netherworld of derealized limbo and breathe into them a dignity of having an inclusive life within.

Mourning thus necessitates the inclusive acceptance of all our thoughts, feelings, wishes, and imaginings within, regardless of whether they will ever come true. Elsewhere (Shabad, 2001), I have suggested that we view a person's inner life of diverse voices metaphorically as an extended family. All the wayward children and relatives who had been disowned and evicted must be welcomed back into the lifeblood of the family. It is especially the black-sheep children—one's disillusioned desires—who never found a niche in the real world that must be welcomed back into the family.

It is only after genuinely becoming receptive to and affirming one's own disillusioned, shamed desires for what could have been or should have been that we can learn to relinquish the omnipotence of necessarily being responsible for making those wishes come true. In a sense, the inclusion of one's wishes facilitates a paradoxical sense of generosity, in which we give away or let go of our stranglehold on what had been disavowed.

The process of mourning one's limitations as a human being, of de-linking the affirmation of one's wishes to change a frustratingly real parent into a fantasied ideal parent from the necessity that those wishes actually be realized, also modifies the omnipotent burden of responsibility for all that goes on from both ends in a relationship with other individuals. The disentanglement of our desires from the necessity that those desires come true also delineates boundaries between where the controlling reach of one's individuality ends and the world of otherness begins.

Each of us is responsible for how we express ourselves to the world in words and in actions. In a relationship with another person, we are responsible to our own conscience for our expressive end of the relationship, including demonstrating empathy and respect for the other person, but we are not omnipotently responsible how our expressions are received by the other person.

Perhaps not surprisingly, the mourning process of helping a patient illuminate, accept, and relinquish the omnipotent responsibility for ensuring the perfectibility of impossible-to-fulfill hopes coming true often leads to a sense of relief rather than great suffering and a sense of loss. Letting reality be reality and accepting one's limitations as an individual also allows us more readily to accept death, suffering, and the unpredictability of our futures without transforming those limitations into the shame of our fault or fatal flaw. Nietzsche's (1882) concept of *amor fati*, or love of one's fate, challenges us all to embrace and not just resign ourselves to the actuality of one's entire existence.

## Seizing the Moment: Overcoming Anticipatory Dread and Letting the Future Be the Future

Much of what we do through the talking cure of psychoanalytic psychotherapy is to help patients speak through and gain insight into their varied experiences of depression, anxiety, regret, and problems in human relationships. During this process, therapists cannot and should not pressure any of their patients to change according to their specifications, of how and when they grow and change, or indeed, whether they grow or change at all. Those choices to act or not to act, to move or not to move, ultimately are up to our patients as agents of their own lives.

One of the most impactful lessons I have learned in my life is that there is a radical discontinuity between the anxious anticipation of what one predicts about the future and the way the future actually unfolds in its specificity. No matter how much we think we know what will happen in the future, we will always be wrong in exactly how life unwinds itself.

Much anticipatory dread derives from transposing dissociated, unmetabolized experiences of trauma and disillusionment from the past onto the blank canvas of a yet-to-be-lived future. Our shames often paralyze our passionate resolve to move toward a future that we anticipate with dread, so we retreat to the apparent sanctuary of what is familiar only to discover that our inertia leaves us with a despairing emptiness.

Here it is not our omnipotence per se, but our omniscient need to know more than we can know, to control a fundamentally unpredictable future in order not to be taken by surprise by trauma again, that entraps us in a stultified life. Through the filter of omniscience, there is a relationship between who we are in the present and a *fantasy* of an often threatening, dangerous future for which we anxiously brace in our dread or from which we recoil. It is ironic though that the actuality of an unfolding life would often be a welcome awakening from the nightmares that we often project into the future, if only we could keep forging ahead.

If one were to think of the changes needed to move courageously into the future as analogous to jumping into a cold swimming pool, then thinking, speaking, and forever preparing to move toward the feared future are analogous to repeatedly walking around the pool indefinitely in order to summon the courage to take the plunge. This individual continues not to dive because his mind is preoccupied with fantasies of how cold the water is. Yet if he were finally able to take the plunge, he would realize that as he is in the process of diving in, he is no longer imagining the coldness of the water as a concept or fantasy because he is now directly bracing for its actual impact. Once in the water, he is again not thinking about the cold water ahead of time, but he is actually in the cold water and figuring out how to move and stay warm. The anticipatory dread of a fantasied cold water is no longer relevant, because he now is on to the next moment of getting used to the coldness.

There is a radical discontinuity between endlessly circling around the pool and finally leaping into its bracingly cold waters that cannot be bridged by rationality. Perhaps what enables us to finally take the courageous "leap of faith" (to appropriate a phrase of Kierkegaard's) of letting go of the safe periphery around the pool (of who one is now) into the "stranger" or otherness of the cold pool itself (who one could be differently in the future) is a generosity that is central to the mourning process.

The therapist's ability to bear witness and validate the actuality of a patient's traumatic experience helps modify omniscience by diluting the urgency of the patient's mandate to continually bring forward action proof of his traumatic experience through the nonverbal communications of his symptomatology. Here, mourning occurs by specifically disentangling the trauma that already occurred from its projection into the future. In modifying the urgent need to predict and to control the future, one gains a relief in the humility of accepting one's limitations of all-knowingness. In this sense, we can join with Camus (1951) in the epigraph to this chapter in emphasizing the importance of generously surrendering to the present. Mourning involves the generosity of learning to be present in the current moment and relinquishing an anxious and tenacious control over one's future life. It entails a letting go, in which one lets life be life in its own unpredictable and unfolding ways.

It has only been relatively late in life that I have acquired the wisdom of humility in not getting so far ahead of where my body can take me and learning to live instead in the embodied present moment. As with much acquired wisdom, it was gained only at the price of missing out on precious life opportunities because of separation fears.

When I was an undergraduate student at my university, many of my classmates were seizing opportunities to do foreign exchange programs abroad and excitedly embarking on their adventures. In contrast, when I imagined traveling to Europe, I retreated immediately from the images I conjured up. I became intimidated by the idea that I would somehow get lost in the "wilds" of Europe, never to be heard from again. In my mind, I was going to be on an airplane that paradoxically would take off without me. It was as if there was a future without me inhabiting it. In retrospect, I most probably was transposing my traumatic experience of being left alone in Moscow at the age of 13 (see Introduction) onto a future where I would become anonymous and get lost in a sea of strangers.

As with much fear, I was paralyzed by this first intimidating image and never thought through how actually I would disappear. I did not realize I would be present in the embodied moment every step of the way on my trip, and I would know how to cope with what life brought me at that time. What I have learned is not to rush the future before it arrives here and now, to live life one step at a time, to seize the moment, and to have the confidence I will be able to cope with life when it gets here.

# References

Angyal, A. (1965). *Neurosis and treatment*. Viking.

Aristotle (332 BCE). *Nichomachean ethics*. (H. Tredenneck, Trans.). Penguin.

Aron, L. (1996). *A meeting of minds: Mutuality in psychoanalysis*. The Analytic Press.

Augustine of Hippo (397–400). *Confessions*. (R. S. Pine-Coffin, Trans.). Penguin.

Bachelard, G. (1932). *Intuition of the instant*. (E. Rizo-Patron, Trans.). Northwestern University Press.

Bakan, D. (1966). *The duality of human existence: An essay on psychology and religion*. Rand McNally.

Balint, M. (1968). *The basic fault*. Brunner Mazel.

Barfield, O. (1973). *The rediscovery of meaning and other essays*. Wesleyan University Press.

Baring, A., & Cornford, J. (1991). *The myth of the goddess*. Penguin.

Becker, E. (1964). The great historical convergence on the problem of alienation. In D. Liechty (Ed.), *The Ernest Becker reader* (pp. 95–105). University of Washington Press.

Becker, E. (1968). The second great step in human evolution. In D. Liechty (Ed.), *The Ernest Becker reader*. (pp. 140-144).University of Washington Press.

Becker, E. (1973). *The denial of death*. The Free Press.

Becker, E. (1975). *Escape from evil*. The Free Press.

Becker, E. (2005). *The Ernest Becker reader* (D. Liechty, Ed.). University of Washington Press.

Benjamin, J. (1988). *The bonds of love*. Pantheon.

Benjamin, J. (1995). *Like subjects, love objects*. Yale University Press.

Bergson, H. (1889). *Time and free will: An essay on the immediate data of consciousness*. Dover Publications.

Bergson, H. (1907). *Creative evolution*. Modern Library.

Bollas, C. (1987). *The shadow of the object*. Columbia University Press.

Boris, H. (1994). *Envy*. Jason Aronson.

Bowlby, J. (1975). *Attachment and loss (Vol 2): Separation, anxiety, and anger*. Hogarth Press.

Bromberg, P. M. (1998). *Standing in the spaces: Essays on clinical process, trauma, and dissociation*. The Analytic Press.

Broucek, F. (1991). *Shame and the self*. Guilford Press.

Brown, N. (1959). *Life against death*. Wesleyan University Press.

Buber, M. (1965). Guilt and guilt feelings. In M. Friedman & R. G. Smith (Trans.), *The knowledge of man* (pp. 111–138). Humanities Press International.

Buechler, S. (2004). *Clinical values: Emotions that guide psychoanalytic treatment*. The Analytic Press.

Camus, A. (1942). *The stranger*. (M. Ward, Trans.). Viking.

Camus, A. (1951). *The rebel*. (A. Bower, trans). Vintage International.

Camus, A. (1955). *The myth of Sisyphys and other essays*. (J. O'Brian, Trans.). Viking

Carlisle, C. (2006). *Kierkegaards's philosophy of becoming: Movements and positions*. State University Press of New York.

Carse, J. (1980). *Death and existence*. Wiley.

Cartwright, D. (1988). Schopenhauer's compassion and Nietzsche's pity. *Schopenhauer Jahrbuch, 69*, 557–567.

Cassirer, E. (1946). *Language and myth*. (S. Langer, Trans.). Dover Publications.

Cooper, S. (2010). *A disturbance in the field: Essays in transference-countertransference engagement*. Routledge.

Crastnopol, M. (2015). *Micro-trauma: A psychoanalytic understanding of cumulative psychic injury*. Routledge.

Critchley, S. (2015). *The problems with Levinas*. (A. Dianda, Ed.). Oxford University Press.

Dalton, D. (2009). *Longing for the other: Levinas and metaphysical desire*. Duquesne University Press.

Darwin, C. (1872). *Expression of the emotions in men and animals*. University of Chicago Press.

Deleuze, G. (1983). *Nietzsche and philosophy*. Columbia University Press.

Derrida, J. (1995). *The gift of death and literature in secret*. (D. Wills, Trans.). University of Chicago Press.

Derrida, J. (2000). *Of hospitality (cultural memory of the present)*. (R. Bowlby, Trans.). Stanford University Press.

Derrida, J. (2008). *The animal that therefore I am*. (D. Wells, Trans.). Fordham University Press.

Dewey, J. (1980). *The quest for certainty: A study of the relation of knowledge and action*. Capricorn Press.

Dickens, C. (1850). *David Copperfield*. Penguin Classics.

Dostoevsky, F. (1864). Notes from the underground. In D. Magarshack (Trans.), *Great short works of Fyodor Dostoevsky* (pp. 261–277). Harper Perennial.

Dostoevsky, F. (1880). *The grand inquisitor*. Continuum.

Douglas, M. (1966). *Purity and danger*. Routledge.

Drozek, R. (2015). The dignity in multiplicity: Human value as a foundational concept in relational thought. *Psychoanalytic Dialogues, 25*, 431–451.

Dupont, J. (Ed.) (1988). *The clinical diary of Sandor Ferenczi*. (M. Balint & N. Jackson, Trans.). Harvard University Press.

Eigen, M. (1981). The area of faith in Winnicott, Lacan and Bion. *International Journal of Psychoanalysis, 62*, 412–433.

Eliade, M. (1954). *The myth of the eternal return*. Princeton University Press.

Elias, N. (1939). *The civilizing process: Sociogenetic and psychogenetic investigations*. Blackwell Publishing.

Erikson, E. (1950). *Childhood and society*. Norton.

Erikson, E. (1964). *Insight and responsibility*. Norton.

Erikson, E. (1977). *Toys and reasons*. W. W. Norton.

Fairbairn, W. R. D. (1941). *An object-relations theory of the personality*. Basic Books.

Fairbairn, W. R. D. (1952). *Psychoanalytic studies of the personality*. Routledge.

Farber, L. (1966). *The ways of the will.* Basic Books.

Fenichel, O. (1945). *The psychoanalytic theory of neurosis.* W. W. Norton.

Fenichel, O. (1954). *The collected papers of Otto Fenichel: Second series.* (H. Fenichel & D. Rapaport, Eds.). W. W. Norton.

Ferenczi, S. (1909). Introjection and transference. In *First contributions to psychoanalysis* (pp. 35–93). No 45 of the *International Psychonalaytical Library.* Brunner-Mazel.

Ferenczi, S. (1932). *The clinical diary of Sandor Ferenczi.* (J. Dupont, Trans.). Harvard University Press.

Foss, M. (1949). *Death, sacrifice, and tragedy.* University of Nebraska Press.

Foster, G. (1965). Peasant society and the image of limited good. *American Anthropologist, 67,* 297–315.

Fraser, J. (1890). *The magic art and the evolution of kings.* Forgotten Books.

Freud, S. (1905a). Three essays on the theory of sexuality. In J. Strachey (Ed. & Trans.), *The standard edition of the complete psychological works of Sigmund Freud* (Vol. 7, pp. 125–145). Hogarth Press.

Freud, S. (1905b). On psychotherapy. In J. Strachey (Ed. & Trans.), *The standard edition of the complete psychological works of Sigmund Freud* (Vol. 7, pp. 257–268). Hogarth Press.

Freud, S. (1911). Formulations on the two principles of mental functioning. In J. Strachey (Ed. & Trans.), *The standard edition of the complete psychological works of Sigmund Freud* (Vol. 12, pp. 218–226). Hogarth Press.

Freud, S. (1912). The dynamics of transference. In J. Strachey (Ed. & Trans.), *The standard edition of the complete psychological works of Sigmund Freud* (Vol. 12, pp. 97–108). Hogarth Press.

Freud, S. (1913a). Formulations on the two principles of mental functioning. In J. Strachey (Ed. & Trans.), *The standard edition of the complete psychological works of Sigmund Freud* (Vol. 12, pp. 18–266). Hogarth Press.

Freud, S. (1913b). Totem and taboo. In J. Strachey (Ed. & Trans.), *The standard edition of the complete psychological works of Sigmund Freud* (Vol. 13, pp. 1–161). Hogarth Press.

Freud, S. (1914). Remembering, repeating and working through. In J. Strachey (Ed. & Trans.), *The standard edition of the complete psychological works of Sigmund Freud* (Vol. 12, pp. 145–156). Hogarth Press.

Freud, S. (1916). On transience. In J. Strachey (Ed. & Trans.), *The standard edition of the complete psychological works of Sigmund Freud* (Vol. 14, pp. 303–307). Hogarth Press.

Freud, S. (1917). Mourning and melancholia. In J. Strachey (Ed. & Trans.), *The standard edition of the complete psychological works of Sigmund Freud* (Vol. 14, pp. 243–258). Hogarth Press.

Freud, S. (1920). Beyond the pleasure principle. In J. Strachey (Ed. & Trans.), *The standard edition of the complete psychological works of Sigmund Freud* (Vol. 18, pp. 7–34). Hogarth Press.

Freud, S. (1921). Group psychology and the analysis of the ego. In J. Strachey (Ed. & Trans.), *The standard edition of the complete psychological works of Sigmund Freud* (Vol. 18, pp. 1–127). Hogarth Press.

Freud, S. (1923). The ego and the id. In J. Strachey (Ed. & Trans.), *The standard edition of the complete of Sigmund Freud* (Vol. 19, pp. 3–166). Hogarth Press.

Freud, S. (1930). Civilization and its discontents. In J. Strachey (Ed. & Trans.), *The standard edition of the complete psychological works of Sigmund Freud* (Vol. 21, pp. 59–145). Hogarth Press.

Freud, S. (1933). New introductory lectures on psychoanalysis. In J. Strachey (Ed. & Trans.), *The standard edition of the complete psychological works of Sigmund Freud* (Vol. 22, pp. 1–267). Hogarth Press.

Freud, S. (1936). A disturbance of memory on the Acropolis. In J. Strachey (Ed. & Trans.), *The standard edition of the complete psychological works of Sigmund Freud* (Vol. 23, pp. 275–278). Hogarth Press.

Freud, S. (1937). Analysis terminable and interminable. In J. Strachey (Ed. & Trans.), *The standard edition of the complete psychological works of Sigmund Freud* (Vol. 23, pp. 141–207). Hogarth Press.

Freud, S., & Breuer, J. (1895). *Studies in hysteria.* (N. Luckhurst, Trans.). Penguin Classics.

Fromm, E. (1941). *Escape from freedom.* Avon Books.

Fromm, E. (1997). *To have or to be.* Bloomsbury Academic.

Ghent, E. (1990). Masochism, submission, surrender: Masochism as a perversion of surrender. *Contemporary Psychoanalysis, 26,* 108–136.

Gilman, S. (1985). *Difference and pathology.* Cornell University Press.

Girard, R. (1979). *Violence and the sacred.* Johns Hopkins University Press.

Goethe, J. W. (1817). The holy longing. In R. Bly (Trans.), *News of the universe: Poems of twofold consciousness* (p. 61). Counterpoint Press.

Goffman, E. (1963). *Stigma: Notes on the management of spoiled identity.* Touchstone.

Greene, G. (2006). A Catholic novelist? In B. Bergonzi (Ed.), *A study in Greene: Graham Greene and the art of the novel.* Oxford University Press.

Groddeck, G. (1923). *The book of the it.* New American Library.

Gusdorf, G. (1965). *Speaking.* (P. Brockelman, Trans.). Northwestern University Press.

Heraclitus (500 BCE). *Fragments.* (T. M. Robinson, Trans.). University of Toronto Press.

Hoffman, I. Z. (1998). *Ritual and spontaneity in the psychoanalytic process.* The Analytic Press.

Horney, K. (1950). *Neurosis and human growth.* Norton.

Hyde, L. (1979). *The gift: Imagination and the erotic life of property.* Vintage.

Ionesco, E. (1959). *Rhinoceros.* Vintage.

James, W. (1890). *The principles of psychology* (Vol. I). Dover Publications.

Jaspers, K. (1933). *Man in the modern age.* Doubleday.

Kant, I. (1785). *Groundwork of the metaphysics of morals.* Cambridge University Press.

Kearney, R. (2003). *Strangers, gods, and monsters: Interpreting otherness.* Routledge.

Kierkegaard, S. (1843a). *Fear and trembling.* (H. V. Hong & E. H. Hong, Trans.). Princeton University Press.

Kierkegaard, S. (1843b). *Repetition.* (W. Lowrie, Trans.). Harper & Row.

Kierkegaard, S. (1843c). *Either/or I.* (D. Swenson & L. Swensen, Trans.). Doubleday.

Kierkegaard, S. (1844). *The concept of anxiety.* (R. Thomte, Trans.). Princeton University Press.

Kierkegaard, S. (1846). *The present age.* (A. Dru, Trans.). Torchbooks.

Kierkegaard, S. (1847a). *Works of love.* Harper & Row.

Kierkegaard, S. (1847b). *Edifying discourses in diverse spirits.* Augsburg Publishing House.

Kierkegaard, S. (1849). *The sickness unto death.* (A. Hannay, Trans.). Penguin.

Kierkegaard, S. (1967). *Soren Kierkegaards's journals and papers* (Vol. 3). (H. Hong & E. Hong, Eds. & G. Malantschuck, Trans.). Indiana University Press.

Klein, M. (1937). *Love, guilt and reparation and other works 1921–1945 (The writings of Melanie Klein, Volume I).* The Free Press.

Klein, M. (1957). *Envy and gratitude and other works, 1946–1963.* Dell.

Koestler, A. (1978). *Janus: A summing up*. One 70 Press.

Kramer, R. (Ed.) (1996). *A psychology of difference: Lectures by Otto Rank*. Princeton University Press.

Lacan, J. (1964). *The seminar, book XI: The four fundamental concepts of psychoanalysis*. (A. Sheridan, Trans.). Hogarth Press.

Lacan, J. (1966). *Ecrits: The complete edition in English*. (B. Fink, Trans.). Norton.

LeBon, G. (1895). *The crowd: A study of the popular mind*. Cherokee Publishing.

Levinas, E. (1969). *Totality and infinity*. Duquesne University Press.

Lewis, H. (1971). *Shame and guilt in neurosis*. International Universities Press.

Loewald, H. (1980). The waning of the Oedipus complex. In *Papers on psychoanalysis* (pp. 384–404). Yale University Press.

Lynch, W. (1965). *Images of hope*. University of Notre Dame Press.

Lynd, H. M. (1958). *On shame and the search for identity*. Harcourt, Brace & Company.

Macalpine, I. (1950). The development of the transference. *Psychoanalytic Quarterly, 19*, 501–539.

Mahler, M., Pine, F., & Bergman, A. (1975). *The psychological birth of the human infant*. Basic Books.

Margolis, D. (1998). *The fabric of self*. Yale University Press.

Maroda, K. (2021). *The analyst's vulnerability: Impact on theory and practice*. Routledge.

Maslow, A. (1962). *Toward a psychology of being*. Wiley.

Mauss, M. (1924). *The gift: Forms and functions of exchange in archaic societies*. (I. Cunnison, Trans.). Norton.

May, R. (1969). *Love and will*. Norton.

Merleau-Ponty, J. (1964). *The primacy of perception*. Northwestern University Press.

Merleau-Ponty, M. (1945). *The phenomenology of perception*. (D. Landes, Trans.). Routledge.

Miller, J. (1988). *The way of suffering: A geography of crisis*. Georgetown University Press.

Miller, S. (1985). *The shame experience*. The Analytic Press.

Milton, J. (1667). *Paradise lost*. Chelsea House.

Mitchell, S. A. (1984). Object relations theories and the developmental tilt. *Contemporary Psychoanalysis, 20*, 473–489.

Mitchell, S. A. (1988). *Relational concepts in psychoanalysis*. Harvard University Press.

Mitchell, S. A. (2000). You've got to suffer the blues: Psychoanalytic reflections on guilt and self-pity. *Psychoanalytic Dialogues, 10*, 713–733.

Mitscherlich, A. (1975). *The inability to mourn: Principles of collective behavior*. Grove Press.

Morrison, A. (1989). *Shame: The underside of narcissism*. The Analytic Press.

Murgoci, A. (1923). The evil eye in Romania and its antidotes. *Folklore, 34*(4), 357–362.

Nietzsche, F. (1873). *Schopenhauer as educator*. (A. Collins, Trans.). CreateSpace Independent Publishing Forum.

Nietzsche, F. (1878). *Human, all too human: A book for free spirits*. Cambridge University Press.

Nietzsche, F. (1882). *The gay science*. Cambridge University Press.

Nietzsche, F. (1887). *The genealogy of morals*. Doubleday.

Nietzsche, F. (1889). *Thus spake Zarathustra*. (R. Hollingdale, Trans.). Penguin.

Nietzsche, F. (1908). *Ecce homo*. Vintage Books.

Nietzsche, F. (1909). *Early Greek philosophy and other essays: Collected works* (Vol II). (M. Mugge, Trans.). CreateSpace Independent Platform.

Orange, D. (2011). *The suffering stranger*. Routledge.

Ovid (8 A.D.). *Metamorphoses*. (D. Raeburn, Trans.). Penguin.

Pagels, E. (1988). *Adam, Eve, and the serpent*. Penguin.

Pascal, B. (1670). *Pensees*. (G. Rawlings, Ed. & Trans.). Peter Pauper Press.

Pattison, S. (2000). *Shame: Theory, therapy, theology*. Cambridge University Press.

Perls, F. (1969). *Ego, hunger, and aggression*. Vintage.

Phillips, A. (1993). *On kissing, tickling and being bored*. Harvard University Press.

Phillips, A. (1995). The story of the mind. In E. Corrigan & P. E. Gordon (Eds.), *The mind object* (pp. 229–240). Jason Aronson.

Phillips, A. (2002). Equals. Perseus.

Piers, G., & Singer, M. (1953). *Shame and guilt: A psychoanalytic and cultural study*. Norton.

Plato (360 BCE). *Timaeus*. (H. D. P. Lee, Trans.). Penguin.

Punter, D. (2014). *The literature of pity*. Edinburgh University Press.

Rank, O. (1927). Love, guilt, and denial. In R. Kramer (Ed.), *A psychology of difference* (pp. 153–165). Princeton University Press.

Rank, O. (1936). *Will therapy and truth and reality*. Knopf.

Rank, O. (1941). *Beyond psychology*. Dover Publications.

Ricoeur, P. (1967). *The symbolism of evil*. Beacon Press.

Ricoeur, P. (1970). *Freud and philosophy: An essay on interpretation*. (D. Savage, Trans.). Yale University Press.

Ricoeur, P. (2005). *The course of recognition*. (D. Pellauer, Trans.). Harvard University Press.

Rilke, R. M. (1907). Quoted in *Love and will*, R. May. Norton.

Rilke, R. M. (1923). *Duino elegies*. (C. F. MacIntyre, Trans.). University of California Press.

Rilke, R. M. (1934). *Letters to a young poet*. Norton.

Roheim, G. (1934). The evolution of culture. *International Journal of Psychoanalysis, 15*, 487–518.

Romanyshyn, R. (1989). *Technology and dream as symptoms*. Routledge.

Rousseau, J. (1755). *First and second discourses* (R. D. Masters, Ed.). St. Marks Press.

Russell, P. (1993). The essential invisibility of trauma and the need for repetition. Commentary to "Resentment, indignation, entitlement: The transformation of unconscious wish into need." *Psychoanalytic Dialogues, 3*(4), 515–522.

Sartre, J. P. (1956). *Being and nothingness*. (S. Richmond, Trans.). Washington Square Press.

Schafer, R. (1978). *Language and insight*. Yale University Press.

Schafer, R. (1983). *The analytic attitude*. Basic Books.

Scheler, M. (1912). *Ressentiment*. (L. Coser & W. Holdheim, Trans.). Marquette University Press.

Schneider, C. (1977). *Shame, exposure and privacy*. Beacon Press.

Searles, H. (1975). The patient as therapist to the analyst. In *Countertransference and related subjects* (pp. 380–459). International Universities Press.

Seneca (60 A.D.). *On the shortness of life*. Penguin.

Shabad, P. (1987). Fixation and the road not taken. *Psychoanalytic Psychology, 4*, 187–205.

Shabad, P. (1989). Vicissitudes of psychic loss of a physically present parent. In D. Dietrich & P. Shabad (Eds.), *The problem of loss and mourning: Contemporary perspectives* (pp. 101–126). International Universities Press.

Shabad, P and Selinger, S.(1995). Bracing for disappointment and the leap into the future. 209-228. In E. Corrigan & and P. Gordon (Eds). *The mind object*. Jason Aronson.

Shabad, P. (2001). *Despair and the return of hope: Echoes of mourning in psychotherapy.* Jason Aronson.

Shabad, P. (2008). Of woman born: The male struggle for significance in the eyes of the cosmos. In L. Wurmser & H. Jarass (Eds.), *Jealousy and envy* (pp. 75–89). The Analytic Press.

Shabad, P. (2010). The suffering of passion: Metamorphoses and the embrace of the stranger. *Psychoanalytic Dialogues, 20,* 710–729.

Shabad, P. (2017). The vulnerability of giving: Ethics and the generosity of receiving. *Psychoanalytic Inquiry, 37*(6), 359–374.

Shakespeare, W. (1599). *Julius Caesar.* Penguin.

Spinoza, B. (1677). *Ethics.* (E. Curley & S. Hampshire, Trans.). Penguin.

Spitz, R. (1959). *A genetic field theory of ego formation.* International Universities Press.

Stern, D. *Relational freedom.* Routledge.

Symington, N. (1983). The analyst's act of freedom as agent of therapeutic change. *The International Review of Psychoanalysis, 10,* 283–291.

Symington, N. (1997). *The making of a psychotherapist.* Routledge.

Tennyson, A. L. (1850). *In Memoriam A. H. H.* Knight & Millett.

Theleweit, K. (1987). *Male fantasies (Vol. 1): Women, floods, bodies, history.* (S. Conway, Trans.). University of Minnesota Press.

Tillich, P. (1952). *The courage to be.* Yale University Press.

Tolpin, M. (2002). Doing psychoanalysis of normal development: Forward edge transferences. In A. I. Goldberg (Ed.), *Progress in self psychology* (Vol. 18, pp. 167–190). The Analytic Press.

Tolstoy, L. (1887). *The death of Ivan Ilych and other stories.* (L. Maude & A Maude, Trans.). Borders Classics.

Tomkins, S. (1963). *Affect, imagery, consciousness: The negative affects* (Vol II). Springer.

Tomkins, S. (1982). Affect theory. In P. Ekman (Ed.), *Emotion in the human face* (pp. 353–395). Cambridge University Press.

Van Gennep, A. (1908). *The rites of passage.* University of Chicago Press.

Wilde, O. (1891). *The soul of man under socialism.* John Luce and Company.

Winnicott, D. W. (1949a). Birth memories, birth trauma, and anxiety. In *Through paediatrics to psychoanalysis* (pp. 174–193). Edited by D.W. Winnicott. Basic Books.

Winnicott, D. W. (1949b). Mind and its relation to psyche-soma. In *Through paediatrics to psychoanalysis* (pp. 243–254). Basic Books.

Winnicott, D. W. (1950). Aggression in relation to emotional development. In *Through paediatrics to psychoanalysis* (pp. 204–218). Basic Books.

Winnicott, D. W. (1951). Transitional objects and transitional phenomena. In *Through paediatrics to psychoanalysis* (pp. 229–242). Basic Books.

Winnicott, D. W. (1954–1955). The depressive position in normal emotional development. In *Through paediatrics to psychoanalysis* (pp. 262–276). Basic Books.

Winnicott, D. W. (1956a). Primary maternal preoccupation. In *Through paediatrics to psychoanalysis* (pp. 300–305). Basic Books.

Winnicott, D. W. (1956b). The antisocial tendency. In *Through paediatrics to psychoanalysis* (pp. 306–315). Basic Books.

Winnicott, D. W. (1960a). Ego distortion in terms of true and false self. In *The maturational process and the facilitating environment* (pp. 140–152). Edited by D.W. Winnicott. International Universities Press.

Winnicott, D. W. (1960b). The theory of the parent-infant-relationship. In *The maturational process and the facilitating environment* (pp. 37–55). Edited by D.W. Winnicott. International Universities Press.

Winnicott, D. W. (1967a). The location of cultural experience. In *Playing and reality* (pp. 95–103). Tavistock.

Winnicott, D. W. (1967b). Mirror role of mother and family in child development. In *Playing and reality* (pp. 111–118). Tavistock.

Winnicott, D. W. (1968). Communication between infant and mother, and mother and infant, compared and contrasted. In W. Joffe (Ed.), *What is psychoanalysis?* (pp. 89–101). The Institute of Psychoanalysis.

Winnicott, D. W. (1969). The use of an objects and relating through identifications. In *Playing and reality* (pp. 86–94). Tavistock.

Winnicott, D. W. (1971). Playing: A theoretical statement. In *Playing and reality* (pp. 51–69). Tavistock.

Winnicott, D.W. (1974) Fear of breakdown. *International Review of Psycho-Analysis*, 1, 103-107.

Wright, R. (1991). *Vision and separation*. Jason Aronson.

Wurmser, L. (1981). *The mask of shame*. Johns Hopkins University Press.

# Index

superego: and introjection of shame 83, 196; as mask to placate parental envy 109; and punishment 83, 84

symptoms: as action proof 126–129; as memorials to lonely suffering 191; as non-verbal communication 194

talking cure 8, 199, 234, 248

thinking in: cycles of and action proof of symptoms 126–129; and derealization of trauma 63

tradition 6, 29, 110, 124, 152, 167, 201; external authority of 110

transcendence 17, 239; and devotion to an other 18

transference 20, 40, 57, 101, 129, 130, 188, 192, 201, 203–224, 239, 241

transience 6

transitions 4, 11, 17, 21–25, 30, 38, 43–46, 49, 50, 54, 65, 88, 95, 97, 103, 107, 116, 118, 136, 183, 186, 197, 204, 238

tyranny of should 189–193

"us" vs. "them": and externalization of shame 178; pure vs. impure 178

waiting 3, 49, 50, 56, 59, 114, 131, 150–153, 158, 163, 208, 245

"waiting at the end of the block" 152

will: of first realm and second realm 221; manifest in action 25; and unconscious intentionality 13, 124, 221

Winnicott, Donald 2, 9, 16, 20–22, 31–35, 39, 41, 50, 51, 63, 78, 92, 117, 118, 123, 130, 140, 148, 156, 163, 239

wished-for parent: fixation on 243, 244; and incomplete mourning 75

wish magic: as motor hallucinations 94

word magic: in countertransference 211

For Product Safety Concerns and Information please contact our EU
representative  GPSR@taylorandfrancis.com
Taylor & Francis Verlag GmbH, Kaufingerstraße 24, 80331 München, Germany

9 780415 703949